ALSO BY W. B. YEATS

The Poems of W. B. Yeats: A New Edition
The Variorum Edition of the Poems of W. B. Yeats
Autobiography
Explorations
Mythologies
A Vision
Collected Plays
Eleven Plays by W. B. Yeats
The Variorum Edition of the Plays of W. B. Yeats
Fairy and Folk Tales of Ireland

SELECTED POEMS
AND
FOUR PLAYS
OF
William Butler Yeats

FOURTH EDITION

*Edited and with a New Foreword
and Revised Introduction and Notes
by* **M. L. ROSENTHAL**

SCRIBNER PAPERBACK POETRY

SCRIBNER PAPERBACK POETRY

SCRIBNER

1230 Avenue of the Americas
New York, NY 10020

First Scribner Paperback Poetry edition 1996

SCRIBNER PAPERBACK POETRY and design are
trademarks of Simon & Schuster Inc.

Designed by Jack Mesarole
Manufactured in the United States of America

1   3   5   7   9   10   8   6   4   2

Library of Congress Cataloging-in-Publication Data is available.

ISBN 0-684-82646-1

Contents

Foreword to the Fourth Edition   xvii

Introduction: The Poetry of Yeats   xix

FROM Crossways (1889)

The Cloak, the Boat, and the Shoes   1
Ephemera   1
The Stolen Child   2
To an Isle in the Water   4
Down by the Salley Gardens   5

FROM The Rose (1893)

To the Rose upon the Rood of Time   6
Fergus and the Druid   7
Cuchulain's Fight with the Sea   8
The Rose of the World   11
A Faery Song   12
The Lake Isle of Innisfree   12
The Pity of Love   13
The Sorrow of Love   13
When You Are Old   14
A Dream of Death   14
Who Goes with Fergus?   15
The Man Who Dreamed of Faeryland   15
The Two Trees   17
To Ireland in the Coming Times   18

FROM The Wind Among the Reeds (1899)

The Hosting of the Sidhe   20
The Moods   20

The Unappeasable Host   21
Into the Twilight   21
The Song of Wandering Aengus   22
The Song of the Old Mother   23
He Bids His Beloved Be at Peace   23
He Reproves the Curlew   23
To His Heart, Bidding It Have No Fear   24
The Cap and Bells   24
The Valley of the Black Pig   25
He Hears the Cry of the Sedge   26
The Lover Pleads with His Friends for Old Friends   26
He Wishes His Beloved Were Dead   27
He Wishes for the Cloths of Heaven   27

FROM In the Seven Woods (1904)

The Folly of Being Comforted   28
Adam's Curse   28
Red Hanrahan's Song About Ireland   30
The Old Men Admiring Themselves in the Water   30

FROM The Green Helmet and Other Poems (1910)

A Woman Homer Sung   31
Words   32
No Second Troy   32
Against Unworthy Praise   33
The Fascination of What's Difficult   33
A Drinking Song   34
On Hearing That the Students of Our New University Have Joined
   the Agitation Against Immoral Literature   34
To a Poet, Who Would Have Me Praise Certain Bad Poets, Imitators
   of His and Mine   34
The Mask   35
Upon a House Shaken by the Land Agitation   35
These Are the Clouds   36
All Things Can Tempt Me   36
Brown Penny   36

FROM Responsibilities (1914)

[Pardon, Old Fathers]   38
September 1913   38
To a Friend Whose Work Has Come to Nothing   39
Paudeen   40
To a Shade   40
When Helen Lived   41
The Three Hermits   42
Beggar to Beggar Cried   43
Running to Paradise   43
 I. The Witch   44
 II. The Peacock   45
 I. To a Child Dancing in the Wind   45
 II. Two Years Later   46
A Memory of Youth   46
Fallen Majesty   47
The Cold Heaven   47
That the Night Come   48
The Magi   48
The Dolls   49
A Coat   49

FROM The Wild Swans at Coole (1919)

The Wild Swans at Coole   51
In Memory of Major Robert Gregory   52
An Irish Airman Foresees His Death   55
The Collar-Bone of a Hare   56
Solomon to Sheba   56
To a Young Beauty   57
The Scholars   58
Tom O'Roughley   58
Lines Written in Dejection   59
The Dawn   59
On Woman   60
The Fisherman   61
The Hawk   62

Memory   63
The People   63
A Thought from Propertius   64
A Deep-Sworn Vow   65
Presences   65
On Being Asked for a War Poem   66
UPON A DYING LADY: 66
    I. *Her Courtesy*   66
    II. *Certain Artists Bring Her Dolls and Drawings*   66
    III. *She Turns the Dolls' Faces to the Wall*   67
    IV. *The End of Day*   67
    V. *Her Race*   67
    VI. *Her Courage*   68
    VII. *Her Friends Bring Her a Christmas Tree*   68
Ego Dominus Tuus   68
The Phases of the Moon   71
The Cat and the Moon   75
The Saint and the Hunchback   76
Two Songs of a Fool   77
The Double Vision of Michael Robartes   78

FROM Michael Robartes and the Dancer (1921)
Solomon and the Witch   81
An Image from a Past Life   82
Easter, 1916   83
On a Political Prisoner   86
The Leaders of the Crowd   86
Towards Break of Day   87
Demon and Beast   88
The Second Coming   89
A Prayer for My Daughter   90
A Meditation in Time of War   92

Calvary (1921)   94

FROM The Tower (1928)
Sailing to Byzantium   102

xii

The Tower   103
MEDITATIONS IN TIME OF CIVIL WAR: 109
    I. *Ancestral Houses*   109
    II. *My House*   110
    III. *My Table*   111
    IV. *My Descendants*   112
    V. *The Road at My Door*   113
    VI. *The Stare's Nest by My Window*   113
    VII. *I See Phantoms of Hatred and of the Heart's Fullness and of the Coming Emptiness*   114
NINETEEN HUNDRED AND NINETEEN   115
Two Songs from a Play   119
Fragments   120
Leda and the Swan   121
Among School Children   121
from A MAN YOUNG AND OLD: 124
    I. *First Love*   124
    IV. *The Death of the Hare*   124
    IX. *The Secrets of the Old*   125
All Souls' Night   125

FROM The Winding Stair and Other Poems (1933)

In Memory of Eva Gore-Booth and Con Markievicz   129
Death   130
A Dialogue of Self and Soul   130
Blood and the Moon   133
Veronica's Napkin   135
The Nineteenth Century and After   135
Three Movements   135
Coole and Ballylee, 1931   136
For Anne Gregory   137
Swift's Epitaph   138
The Choice   138
Byzantium   138
The Mother of God   140
Vacillation   140
Quarrel in Old Age   143

Remorse for Intemperate Speech   144
from WORDS FOR MUSIC PERHAPS: 145
    I. *Crazy Jane and the Bishop*   145
    II. *Crazy Jane Reproved*   146
    III. *Crazy Jane on the Day of Judgment*   146
    IV. *Crazy Jane and Jack the Journeyman*   147
    V. *Crazy Jane on God*   148
    VI. *Crazy Jane Talks with the Bishop*   148
    VII. *Crazy Jane Grown Old Looks at the Dancers*   149
    VIII. *Girl's Song*   150
    IX. *Young Man's Song*   150
    X. *Her Anxiety*   151
    XV. *Three Things*   151
    XVI. *Lullaby*   152
    XVII. *After Long Silence*   153
    XX. *'I Am of Ireland'*   153
    XXII. *Tom the Lunatic*   154
    XXV. *The Delphic Oracle upon Plotinus*   155
from A WOMAN YOUNG AND OLD: 155
    III. *A First Confession*   155
    VI. *Chosen*   156
    IX. *A Last Confession*   156

The Words Upon the Window-Pane (1934)   158

FROM A Full Moon in March:
"Parnell's Funeral" and Other Poems (1935)
Parnell's Funeral   172
Church and State   173
from SUPERNATURAL SONGS: 174
    I. *Ribh at the Tomb of Baile and Aillinn*   174
    III. *Ribh in Ecstasy*   175
    IV. *There*   175
    VI. *He and She*   175
    VIII. *Whence Had They Come?*   176

IX. *The Four Ages of Man* 176
XII. *Meru* 177

FROM New Poems (1938)

The Gyres 178
Lapis Lazuli 179
The Three Bushes 180
The Lady's First Song 183
The Lady's Second Song 183
The Lady's Third Song 184
The Lover's Song 184
The Chambermaid's First Song 185
The Chambermaid's Second Song 185
An Acre of Grass 185
What Then? 186
Beautiful Lofty Things 187
Come Gather Round Me, Parnellites 188
The Wild Old Wicked Man 189
The Great Day 190
Parnell 191
The Spur 191
A Model for the Laureate 191
The Old Stone Cross 192
Those Images 193
The Municipal Gallery Revisited 193

FROM On the Boiler (1939)

Why Should Not Old Men Be Mad? 196
Crazy Jane on the Mountain 196
A Statesman's Holiday 197

FROM Last Poems and Two Plays (1939)

Under Ben Bulben 199
The Black Tower 202

Cuchulain Comforted   203
from Three Marching Songs   204
The Statues   205
News for the Delphic Oracle   206
Long-legged Fly   207
John Kinsella's Lament for Mrs. Mary Moore   208
The Apparitions   209
Man and the Echo   210
The Circus Animals' Desertion   212
Politics   213

The Death of Cuchulain (1939)   215

Purgatory (1939)   225

Notes   233

Glossary of Names and Places   251

Selective Bibliography   259

Index to Titles   263

Index of First Lines of Poems   267

Foreword to the Fourth Edition

Like its predecessors, this edition aims to present a responsible, attractive selection of Yeats's poems and plays. Over the years, scholarly studies have achieved ever more dependable texts. Hence the welcome revisions in our successive printings.

It was a special joy in the 1986 "Revised Edition" to present the poems appearing after *A Full Moon in March* (1935) in their proper groupings and order. This major change had been deferred in earlier printings to avoid confusion, since the *Collected Poems* of 1956, then current, still lumped together arbitrarily as "Last Poems" the poetry in *New Poems* (1938), the posthumous *On the Boiler*, and *Last Poems and Two Plays* (both 1939). But in 1983 Richard Finneran's *The Poems of W. B. Yeats: A New Edition* had sorted out the order correctly. We could finally, without being at odds with this improved collected edition, close the selected volume with key poems and both plays from *Last Poems and Two Plays*: a powerful sequence showing the continued vitality of Yeats's tragic imagination despite his failing health. Yeats's climactic pairing of the plays *The Death of Cuchulain* and *Purgatory* stunningly reveals the subtle intelligence informing his art to the very end.

The 1986 edition included a few poems I had ruefully omitted originally, and the present edition adds an extraordinary play, *The Words Upon the Window-Pane* (1934), I have long felt was needed. For one thing, the play throws a vivid theatrical light on the poet's typically paradoxical attraction to supernaturalism and "psychic research" and to certain Anglo-Irish figures of the eighteenth century: chiefly, Burke, Goldsmith, Berkeley, and especially Swift. For another, it employs a realistic style unique in Yeats's writing to bring us into a visionary realm of violent psychological torment beyond the grave.

In general, my texts are based on *The Variorum Edition of the Poems*, *The Variorum Edition of the Plays*, *The Poems of W. B. Yeats: A New Edition*, and the redactions of *The Death of Cuchulain* and *Purgatory* by Phillip R. Marcus and Sandra F. Siegel, respectively. The texts here represent as sensibly readable a conflation as I can manage. (For further discussion, see the note "On the Text," pages 247–249.)

The date printed for each poem or play is that of first publication as given in Allan Wade's *A Bibliography of the Writings of W. B. Yeats*. In the Notes section at the back, I have drawn on Yeats's notes and added my own critical and interpretive suggestions sparingly, to clarify an allusion or provide a hint about a work's organizing perspective. For the poems (but not the plays), I have usually for simplicity listed names of people and places, both historical and mythical, in the alphabetical glossary rather than in the Notes. My main factual sources are the books listed in the brief Bibliography: either Yeats's own works or those by such pioneering scholars as Richard Ellmann, George Brendan Saul, T. R. Henn, and A. Norman Jeffares. For extended criticism and treatment of the poet's many-faceted life and work, one must turn to those books and to others that one's interests may lead one to seek out. My introductory essay proposes some of the relevant considerations and discusses the purely poetic character of Yeats's achievement.

Introduction:
The Poetry of Yeats

I

William Butler Yeats is the most widely admired, by common reader and sophisticate alike, of all modern poets who have written in English. Early and late he has the simple, indispensable gift of enchanting the ear:

> In pools among the rushes
> That scarce could bathe a star
> ("The Stolen Child," 1886)

> *Cast a cold eye*
> *On life, on death,*
> *Horseman, pass by!*
> ("Under Ben Bulben," 1938)

It was not this gift alone which made Yeats the poet he was, though without it no poet can be great. He was also the poet who, while very much of his own day in Ireland, spoke best to the people of all countries. And though he plunged deep into arcane studies, his themes are most clearly the general ones of life and death, love and hate, man's condition, and history's meanings. He began as a sometimes effete post-Romantic, heir to the pre-Raphaelites, and then, quite naturally, became a leading British Symbolist; but he grew at last into the boldest, most vigorous voice of this century:

> Now days are dragon-ridden, the nightmare
> Rides upon sleep; a drunken soldiery
> Can leave the mother, murdered at her door,
> To crawl in her own blood, and go scot-free;
> The night can sweat with terror as before
> We pieced our thoughts into philosophy,
> And planned to bring the world under a rule,
> Who are but weasels fighting in a hole.
> ("Nineteen Hundred and Nineteen")

These lines grew directly out of "the Troubles" in Ireland following upon the 1916 Rebellion and preceding the establishment of the new Irish state then coming to birth. Irish history aside, however, one could hardly ask for a clearer, more bitter statement of the problem of contemporary man face to face with the rebirth of naked violence. "Violence upon the roads: violence of horses," Yeats says later on in the same work. Or, as he puts it in four more famous lines elsewhere:

> The blood-dimmed tide is loosed, and everywhere
> The ceremony of innocence is drowned;
> The best lack all conviction, while the worst
> Are full of passionate intensity.
> ("The Second Coming")

This passage, in turn, is intimately an expression of Yeats's theory of history and of the aristocratic ideal he cherished. But no one needs a gloss to see its relevance to the flood of war and terror in our century, with murderous fanaticism overruling skeptical intelligence.

I do not wish to oversimplify matters. Yeats sometimes demands a knowledge of his special interests and at least a momentary sympathy with them. Read a line like "Hunchback and Saint and Fool are the last crescents" (in "The Phases of the Moon") or lines like

> Had De Valéra eaten Parnell's heart
> No loose-lipped demagogue had won the day,
> ("Parnell's Funeral")

and at least at first you will feel meanings here beyond what is given. Yeats sometimes made the assumption, flattering both to himself and to his readers, that because he had something intensely felt to say it must somehow be understood. When in "Sailing to Byzantium" he begs the "sages standing in God's holy fire" to "perne in a gyre" few readers can follow him to his literal meaning. Yet these three poems have an overriding beauty and power that give him the right to make his assumption. In these instances the meaning does make itself manifest with attention, but in any case the poems present images and "magical" incantations with a tremendous magnetism apart from their literal meaning.

Still, Yeats is not the poet mainly of mystics and scholars.

Anyone can read and follow most of his poems, hear their music, visualize the pictures they project. I mean this in the sense that "anyone" can read Shakespeare or Keats or Tennyson. Yeats called himself one of the "last Romantics." He was intrigued by the thought that in India one might hear peasant women in the fields singing the songs of the Bengal poet Tagore. The women were illiterate and ignorant of whose poem they sang; perhaps they did not even know a poem must have an author. Such a thing could hardly happen in the English-speaking countries, at all events now. We have no illiterate peasantries to speak of, and poets "hear" their first romantic lyrics on the printed page (unless they are the mass-produced, copyrighted songs of popular tapes and recordings). In Ireland, Yeats was still in touch with an earlier day:

> Some few remembered still when I was young
> A peasant girl commended by a song,
> Who'd lived somewhere upon that rocky place,
> And praised the colour of her face,
> And had the greater joy in praising her,
> Remembering that, if walked she there,
> Farmers jostled at the fair
> So great a glory did the song confer.
> ("The Tower")

Like Wordsworth, Yeats turned to folk sources to give his work the grain of ordinary humanity and the direct appeal of ballads and other popular traditional forms. One poem, for instance, was "an extension of three lines sung to me by an old woman at Ballisodare." Another was "developed from three or four lines of an Irish fourteenth-century dance song." A third was "founded on a West of Ireland legend." The element of song is always present in this poet's work, not only in his purely lyrical writing with obvious roots in folksong but also in his more intellectual and rhetorical writing. Everywhere, too, the *theme* of music and singing recurs constantly. Thus, the old man of "Sailing to Byzantium" dreams of the songs he will make if, by studying man's most beautiful creations, he can be lifted beyond the needs and limitations of the flesh:

> Once out of nature I shall never take
> My bodily form from any natural thing,
> But such a form as Grecian goldsmiths make

> Of hammered gold and gold enamelling
> To keep a drowsy Emperor awake;
> Or set upon a golden bough to sing
> To lords and ladies of Byzantium
> Of what is past, or passing, or to come.

In a sense Yeats's own making of a song and his subject are one and the same here. It is not only his alliterations and reverberating disposition of sounds and words (note the echoing of "nature," "form," "gold," "past"). It is his very construction of the stanza and the way it builds up to the image of the golden bird singing its timeless song. As usual with Yeats, he employs a conventional stanza, in this case *ottava rima,* and his syntax is as straightforward as that of good prose. The conventionality allows his reader to expect the working out of a known pattern as a sustained unit of composition. Yeats's originality and daring lie in the force of what is wrought from these conventional formal qualities, and in the paradoxical insights the poems unfold. Also, he can make a slight distortion or variation—an off-rhyme or grammatical ambiguity—count for a great deal.

Yeats was sixty-two when he wrote "Sailing to Byzantium." He was in the midst of that wonderful period when his powers seemed unbounded. It is curious to speculate about how predictable this future would have seemed in the eighties and nineties when he first won recognition as a young exquisite. In 1885, at twenty, he published "The Cloak, the Boat, and the Shoes," a lovely, "strange," perfect poem of its kind whose delicate poignancy betokened a coming de La Mare much more than the author of "Sailing to Byzantium." As it first appeared, one section read:

> 'What do you build with sails for flight?'
>
> 'A boat I build for Sorrow:
> O swift on the seas all day and night
> Saileth the rover Sorrow,
> All day and night.'

Nor could we have foreseen the mature Yeats from the original form of "Cuchulain's Fight with the Sea," published in 1892. Even the briefest passage from that sad adventure in mechanical rhyme is well-nigh unbearable:

> A man came slowly from the setting sun
> To Emer of Borda, in her clay-piled dun,

And found her dyeing cloth with subtle care
And said, casting aside his draggled hair,
'I am Aleel, the swineherd, whom you bid
Go dwell upon the sea cliffs, vapour hid,
But now my years of watching are no more.'

Despite the excellent ear that produced the quick, light modulations of "The Cloak, the Boat, and the Shoes," the young poet could not yet handle the more intransigent problems of a narrative poetry hagridden by the twin conventions of the iambic pentameter line and the heroic couplet.[1] At the same time, we can see even from this sample that he lacked neither invention nor a lively fancy. He had also the simple virtue of being able to carry through an extended piece of writing. Yeats showed unusual energies in this respect, unlike the many young poets whose paths are strewn with unfinished masterpieces. In the long run his persistence helped him make poetry his natural means of expression.

But many a poor poet perseveres and writes his roomful of wretched verse without rising an inch toward Heaven. *Audacity* is another thing, and it seems to me the early Yeats had this quality to a marked degree. He was not afraid to juggle with ideas and adumbrations or to risk ambiguity for the sake of the main chance. His boldness undoubtedly had much to do with his excursions into Irish faery lore and into the self-hypnotic realms of occultism. He tried to look at the world through a seer's eye, and to see reflected in one another that world's sense-realities and the evocative, symbolic forms of the dreaming mind that draws endlessly on a stock of archetypal images and memories. As the hero of "Fergus and the Druid" suggests, all that has ever been is contained within that mind. He says, at the close of the poem as it first appeared in 1892:

I see my life go dripping like a stream
From change to change! I have been many things:
A green drop in the surge, a gleam of light
Upon a sword, a fir tree on a hill,

[1] The final "definitive" version of one of Yeats's poems is often deceptive in the sense that it represents a recasting over the years which may have changed it drastically from its form at first publication. Thus, "Cuchulain's Fight with the Sea" (p. 8) reached its final form in 1933, forty-one years after the version whose opening stanza is quoted above.

An old slave grinding at a heavy quern,
A king sitting upon a chair of gold;
And all these things were wonderful and great.
But now I have grown nothing, being all:
The sorrows of the world bow down my head,
And in my heart the daemons and the gods
Wage an eternal battle, and I feel
The pain of wounds, the labour of the spear,
But have no share in loss or victory.

Although it was not until 1925 that he made the last important changes in this poem, Yeats's most brilliant revisions took place in the very next printing, the same year as the original publication. The same passage in its present version is very close to the revision of 1892, and shows how quick he was in learning to gain greater lyric swiftness and variation and greater dramatic impact through concentration and a shift of tone or emphasis:

I see my life go drifting like a river
From change to change; I have been many things—
A green drop in the surge, a gleam of light
Upon a sword, a fir-tree on a hill,
An old slave grinding at a heavy quern,
A king sitting upon a chair of gold—
And all these things were wonderful and great;
But now I have grown nothing, knowing all.
Ah! Druid, Druid, how great webs of sorrow
Lay hidden in the small slate-coloured thing!

Yeats made many subtle changes in punctuation and phrasing between 1892 and 1925, but the most striking alteration comes in the replacing of the five lines at the end of the original version by the two that now close the poem. (The later 1892 printing made this basic change, though it retained one line of the original ending and had other differences from the final form as well.) The ending underlines the situation of the poem, for the "small slate-coloured thing" that Fergus holds is a "little bag of dreams" given him by a Druid to make him forget he was once "king of the proud Red Branch kings." He has given up his power to the more worldly Conchubar and seeks to learn the "dreaming wisdom," both intoxicating and bitter, which is poet's wisdom also and in which by his late twenties Yeats had diligently schooled himself. The vocabulary remains very much of the nineties, but the poet was even then beginning to use it in new ways. He manages to imply strongly through it the self-tormenting, restless intelligence behind the silently lush phrasing.

Fergus stands forth ambiguously, a mythical, yearning presence. He is from one point of view a half-king, and from another a double king, poised hesitatingly between two realms. He cannot quite give up what he has forsworn, nor does he quite possess the ideal realm of desire and imagination he has turned to. That no one can choose absolutely between opposites is one of the major motifs of the whole of Yeats's poetry, and so is the further complication that the two realms depend on one another for whatever it is they signify. Thus, Fergus prefigures many another character of Yeats's poetry and drama such as the old man of "Sailing to Byzantium," the beings out of the world of spirit and imagination who in "The Magi" haunt the "bestial floor" of human life to search out their meanings, and the baffled hero of *Purgatory*. He appears again in the brief, disturbing "Who Goes with Fergus?" This is one of the loveliest of the early pieces, whose most seductive and at the same time most sinister phrase ("white breast of the dim sea") we hear Joyce's Stephen Dedalus repeating to himself in *Ulysses*.

Indeed, the whole of the poem is seductive and sinister. Fergus (or the poet as his wry spokesman) seeks to lure the young to his dream dominion whose "woven shade" and "level shore" suggest the triumph of aesthetic vision over life's disorder. No longer will melancholy, like Blake's "invisible worm," assail and corrupt their joy.

> Young man, lift up your russet brow,
> And lift your tender eyelids, maid,
> And brood on hopes and fear no more.
>
> And no more turn aside and brood
> Upon love's bitter mystery.

Yet the fear and bitter mystery and ruthlessness of reality cannot be escaped. "Brazen cars," "shadows of the wood," "dim sea," "dishevelled wandering stars"—all are images to trouble the imagination. Neither Faerie nor art, it is implied, can be free of the sickness of unfulfilled yearning; one might easily, bringing many other poems to witness, press the thought to the idea that Paradise itself could not be free of it unless through the harshest impersonality (a view Yeats embodies most specifically in the late poem "News for the Delphic Oracle").

Throughout his career Yeats wove certain hoary systems of philosophical symbolism into his poetry. "With them," writes Richard Ellmann, referring specifically to the symbolism of the four elements earth, air, fire, and water, "he was able to enlarge his context steadily. . . . By couching his feelings in the framework of the elements, he anchored them in universal forces and lent them added dignity and sanction."[2] By the same token, we can add, he gave to the universal symbolism he employed the coloration of his private feelings. This happens literally in "Who Goes with Fergus?"—in which the impersonal sea and stars, for example, are made to seem distraught and erotically perturbed by the figurative language that associates them with white breasts and "dishevelled wandering" lovers. In poetry an image or figure brought in to illuminate a subject is itself inevitably illuminated by the subject; it is not a matter of logic but of transferred association, as in the subconscious life of the mind and emotions. Yeats wove his symbolic effects into his writing subtly, at times almost invisibly; the more subtly, the more effective the transference. I say "effects," but what he did was more than a technique. It approached an *experiencing* of relationships and insights at many different levels—of *correspondences,* to go back to the way of thinking we associate with Boehme, Blake, and Swedenborg, which so influenced him in his youth.

That influence had extraordinary results for Yeats's early poetry, as did his involvement with Rosicrucianism, theosophy, and spiritualism. Not only did it lend authority to what might otherwise have been vague sentimentality; it also made him at home, as it were, among the "universal forces" of magical and religious tradition that have stored up—whatever their objective validity—certain explosive symbols of tremendous psychic power. No poet since Blake has succeeded like Yeats in bringing this tradition and the sense of ordinary mortality to bear on one another. Among simpler examples we have poems like "The

[2]Richard Ellmann, *The Identity of Yeats* (New York: Oxford University Press, 1964), p. 35. [second edition].

Stolen Child" and "The Man Who Dreamed of Faeryland." The former poem is unspeakably touching in its evocation of the uneasy world into which the child is beguiled by the faeries to abandon its parents' warm hearth-and-oatmeal world for their mysteriously sad one. In the second of these poems the hero would have known a few good, "normal" things in his life had he not been led into impossible visions that mocked him and cheapened everything he actually had in his grasp. He is seduced by the song of things below the level of human consciousness that speak for the elements themselves and cry out the longing of all mortality for eternity. The "singers" are a pile of dead fish in the market-place, a lug-worm in the mud, a common weed, and finally the worms that "spired" about his body in the grave so that he could not even have his death in peace. (The complaint, incidentally, is the same that Lazarus raises against Jesus in Yeats's play *Calvary*.) Students of Yeats will see in the word "spired" that pervasive gyre-symbol that appears in so many later poems and is so important in his prose work *A Vision*, but the poem gives us a clear enough picture in itself; as with its use of the four elements, it absorbs the further symbolism into its primary effect. Even when he introduced such symbolism much more dramatically and forcefully, Yeats usually was able to keep it in human perspective and, as I have suggested, give it a human coloration:

> *Until the axle break*
> *That keeps the stars in their round,*
> *And hands hurl in the deep*
> *The banners of East and West,*
> *And the girdle of light is unbound,*
> *Your breast will not lie by the breast*
> *Of your beloved in sleep.*
>
> ("He Hears the Cry of the Sedge")

Yeats's earlier poetry is to some extent obscured by the thunder of his last three decades; he seemed to advance in power almost to the day of his death. But we have seen that the later achievement is foreshadowed not only in its themes but also in certain qualities of imagination and style by the work he did before 1900, and especially in its treatment of the human vis-à-vis the superhuman, the Here and the There. Leaf through his writing of this period and you will rediscover the germinating passion behind the end-of-century tone: the resentment against "time's bitter flood," as he calls it in "The Lover Pleads with His Friend for Old Friends," with its desolate awareness that the loss is more than a personal one:

> 'Ah, do not mourn,' he said,
> 'That we are tired, for other loves await us;
> Hate on and love through unrepining hours.
> Before us lies eternity; our souls
> Are love, and a continual farewell.'
> ("Ephemera")

What is the difference between this and such harsh later developments of the same motif as "The Second Coming" and "Under Ben Bulben"? The former poem, like "Ephemera," also speaks of the irreversible cycles of eternity but relates them to our specific historical era and to the terrible moments of annunciation that accompany the death of old eras and the birth of new ones. "Under Ben Bulben," written in the poet's last year, tells us that

> Many times man lives and dies
> Between his two eternities,
> That of race and that of soul,
> And ancient Ireland knew it all.
> Whether man dies in his bed
> Or the rifle knocks him dead,
> A brief parting from those dear
> Is the worst man has to fear.
> Though grave-diggers' toil is long,
> Sharp their spades, their muscles strong,
> They but thrust their buried men
> Back in the human mind again.

The difference is important—a matter of cleanness of statement and of liberated stylistic energy. A unique and rich personality has emerged, with a mind full of paradoxes and ranging freely over the fundamental issues of man's existence. The tone is prophetic and incantatory, yet in some fashion these qualities are combined with candor, directness, and something like the flavor of conversational speech. There is far more to the later Yeats, but it was all promised in the poetry before 1900 which looks so intently and with such originality at the predicament of man—the gap between his will and his fate, the tragic impersonality of the universe, and his nagging inability either to accept things as they literally are or to escape them entirely through his dreams.

2

When Yeats received the Nobel Prize for Literature in 1925, he said, in the course of his address to the Swedish Royal Academy:

> When your king gave me medal and diploma, two forms should have stood, one at either side of me, an old woman sinking into the infirmity of age and a young man's ghost. I think when Lady Gregory's name and John Synge's name are spoken by future generations, my name, if remembered, will come up in the talk, and that if my name is spoken first their names will come in their turn because of the years we worked together. I think that both had been well pleased to have stood beside me at the great reception at your palace, for their work and mine has delighted in history and tradition.[3]

Lady Gregory and John Synge came particularly to Yeats's mind on this occasion because his prize was to him not only a recognition of his work but a tribute to the Irish Renaissance in which he, with these two, played his part. The Free State was, in 1925, but a few years old. The memory of terrible struggles was fiercely alive, as we can see from the wholly or partly political poems of this period. (See the 1921 volume *Michael Robartes and the Dancer* and the 1928 volume *The Tower*.) The poems report the hopes and disillusionments of those years, and Yeats's feeling of inadequacy for the physical side of the struggle:

> An affable Irregular,
> A heavily-built Falstaffian man,
> Comes cracking jokes of civil war
> As though to die by gunshot were
> The finest play under the sun. . . .
>
> I count those feathered balls of soot
> The moor-hen guides upon the stream,
> To silence the envy in my thought;
> And turn towards my chamber, caught
> In the cold snows of a dream.
> ("The Road at My Door")

[3] *The Bounty of Sweden*, reprinted in *The Autobiography of William Butler Yeats* (New York: Doubleday Anchor Books, 1958), pp. 373–374.

Earlier, immediately after the Easter Rebellion, he had expressed the ideal of an Ireland that had recaptured the "history and tradition" Yeats said his own work and that of his two friends "delighted in." The Rebellion might have been a needless sacrifice, yet it had transformed a nation of mean-spirited clowns into something glorious:

> All changed, changed utterly:
> A terrible beauty is born.

Then, in "Meditations in Time of Civil War" (of which "The Road at My Door" is one section) and in "Nineteen Hundred and Nineteen," he had seen the transformation apparently undone. Under the impact of the atrocities perpetrated by the "drunken soldiery" of the Black and Tans and other groups, Ireland was once more the home of squalor "where but motley is worn":

> Come, let us mock at the great
> That had such burdens on the mind
> And toiled so hard and late
> To leave some monument behind,
> Nor thought of the levelling wind. . . .

and—

> Violence upon the roads: violence of horses;
> Some few have handsome riders, are garlanded
> On delicate sensitive ear or tossing mane,
> But wearied running round and round in their courses
> All break and vanish, and evil gathers head.

Political struggle, though occasionally inspiring and doubtless necessary, was thus seen by Yeats as not only tragic but by its very nature inimical to uncompromised idealism. Against it he could set the struggle for an Irish art and intellectual life best exemplified by Synge and Lady Gregory. The house of Lady Gregory at Coole he saw as the center of this nobler struggle. A refuge and a meeting place for people like himself, it generated the atmosphere out of which came the Abbey Theatre and the new Irish literature, and in itself it stood for a heritage— aristocratic, disinterested, aesthetic—which was Ireland's true meaning:

Beloved books that famous hands have bound,
Old marble heads, old pictures everywhere;
Great rooms where travelled men and children found
Content or joy; a last inheritor
Where none has reigned that lacked a name and fame
Or out of folly into folly came.

("Coole and Ballylee, 1931")

I have used these tributes to Lady Gregory and the allusions
to the Civil War as a starting point to suggest the complex
subject of the relation between Yeats's private life and his art.
More than most poets of his time, he worked his association
with particular men and women and his personal problems and
predicaments directly into his poetry. Usually he did so quite
deliberately, though he never conceived of a poem simply as a
private mirror—not in the published versions, at any rate. He
read a special symbolism into all his private acts and relation-
ships, so that although he often writes in the first person he
rarely presents himself nakedly in his poems. When we come
across the draft of an unpublished poem which does present him
in this way it is striking because so rare. Here is a stanza from
such a poem in his manuscript book:

Oh my beloved. How happy
I was that day when you
came here from the
railway, and set your hair
aright in my looking glass
and then sat with me at
my table, and lay resting
in my big chair. I am
like the children o my
beloved and I play at
marriage—I play
with images of the life
you will not give to me o
my cruel one.[4]

Compare this poem with almost any of the published poems
in which he speaks of his beloved. The emotion of such poems,
say of the early "He Bids His Beloved Be at Peace" or the much

[4]Richard Ellmann, *The Man and the Masks* (New York: W.W. Norton 1979), p. 161.
[second edition]

later "An Image from a Past Life" or "Among School Children," is no less strongly felt, and the last-named one even describes a real incident in the first person. But all have a protective symbolism and achieve, if not absolute impersonality, some kind of removal from the feeling that first motivated them. The draft poem, on the other hand, is much closer than any printed work of the poet's to the unpretentious immediacies of a whole new school of contemporary American poets.

Be that as it may, some knowledge of Yeats's life and thought is helpful for understanding his poetic personality if only we do not read the private Yeats too literally into his writings. Fortunate in his biographers, such men as A. Norman Jeffares, T. R. Henn, and Richard Ellmann, he has also left us a fascinating *Autobiography* and *Journal*. I can here offer only a few notes. He was born in 1865, the son of John Butler Yeats and Elizabeth Pollexfen Yeats. The father had been educated to go into law but instead became an artist. He was a highly articulate man, deeply involved with his son's upbringing, and doubtless the single individual most important in Yeats's life. He gave him a background of constant discussion of ideas from many viewpoints and an understanding of the seriousness of the arts, especially of poetry, and even left his mark on his prose style. His own father and grandfather had both been rectors of the Church of Ireland, but he had turned against both orthodoxy and a conventional profession. His son went him one better by resisting a conventional education and, after studying art for a short time and turning more and more to writing, by seeking to master occult systems in part at least as a reaction against the father's skeptical and logical turn of mind. Their difference on this last score, as on some others, took on some bitterness, but in fact the father's rationalism was of a rather precarious sort. It centered on words like "personality" and "experience" and "desire" and gave full encouragement to the idea of self-liberation from conventional habits of thought and to introspective pursuits which might well lead one into mystical paths. It was precarious in another way also; his views and interests were forever fluctuating. He could see the various sides of a question and liked considering problems in terms of opposed categories. So in an important sense the son's interests were an extension, with many different points of reference, of those of his father.

The "silent" Pollexfens on his mother's side were much more of the practical and physical world and of the Irish countryside and seaport life in the county of Sligo. They were the antithesis of the father's cosmopolitan intellectualism; he said that in begetting William he had "given a tongue to the sea-cliffs." Much of Yeats's childhood was spent with his mother's family in Sligo; as he describes it, it was not a very happy childhood. He was lonely and felt inferior physically and even mentally. But he gained a lasting sense of common Irish life and speech and attitudes which later guided him toward native themes and toward a committed if very individualistic patriotism. The whole matter of his mother's influence on him is difficult to deal with. She was not at ease with art and ideas or the people attached to them. It would be all too easy to speculate about the connection between her lack of a developed personality and Yeats's uncertainties about himself and later difficulties with women and dependence on Lady Gregory for reassurance as well as patronage. In 1901 a stroke affected her mind. This event may help explain the deepening sadness and tougher fiber of her son's later work, though his poetry virtually never alludes directly to either of his parents. Again, it may be stretching a point, but perhaps his early association with the Hermetic Society and the Society of the Golden Dawn, and his studies in theosophy and magic under the tutelage of Mme. Blavatsky and others, had something to do with a wish to associate himself with his mother's almost instinctive religious, and probably superstitious, feelings.

The woman who does appear most often in his poems, more even than does Lady Gregory, is Maud Gonne. Virtually every poem celebrating a woman's beauty or addressing a beloved woman has to do with her. She is the "Helen" of his poems, the woman with a "Ledaean body," his "phoenix," and perhaps the "sweetheart from another life" whose memory embitters his still-recent marriage to George Hyde-Lees in the poem "An Image from a Past Life."[5] Her beauty, her proud presence, her

[5] But see note, p. 239.

nationalist and leftist ardor, expressed in social work and in political activity of the most devoted kind, and the continued linking of their destinies despite her marriage to another man that shocked Yeats so—all make of her something more than the nostalgically remembered light of his youth. Like Lady Gregory in another way, she became a symbol for him of Ireland; she also came to symbolize conscience, Classical and Renaissance beauty, and heroic energies without an adequate objective in the modern world. Yeats thus attached to the figure of the "beloved" in his poems not only Maud Gonne's own qualities but those of the great heroines of tradition and, very probably, of other women whom he had loved as well.

In short, we need to remind ourselves of the dangers of translating his poems into mere autobiography. We can hardly avoid the temptation in reading a poem like "No Second Troy," which begins:

> Why should I blame her that she filled my days
> With misery, or that she would of late
> Have taught to ignorant men most violent ways . . .

Yet even here we need to remain aware of the poem rather than of the antecedent facts. That is, it is a poem about a woman who has embittered the speaker's life and demeaned herself through unworthy actions—and this woman is doubtless Maud Gonne and the speaker is doubtless Yeats himself. But the poem does not actually make these identifications, and beyond that almost irrelevant point there is one more important. The poem projects (but certainly does not specify) a dramatic situation in which the speaker is a man something like Yeats, the subject a woman something like Maud Gonne. The woman has made the speaker unhappy, and has "taught" violence to others. But *in the poem* who is she? She is a modern Helen, but one without "another Troy for her to burn." Did Maud Gonne herself have "nobleness made simple as a fire" and "beauty like a tightened bow," beauty that was "high and solitary and most stern"? Was she truly a Helen who must make men suffer because ours is an age without a Paris, and must turn to the politics of street fighting and petty hatreds because the heroic age—her proper phase—is forever lost? We cannot answer questions like this in any objective way, and from this fact we see that although Yeats used real experience for the dramatic situation of the poem he was guided as well by conceptions and symbolic associations not necessarily dependent on that experience. He might have written much the same poem, admittedly with some differences of detail, out of his feeling about the age alone. The specific argument of the poem has an added poignancy for us as a justification of Maud Gonne's kind of life in the face of his own suffering, yet the insight it gives might well have derived from mere observation of a woman of her sort with no relationship to Yeats at all. In fact, of course, it comes from the continuous nurturing of his feeling for her under the pressure of his concerns as a poet, and that is why the problem of the exact relationship of the poet's life to his art is easier to define than it is to settle.

Without attempting to settle it, then, I want only to note that the poem has a life independent of what "really" happened to the poet and of what the "truth" is about Maud Gonne. We are best off taking each poem on its own terms as far as we are able to do so; artistically, nearly all Yeats's work is self-sufficient. Even with "No Second Troy" we do not *need* biography; we are told enough to set up the situation of the poem. And with other poems, such as the beautifully and subtly developed "Adam's Curse," it would be a positive interference to try to trace the poem back to its true-life origins. All we would find out would be that a remark Yeats attributes to his beloved's "close friend" in the poem was actually made by her sister. Although the cavalier transference might teach us something about the difference between literal truth and art, should we not have absorbed this distinction with our mothers' milk anyway? The poem describes a conversation between the poet and this close friend, herself a lovely woman, while the beloved sits silently by. He speaks rather bitterly of how lightly the world regards his very difficult labors, and the friend replies that women too "must labour to be beautiful." The world, it is clear, does not realize that behind the seeming spontaneity of a line of verse or casualness of a woman's presence lies much effort, thought, dedication, and even sacrifice. (The word "labour," of course, has connotations for womanliness that go beyond mere appearance.) The poet generalizes on the theme: *all* fine things "since Adam's fall" need "much labouring." But these things are going out of fashion. Who now believes in the "old high way" of love-making, "compounded of high courtesy" and learned quotations, that now "seems an idle trade enough"? But this thought makes them silent "at the name of love." They look at the fragile moon just appearing in the sky, "worn as if it had been a shell" that was "washed by time's waters as they rose and fell." The stillness of the beloved is now felt as a token of the incommunicability of outworn values; they might have been great lovers, but that possibility has been eroded away and is but an anachronism. This is not autobiography but a desolate insight arranged rhetorically and dramatically.

Similarly, we may be moved to think the poet wrote out of a very specific motivation in "A Dialogue of Self and Soul" when he spoke of

> that most fecund ditch of all,
> The folly that man does
> Or must suffer, if he woos
> A proud woman not kindred of his soul.

No doubt he did have Maud Gonne in mind, but the true context of the lines is the brilliant debate in the poem between Soul and Self, and the praise of life in the Self's audacious, rapturous, and triumphant peroration. Considered purely as a poetic symbol, however, the "Maud Gonne figure" in Yeats's poems is important in bringing into a single focus a number of diverse aspects of his mentality. To the other connotations I have already mentioned, we should add the almost desperate worship of erotic love and beauty, a Romantic motif Yeats inherited by way of the pre-Raphaelites, the atmosphere of the nineties, and his own studies of Blake (whose works he edited with E. J. Ellis in 1893, providing a detailed interpretative commentary). It led him to an ever-increasing interest in sexual realism and conviction of a sexual principle at the heart of all existence and all history.

Yeats was well prepared to make of the disparate interests of his life a unity through such combining symbols as this of the Beloved. He had given his entire adult life to the study of mystical symbolism, not only from a poet's point of view but also from that of one who has crossed the line into the realm of belief. We are nowadays quite familiar with the kind of mentality that is tremendously interested in religion and mysticism and magic on intellectual grounds but never steps over that line of commitment in any way. Yeats had something of this in him also but really went beyond its limits. Though he used his skeptical intelligence as a check on himself, he did "step over." It was the difference of a single notch, perhaps, but that was the difference between conviction and resistance to it. Yeats believed that the power of his later writing owed a great deal to this commitment as he codified it in A Vision in the years between his marriage in 1917 and the book's first publication in 1925. (It was thoroughly revised for the 1937 edition.) I would be willing to argue that, having made this great commitment, he found ways of taking nearly all of it back—that his strength lies in this side of him also. But it had to be made if the balance was to count for anything. The reader who takes up such works of his written before 1900 as *Rosa Alchemica, The Adoration of the Magi,* and *The Tables of the Law* and such later ones as *Per Amica Silentia Lunae* (1917), *A Vision,* and "Vacillation" (1932) will observe a constant poise within them of their mystical, schematic message, their rationalistic notes in spite of that message, and their extremely personal tone. We do not expect a prophet to confide to us, as Yeats does in *Per Amica Silentia Lunae,* that "when I come home after meeting men who are strange to me, and sometimes even after talking to women, I go over all I have said in gloom and disappointment." Nor do we expect anything like this, from the same book: "All souls have a vehicle or body, and when one has said that . . . one has escaped from the abstract schools who seek always the power of some Church or institution, and found oneself with great poetry, and superstition which is but popular poetry, in a pleasant, dangerous world." Least of all would a man blind to all but the revelation that possesses him say, as Yeats does in a famous passage of *A Vision:*

Some will ask whether I believe in the actual existence of my circuits of sun and moon. . . . I can but answer that if sometimes, overwhelmed by miracle as all men must be when in the midst of it, I have taken such periods literally, my reason has soon recovered. . . . I regard them as stylistic arrangements of experience comparable to the cubes in the drawing of Wyndham Lewis and to the ovoids in the sculpture of Brancusi. They have helped me to hold in a single thought reality and justice.

In a large sense, then, though his thought has its genuinely arcane side, that aspect is leavened by the exploratory, self-conscious, self-questioning side of his poetic personality. Look for example at the poem "The Phases of the Moon," one of the poems which he said he had written "to explain my philosophy of life and death." The poem gives us, in compressed form, the theory of *A Vision*—the secret of human destiny, imaged in the phases of the moon. But if we examine the picture the poem presents, it is of two figures in the night under a "dwindling or late-risen moon" carrying the knowledge of this secret with them. They are creatures of his own making, characters he has used in other works, but now they mockingly contemplate the lighted window in the tower where he sits trying to fathom ultimate meanings. The whole thing amounts to a self-irony on Yeats's part—that he should be the vehicle of the revelation they refuse to explain to him; and more, that the elusiveness of the symbolism itself prevents there being any conclusive answers. It is notable also that the language the speaker employs who explains the lunar process of history is fraught with tragic overtones such as

> And after that the crumbling of the moon:
> The soul remembering its loneliness
> Shudders in many cradles . . .

The whole poem betokens the helplessness of man to control his destiny, or even to comprehend anything beneath its surface. Turn now to the poem Yeats placed directly after this one, "The Cat and the Moon." Here the carrier of transcendent meanings is not a figure from the image world but "wise Minnaloushe" the cat. At night the changing moon is reflected in his innocent mammal's eyes; he is as unaware of the terror of being as Robartes and Aherne, the speakers of the previous poem, were indifferent to it. The second poem simplifies and clarifies the first and shows that Yeats's most central concern was with the mortal condition in its basic, sensed mystery. It is useful (though not the whole relevance they have) to see his theories in relation to this ultimate concern, when they are brought into his poetry. Thus, his interest in the ancient concept of the Great Year—and within it the lesser cycles of civilization which, like the moon, increase to the full and then decline—led him to an important organizing conception for his poetry. It enabled him to see the irrational pre-Grecian, the Grecian, and the Christian eras as all part of a recurring pattern that is entirely indifferent to human suffering and faith. History, like art, teaches us that only through identification with the impersonal can we transcend our human suffering and limitations:

> And then did all the Muses sing
> Of Magnus Annus at the spring,
> As though God's death were but a play.
> ("Two Songs from a Play")

Another symbol of this transcendence in the poems is Byzantine civilization, with the cathedral of Sancta Sophia—a "starlit or moonlit dome"—as its great central point of reference. Ancient Byzantium became for Yeats the purest embodiment of the union and subsequent transfiguration through art of the fleshly condition and the ideal of holiness. Even more inclusive was his conception of a universal system of interpenetrating opposites, pictured as rotating gyres forever whirling into one another's centers, merging, and then separating.[6] The process, with its obviously sexual dimensions, involves all facets of being: the historical phases, the interrelation of man's subjective mind and will and the objectivity of nature and fatality, and even the series of reincarnations every soul must undergo. Moreover, the dominant personalities in succeeding phases of a civilization are related to one another in terms of the stages of engagement and disengagement of the historical gyres. An incidental facet is the poet's highly personal conception of Purgatory as a condition in which the progress of a soul is interrupted while it relives, again and again, a stage in which it violently outraged another soul or was violently outraged by it, until at last the crime is expiated. The expiation, however, cannot be contrived by human will alone, as the play *Purgatory* tragically shows. Here again Yeats pushes at the mystery of the gap between human understanding (and ability to act on it) and ultimate reality.

At some time the reader of Yeats must come up against

---

[6] See notes and diagrams in *The Variorum Edition of the Poems of W. B. Yeats* (New York: Macmillan, 1957), pp. 823–825, and in *A Vision* (New York: Macmillan, 1956), pp. 66, 68, 71–72, 74–81, 199–201, and 266. Some further comments will be found in the Notes to individual poems, pp. 233 ff.

these knottier aspects of his thought. It is possible, and exciting if one becomes absorbed enough, to go into them very deeply, as a good deal of Yeatsian scholarship has done, and become happily lost in the sources and convolutions of his theoretical spinnings. (T. R. Henn, to indicate what this pursuit involves, lists among other works Yeats was familiar with "much esoteric literature, including the *Kabala* and Boehme; Spenser, Swift, Berkeley, Burke; . . . Plato, Plotinus, Julian, Vico, Gentile, McTaggart, Croce, von Hügel, Spengler, Whitehead. . . ."[7]) What we must guard against is imagining that knowledge of this sort is knowledge of his artistic achievement. It is like the bio-graphical information, useful only if reassimilated into our aes-thetic awareness of the poems—and that reassimilation raises baffling questions in both cases. Study Yeats's life and thought as you may, you are still looking at something else when you lift your head and read a poignant little bit of whimsy like "Brown Penny" or a rollicking, hardheaded, yet savage piece like "A Statesman's Holiday" or "John Kinsella's Lament for Mrs. Mary Moore" or a marvel of pure realization like "Byzantium." But external knowledge may help us see relationships—how, for in-stance, early pieces like the Fergus poems and "The Man Who Dreamed of Faeryland" anticipate the more complex confron-tations of the Byzantium poems and the great plays of later years. It may help us, too, to see how the fastening together of many threads of interest in *A Vision* enabled the poet, using his own personality increasingly as the major symbol of his art, to work with many more elements at once than he had done previously.

On this last point a whole book needs to be written. All of Yeats's great poems are involved with it. Often we seem to hear the poet speaking in his own right, as in that most brilliantly yet elusively self-analytical of his poems, "The Circus Animals' Desertion." Or he may project a supposed character, a Crazy Jane or a Ribh, who can present the crucial issues of the Self differently from the literal "I" because of the particular dramatic disguise offered. Yeats became the great poetic spokesman of the modern sensibility not because of his "system" and his ec-centrically specialized interests in themselves, but in part because of the way they helped him encompass the many possibilities of

[7] T. R. Henn, *The Lonely Tower* (London: Methuen, 1950), p. xvi.

xl

the Self and therefore reach deeply into the soul of our century. What else made him the poet he was? For one thing, the fact that although he had the tentativeness, the uncommitted responsiveness, of a contemporary intellectual, he had also within himself a will to commitment, and that he trained himself to use that will. Out of this double personality comes his constant self-examination based on his recognition of his own weaknesses and inconsistencies and on the desire for a transforming vision. But finally, after we have said all this, it was his cultivation of a graceful yet muscular style, at once colloquial and formal, at once serious and boisterous, prophetic and worldly, that enabled him to write a poetry matching in its impact on the reader the rigorous humanity of its conception.

It also enabled him to become one of the pioneers of the modern lyrical sequence, that revolutionary turn in the nature of longer verse-structures that has dominated poetic art in this century. Essentially, the sequence deploys groupings of whole poems and fragments as if they were parts of a single poem in the Symbolist tradition, related by the interaction of resonant centers of subjective tonality with varying degrees of intensity. Unhampered by requirements of narrative, discursive, or "voice" continuity, the sequence can be both simple in its immediacies and complex (without clutter) in its associative dynamics. But its success does require high virtuosity combined with the ability to hold in suspension varied psychological pressures and centers of feeling and awareness. A number of Yeats's sequences are represented here, of which the richest are the double sequence "Meditations in Time of Civil War" and "Nineteen Hundred and Nineteen"; "Words for Music Perhaps" (centered largely in imagined female sensibility); and the doughtily tragic Last Poems and Two Plays, a unique turn in sequence-structure because of its culmination in two powerful verse-plays.

3

In a selected edition one must seek first of all to choose a poet's best work, the poems that stand up entirely on their own merit. Admittedly an impossible aim, but unless one keeps it in view the book will bog down in other considerations: in this instance the poet's occultism, his politics, his controversies and

xli

allegiances, his loves and friendships, and the place of lesser poems in his long artistic development. As we are speaking of a great poet, these considerations are indeed pressing. If I may be allowed a feeble "witticism," I have toyed with the idea of quoting in full in this introduction every poem omitted from the selection that follows. Fortunately, though, the selection does amply represent the wide range of reference underlying Yeats's work. All will be justified if this book brings him still more readers—and its very compression may well help them appreciate him more quickly.

I have included four of his plays: *Calvary, The Words Upon the Window-Pane, The Death of Cuchulain,* and *Purgatory.* Brief as they are, they demonstrate his genius as a poetic dramatist. *Calvary*'s impact is by far the simplest. Yeats's use of the three Musicians enables him to mingle lyric and dramatic verse quite "naturally," and also to contrast sharply two incommensurable worlds: that of the intractable, impersonal, mythopeic realm of art, which is allied in this play to the rhythms and transcendences of nature; and that of Christ's demanding vision. Lazarus' resentment, Judas' defiance, and the Roman soldiers' friendly indifference all either resist the meaning of the Crucifixion or, like unconscious nature, ignore it: "God has not died for the birds." Christ's frustration, compelling him to realize step by step the loneliness of his burden and sacrifice, is made convincing by the way the songs and other lyrical passages reinforce the dramatic progression.

The Words Upon the Window-Pane, though using verse only at a few points, nevertheless soars from a level of quiet prose dialogue and discourse to a scorching pitch of prose-poetry. The initially rational tone, sometimes dryly expository, sometimes droll or comic, sometimes eloquent, prevails until the characters assemble for a séance. But as the ritual gets under way, with deliberately ludicrous touches that contribute to its uncanny atmosphere, an intrusive spirit in agony destroys any sense of orderly control. It is the spirit of Jonathan Swift, cruelly berating his unhappy Vanessa. Swift, seen in the process of sinking into insanity, now takes over as the play's tragic central figure. *The Words Upon the Window-Pane* has affinities with Ibsen's *Ghosts* and foreshadows Samuel Beckett's plays in important aspects. Also, it brings into a single focus some of Yeats's driving

xlii

preoccupations: especially, his terror of madness, his broodings over the intricacies of sexual entanglement and heredity, and his fascination with Swift as a model of the Irish "men of intellect" in the eighteenth century who embodied "everything great in Ireland and in our character."

Purgatory, one of the great short dramatic works of the century, may be compared with *Oedipus* or *Hamlet* in intensity if not in scope. It too carries a complex social and "Freudian" symbolism centered on familial shame and a double need for revenge and purgation. Swift and stripped-down, its movement— from the short incantatory lines as the characters enter the stark set to the terrifying ending—never falters. Here as in *The Words Upon the Window-Pane*, Yeats fleshes out the idiosyncratic conception of Purgatory proposed in his *A Vision*. The play's psychological resonances are well attuned to modern sensibility, and its dramatic immediacy is sustained despite the mystery of its visionary spectacle and the imagined hoofbeats at the end. With utmost economy, it projects a ruthless sense of humanity's failed efforts to reverse fatality, and of the way human will itself becomes an instrument of karma.

Yeats's last play, *The Death of Cuchulain*, is more challenging and ambiguous, although the succession of confrontations by which it advances is simple enough. The play reaches back to Yeats's earlier poems and plays, many of whose characters reappear here, that have to do with the Cuchulain legend. In his final hours, the hero sees his own nature, actions, and loves fatalistically. He accepts his destiny with a noble gentleness that is the reverse of archetypal heroism. It is more, rather, like the self-readying for death of the poet himself, putting his moment of truth in perspective through the creation of an alternate persona. The work thus achieves a magical distancing, an almost eerie tolerance of the contradictions of life. In planning his final volume, Yeats placed this play just before the end, leaving *Purgatory* to close the book with its sharper delineations and relatively more realistic detail. Mythic and empirical Ireland are thus juxtaposed at the same time as the poet links them with his sense of his own inner realities. All three later plays are charged with the motifs of sexual power and guilt, of love's mazes, and of unresolved meanings *in extremis*.

As a group, these four plays exemplify Yeats's ability to give flesh and blood to abstract thoughts by what, in "The Circus Animals' Desertion," he called "character isolated by a deed." ("Man can embody truth but he cannot know it," he wrote toward the end of his life.) All of them, too, reflect his study of the Noh drama of Japan. They stand with his finest poems as examples of an extraordinarily original, penetrating, and uninhibited imagination.

M. L. ROSENTHAL

Suffern, 1996

SELECTED POEMS

AND

FOUR PLAYS

OF

William Butler Yeats

FROM **Crossways**

(1889)

THE CLOAK, THE BOAT, AND THE SHOES

'WHAT do you make so fair and bright?'

'I make the cloak of Sorrow:
O lovely to see in all men's sight
Shall be the cloak of Sorrow,
In all men's sight.'

'What do you build with sails for flight?'

'I build a boat for Sorrow:
O swift on the seas all day and night
Saileth the rover Sorrow,
All day and night.'

'What do you weave with wool so white?'

'I weave the shoes of Sorrow:
Soundless shall be the footfall light
In all men's ears of Sorrow,
Sudden and light.'

(1885)

EPHEMERA

'YOUR eyes that once were never weary of mine
Are bowed in sorrow under pendulous lids,
Because our love is waning.'

I

And then she:
'Although our love is waning, let us stand
By the lone border of the lake once more,
Together in that hour of gentleness
When the poor tired child, Passion, falls asleep:
How far away the stars seem, and how far
Is our first kiss, and ah, how old my heart!'

Pensive they paced along the faded leaves,
While slowly he whose hand held hers replied:
'Passion has often worn our wandering hearts.'

The woods were round them, and the yellow leaves
Fell like faint meteors in the gloom, and once
A rabbit old and lame limped down the path;
Autumn was over him: and now they stood
On the lone border of the lake once more:
Turning, he saw that she had thrust dead leaves
Gathered in silence, dewy as her eyes,
In bosom and hair.

           'Ah, do not mourn,' he said,
'That we are tired, for other loves await us;
Hate on and love through unrepining hours.
Before us lies eternity; our souls
Are love, and a continual farewell.'

(1889)

THE STOLEN CHILD

Where dips the rocky highland
Of Sleuth Wood in the lake,
There lies a leafy island
Where flapping herons wake
The drowsy water-rats;
There we've hid our faery vats,
Full of berries

And of reddest stolen cherries.
Come away, O human child!
To the waters and the wild
With a faery, hand in hand,
For the world's more full of weeping than you
    can understand.

Where the wave of moonlight glosses
The dim grey sands with light,
Far off by furthest Rosses
We foot it all the night,
Weaving olden dances,
Mingling hands and mingling glances
Till the moon has taken flight;
To and fro we leap
And chase the frothy bubbles,
While the world is full of troubles
And is anxious in its sleep.
Come away, O human child!
To the waters and the wild
With a faery, hand in hand,
For the world's more full of weeping than you
    can understand.

Where the wandering water gushes
From the hills above Glen-Car,
In pools among the rushes
That scarce could bathe a star,
We seek for slumbering trout
And whispering in their ears
Give them unquiet dreams;
Leaning softly out
From ferns that drop their tears
Over the young streams.
Come away, O human child!
To the waters and the wild
With a faery, hand in hand,
For the world's more full of weeping than you
    can understand.

Away with us he's going,
The solemn-eyed:
He'll hear no more the lowing
Of the calves on the warm hillside
Or the kettle on the hob
Sing peace into his breast,
Or see the brown mice bob
Round and round the oatmeal-chest.
For he comes, the human child,
To the waters and the wild
With a faery, hand in hand,
From a world more full of weeping than he can
understand.

(1886)

TO AN ISLE IN THE WATER

Shy one, shy one,
Shy one of my heart,
She moves in the firelight
Pensively apart.

She carries in the dishes,
And lays them in a row.
To an isle in the water
With her would I go.

She carries in the candles,
And lights the curtained room,
Shy in the doorway
And shy in the gloom;

And shy as a rabbit,
Helpful and shy.
To an isle in the water
With her would I fly.

(1889)

4

DOWN BY THE SALLEY GARDENS

Down by the salley gardens my love and I did meet;
She passed the salley gardens with little snow-white feet.
She bid me take love easy, as the leaves grow on the tree;
But I, being young and foolish, with her would not agree.

In a field by the river my love and I did stand,
And on my leaning shoulder she laid her snow-white hand.
She bid me take life easy, as the grass grows on the weirs;
But I was young and foolish, and now am full of tears.

(1889)

TO THE ROSE UPON THE ROOD OF TIME

Red Rose, proud Rose, sad Rose of all my days!
Come near me, while I sing the ancient ways:
Cuchulain battling with the bitter tide;
The Druid, grey, wood-nurtured, quiet-eyed,
Who cast round Fergus dreams, and ruin untold;
And thine own sadness, whereof stars, grown old
In dancing silver-sandalled on the sea,
Sing in their high and lonely melody.
Come near, that no more blinded by man's fate,
I find under the boughs of love and hate,
In all poor foolish things that live a day,
Eternal beauty wandering on her way.

Come near, come near, come near—Ah, leave me still
A little space for the rose-breath to fill!
Lest I no more hear common things that crave;
The weak worm hiding down in its small cave,
The field-mouse running by me in the grass,
And heavy mortal hopes that toil and pass;
But seek alone to hear the strange things said
By God to the bright hearts of those long dead,
And learn to chaunt a tongue men do not know.
Come near; I would, before my time to go,
Sing of old Eire and the ancient ways:
Red Rose, proud Rose, sad Rose of all my days.

(1892)

6

FERGUS AND THE DRUID

Fergus. This whole day have I followed in the rocks,
    And you have changed and flowed from shape to shape,
    First as a raven on whose ancient wings
    Scarcely a feather lingered, then you seemed
    A weasel moving on from stone to stone,
    And now at last you wear a human shape,
    A thin grey man half lost in gathering night.

Druid. What would you, king of the proud Red Branch kings?

Fergus. This would I say, most wise of living souls:
    Young subtle Conchubar sat close by me
    When I gave judgment, and his words were wise,
    And what to me was burden without end,
    To him seemed easy, so I laid the crown
    Upon his head to cast away my sorrow.

Druid. What would you, king of the proud Red Branch kings?

Fergus. A king and proud! and that is my despair.
    I feast amid my people on the hill,
    And pace the woods, and drive my chariot-wheels
    In the white border of the murmuring sea;
    And still I feel the crown upon my head.

Druid. What would you, Fergus?

Fergus.   Be no more a king,
    But learn the dreaming wisdom that is yours.

Druid. Look on my thin grey hair and hollow cheeks
    And on these hands that may not lift the sword,
    This body trembling like a wind-blown reed.
    No woman's loved me, no man sought my help.

Fergus. A king is but a foolish labourer
    Who wastes his blood to be another's dream.

Druid. Take, if you must, this little bag of dreams;
    Unloose the cord, and they will wrap you round.

Fergus. I see my life go drifting like a river
From change to change; I have been many things—
A green drop in the surge, a gleam of light
Upon a sword, a fir-tree on a hill,
An old slave grinding at a heavy quern,
A king sitting upon a chair of gold—
And all these things are wonderful and great;
But now I have grown nothing, knowing all.
Ah! Druid, Druid, how great webs of sorrow
Lay hidden in the small slate-coloured thing!

(1892)

CUCHULAIN'S FIGHT WITH THE SEA

A MAN came slowly from the setting sun,
To Emer, raddling raiment in her dun,
And said, 'I am that swineherd whom you bid
Go watch the road between the wood and tide,
But now I have no need to watch it more.'

Then Emer cast the web upon the floor,
And raising arms all raddled with the dye,
Parted her lips with a loud sudden cry.

That swineherd stared upon her face and said,
'No man alive, no man among the dead,
Has won the gold his cars of battle bring.'

'But if your master comes home triumphing
Why must you blench and shake from foot to crown?'

Thereon he shook the more and cast him down
Upon the web-heaped floor, and cried his word:
'With him is one sweet-throated like a bird.'

'You dare me to my face,' and thereupon
She smote with raddled fist, and where her son

8

Herded the cattle came with stumbling feet,
And cried with angry voice, 'It is not meet
To idle life away, a common herd.'

'I have long waited, mother, for that word:
But wherefore now?'

                          'There is a man to die;
You have the heaviest arm under the sky.'

'Whether under its daylight or its stars
My father stands amid his battle-cars.'

'But you have grown to be the taller man.'

'Yet somewhere under starlight or the sun
My father stands.'

                    'Aged, worn out with wars
On foot, on horseback or in battle-cars.'

'I only ask what way my journey lies,
For He who made you bitter made you wise.'

'The Red Branch camp in a great company
Between wood's rim and the horses of the sea.
Go there, and light a camp-fire at wood's rim;
But tell your name and lineage to him
Whose blade compels, and wait till they have found
Some feasting man that the same oath has bound.'

Among those feasting men Cuchulain dwelt,
And his young sweetheart close beside him knelt,
Stared on the mournful wonder of his eyes,
Even as Spring upon the ancient skies,
And pondered on the glory of his days;
And all around the harp-string told his praise,
And Conchubar, the Red Branch king of kings,
With his own fingers touched the brazen strings.

At last Cuchulain spake, 'Some man has made
His evening fire amid the leafy shade.
I have often heard him singing to and fro,
I have often heard the sweet sound of his bow.
Seek out what man he is.'

                One went and came.
'He bade me let all know he gives his name
At the sword-point, and waits till we have found
Some feasting man that the same oath has bound.'

Cuchulain cried, 'I am the only man
Of all this host so bound from childhood on.'

After short fighting in the leafy shade,
He spake to the young man, 'Is there no maid
Who loves you, no white arms to wrap you round,
Or do you long for the dim sleepy ground,
That you have come and dared me to my face?'

'The dooms of men are in God's hidden place.'

'Your head a while seemed like a woman's head
That I loved once.'

            Again the fighting sped,
But now the war-rage in Cuchulain woke,
And through that new blade's guard the old blade broke,
And pierced him.
              'Speak before your breath is done.'

'Cuchulain I, mighty Cuchulain's son.'

'I put you from your pain. I can no more.'

While day its burden on to evening bore,
With head bowed on his knees Cuchulain stayed;
Then Conchubar sent that sweet-throated maid,

And she, to win him, his grey hair caressed;
In vain her arms, in vain her soft white breast.
Then Conchubar, the subtlest of all men,
Ranking his Druids round him ten by ten,
Spake thus: 'Cuchulain will dwell there and brood˙
For three days more in dreadful quietude,
And then arise, and raving slay us all.
Chaunt in his ear delusions magical,
That he may fight the horses of the sea.'
The Druids took them to their mystery,
And chaunted for three days.

                    Cuchulain stirred,
Stared on the horses of the sea, and heard
The cars of battle and his own name cried;
And fought with the invulnerable tide.

(1892)

THE ROSE OF THE WORLD

WHO dreamed that beauty passes like a dream?
For these red lips, with all their mournful pride,
Mournful that no new wonder may betide,
Troy passed away in one high funeral gleam,
And Usna's children died.

We and the labouring world are passing by:
Amid men's souls, that waver and give place
Like the pale waters in their wintry race,
Under the passing stars, foam of the sky,
Lives on this lonely face.

Bow down, archangels, in your dim abode:
Before you were, or any hearts to beat,

11

Weary and kind one lingered by His seat;
He made the world to be a grassy road
Before her wandering feet.

(1892)

A FAERY SONG

*Sung by the people of Faery over Diarmuid and
Grania, in their bridal sleep under a Cromlech.*

WE who are old, old and gay,
O so old!
Thousands of years, thousands of years,
If all were told:

Give to these children, new from the world,
Silence and love;
And the long dew-dropping hours of the
night,
And the stars above:

Give to these children, new from the world,
Rest far from men.
Is anything better, anything better?
Tell us it then:

Us who are old, old and gay,
O so old!
Thousands of years, thousands of years,
If all were told.

(1891)

THE LAKE ISLE OF INNISFREE

I WILL arise and go now, and go to Innisfree,
And a small cabin build there, of clay and wattles made:
Nine bean-rows will I have there, a hive for the honey-bee,
And live alone in the bee-loud glade.

And I shall have some peace there, for peace comes dropping
   slow,
Dropping from the veils of the morning to where the cricket
   sings;
There midnight's all a glimmer, and noon a purple glow,
And evening full of the linnet's wings.

I will arise and go now, for always night and day
I hear lake water lapping with low sounds by the shore;
While I stand on the roadway, or on the pavements grey,
I hear it in the deep heart's core.

(1890)

THE PITY OF LOVE

A PITY beyond all telling
Is hid in the heart of love:
The folk who are buying and selling,
The clouds on their journey above,
The cold wet winds ever blowing,
And the shadowy hazel grove
Where mouse-grey waters are flowing,
Threaten the head that I love.

(1892)

THE SORROW OF LOVE

THE brawling of a sparrow in the eaves,
The brilliant moon and all the milky sky,
And all that famous harmony of leaves,
Had blotted out man's image and his cry.

A girl arose that had red mournful lips
And seemed the greatness of the world in tears,

Doomed like Odysseus and the labouring ships
And proud as Priam murdered with his peers;

Arose, and on that instant clamorous eaves,
A climbing moon upon an empty sky,
And all that lamentation of the leaves,
Could but compose man's image and his cry.

(1892)

WHEN YOU ARE OLD

WHEN you are old and grey and full of sleep,
And nodding by the fire, take down this book,
And slowly read, and dream of the soft look
Your eyes had once, and of their shadows deep;

How many loved your moments of glad grace,
And loved your beauty with love false or true,
But one man loved the pilgrim soul in you,
And loved the sorrows of your changing face;

And bending down beside the glowing bars,
Murmur, a little sadly, how Love fled
And paced upon the mountains overhead
And hid his face amid a crowd of stars.

(1892)

A DREAM OF DEATH

I DREAMED that one had died in a strange place
Near no accustomed hand;
And they had nailed the boards above her face,
The peasants of that land,
Wondering to lay her in that solitude,

And raised above her mound
A cross they had made out of two bits of wood,
And planted cypress round;
And left her to the indifferent stars above
Until I carved these words:
She was more beautiful than thy first love,
But now lies under boards.

(1891)

WHO GOES WITH FERGUS?

WHO will go drive with Fergus now,
And pierce the deep wood's woven shade,
And dance upon the level shore?
Young man, lift up your russet brow,
And lift your tender eyelids, maid,
And brood on hopes and fear no more.

And no more turn aside and brood
Upon love's bitter mystery;
For Fergus rules the brazen cars,
And rules the shadows of the wood,
And the white breast of the dim sea
And all dishevelled wandering stars.

(1892)

THE MAN WHO DREAMED OF FAERYLAND

HE stood among a crowd at Dromahair;
His heart hung all upon a silken dress,
And he had known at last some tenderness,
Before earth took him to her stony care;
But when a man poured fish into a pile,
It seemed they raised their little silver heads,

And sang what gold morning or evening sheds
Upon a woven world-forgotten isle
Where people love beside the ravelled seas;
That Time can never mar a lover's vows
Under that woven changeless roof of boughs:
The singing shook him out of his new ease.

He wandered by the sands of Lissadell;
His mind ran all on money cares and fears,
And he had known at last some prudent years
Before they heaped his grave under the hill;
But while he passed before a plashy place,
A lug-worm with its grey and muddy mouth
Sang that somewhere to north or west or south
There dwelt a gay, exulting, gentle race
Under the golden or the silver skies;
That if a dancer stayed his hungry foot
It seemed the sun and moon were in the fruit:
And at that singing he was no more wise.

He mused beside the well of Scanavin,
He mused upon his mockers: without fail
His sudden vengeance were a country tale,
When earthy night had drunk his body in;
But one small knot-grass growing by the pool
Sang where—unnecessary cruel voice—
Old silence bids its chosen race rejoice,
Whatever ravelled waters rise and fall
Or stormy silver fret the gold of day,
And midnight there enfold them like a fleece
And lover there by lover be at peace.
The tale drove his fine angry mood away.

He slept under the hill of Lugnagall;
And might have known at last unhaunted sleep
Under that cold and vapour-turbaned steep,
Now that the earth had taken man and all:
Did not the worms that spired about his bones
Proclaim with that unwearied, reedy cry
That God has laid His fingers on the sky,

That from those fingers glittering summer runs
Upon the dancer by the dreamless wave.
Why should those lovers that no lovers miss
Dream, until God burn Nature with a kiss?
The man has found no comfort in the grave.

(1891)

THE TWO TREES

BELOVED, gaze in thine own heart,
The holy tree is growing there;
From joy the holy branches start,
And all the trembling flowers they bear.
The changing colours of its fruit
Have dowered the stars with merry light;
The surety of its hidden root
Has planted quiet in the night;
The shaking of its leafy head
Has given the waves their melody,
And made my lips and music wed,
Murmuring a wizard song for thee.
There the Loves a circle go,
The flaming circle of our days,
Gyring, spiring to and fro
In those great ignorant leafy ways;
Remembering all that shaken hair
And how the wingèd sandals dart,
Thine eyes grow full of tender care:
Beloved, gaze in thine own heart.

Gaze no more in the bitter glass
The demons, with their subtle guile,
Lift up before us when they pass,
Or only gaze a little while;
For there a fatal image grows
That the stormy night receives,
Roots half hidden under snows,

Broken boughs and blackened leaves.
For all things turn to barrenness
In the dim glass the demons hold,
The glass of outer weariness,
Made when God slept in times of old.
There, through the broken branches, go
The ravens of unresting thought;
Flying, crying, to and fro,
Cruel claw and hungry throat,
Or else they stand and sniff the wind,
And shake their ragged wings; alas!
Thy tender eyes grow all unkind:
Gaze no more in the bitter glass.

(1892)

TO IRELAND IN THE COMING TIMES

Know, that I would accounted be
True brother of a company
That sang, to sweeten Ireland's wrong,
Ballad and story, rann and song;
Nor be I any less of them,
Because the red-rose-bordered hem
Of her, whose history began
Before God made the angelic clan,
Trails all about the written page.
When Time began to rant and rage
The measure of her flying feet
Made Ireland's heart begin to beat;
And Time bade all his candles flare
To light a measure here and there;
And may the thoughts of Ireland brood
Upon a measured quietude.

Nor may I less be counted one
With Davis, Mangan, Ferguson,
Because, to him who ponders well,

My rhymes more than their rhyming tell
Of things discovered in the deep,
Where only body's laid asleep.
For the elemental creatures go
About my table to and fro,
That hurry from unmeasured mind
To rant and rage in flood and wind;
Yet he who treads in measured ways
May surely barter gaze for gaze.
Man ever journeys on with them
After the red-rose-bordered hem.
Ah, faeries, dancing under the moon,
A Druid land, a Druid tune!

While still I may, I write for you
The love I lived, the dream I knew.
From our birthday, until we die,
Is but the winking of an eye;
And we, our singing and our love,
What measurer Time has lit above,
And all benighted things that go
About my table to and fro,
Are passing on to where may be,
In truth's consuming ecstasy,
No place for love and dream at all;
For God goes by with white footfall.
I cast my heart into my rhymes,
That you, in the dim coming times,
May know how my heart went with them
After the red-rose-bordered hem.

(1892)

THE HOSTING OF THE SIDHE

THE host is riding from Knocknarea
And over the grave of Clooth-na-Bare;
Caoilte tossing his burning hair,
And Niamh calling *Away, come away:*
Empty your heart of its mortal dream.
The winds awaken, the leaves whirl round,
Our cheeks are pale, our hair is unbound,
Our breasts are heaving, our eyes are agleam,
Our arms are waving, our lips are apart;
And if any gaze on our rushing band,
We come between him and the deed of his hand,
We come between him and the hope of his heart.
The host is rushing 'twixt night and day,
And where is there hope or deed as fair?
Caoilte tossing his burning hair,
And Niamh calling *Away, come away.*

(1893)

THE MOODS

TIME drops in decay,
Like a candle burnt out,
And the mountains and woods
Have their day, have their day;
What one in the rout

Of the fire-born moods
Has fallen away?

(1893)

THE UNAPPEASABLE HOST

THE Danaan children laugh, in cradles of wrought gold,
And clap their hands together, and half close their eyes,
For they will ride the North when the ger-eagle flies,
With heavy whitening wings, and a heart fallen cold:
I kiss my wailing child and press it to my breast,
And hear the narrow graves calling my child and me.
Desolate winds that cry over the wandering sea;
Desolate winds that hover in the flaming West;
Desolate winds that beat the doors of Heaven, and beat
The doors of Hell and blow there many a whimpering ghost;
O heart the winds have shaken, the unappeasable host
Is comelier than candles at Mother Mary's feet.

(1896)

INTO THE TWILIGHT

OUT-WORN heart, in a time out-worn,
Come clear of the nets of wrong and right;
Laugh, heart, again in the grey twilight,
Sigh, heart, again in the dew of the morn.

Your mother Eire is always young,
Dew ever shining and twilight grey;
Though hope fall from you and love decay,
Burning in fires of a slanderous tongue.

Come, heart, where hill is heaped upon hill:
For there the mystical brotherhood

Of sun and moon and hollow and wood
And river and stream work out their will;

And God stands winding His lonely horn,
And time and the world are ever in flight;
And love is less kind than the grey twilight,
And hope is less dear than the dew of the morn.

(1893)

THE SONG OF WANDERING AENGUS

I WENT out to the hazel wood,
Because a fire was in my head,
And cut and peeled a hazel wand,
And hooked a berry to a thread;
And when white moths were on the wing,
And moth-like stars were flickering out,
I dropped the berry in a stream
And caught a little silver trout.

When I had laid it on the floor
I went to blow the fire aflame,
But something rustled on the floor,
And some one called me by my name:
It had become a glimmering girl
With apple blossom in her hair
Who called me by my name and ran
And faded through the brightening air.

Though I am old with wandering
Through hollow lands and hilly lands,
I will find out where she has gone,
And kiss her lips and take her hands;
And walk among long dappled grass,
And pluck till time and times are done
The silver apples of the moon,
The golden apples of the sun.

(1897)

THE SONG OF THE OLD MOTHER

I RISE in the dawn, and I kneel and blow
Till the seed of the fire flicker and glow;
And then I must scrub and bake and sweep
Till stars are beginning to blink and peep;
And the young lie long and dream in their bed
Of the matching of ribbons for bosom and head,
And their day goes over in idleness,
And they sigh if the wind but lift a tress:
While I must work because I am old,
And the seed of the fire gets feeble and cold.

(1894)

HE BIDS HIS BELOVED BE AT PEACE

I HEAR the Shadowy Horses, their long manes a-shake,
Their hoofs heavy with tumult, their eyes glimmering white;
The North unfolds above them clinging, creeping night,
The East her hidden joy before the morning break,
The West weeps in pale dew and sighs passing away,
The South is pouring down roses of crimson fire:
O vanity of Sleep, Hope, Dream, endless Desire,
The Horses of Disaster plunge in the heavy clay:
Beloved, let your eyes half close, and your heart beat
Over my heart, and your hair fall over my breast,
Drowning love's lonely hour in deep twilight of rest,
And hiding their tossing manes and their tumultuous feet.

(1896)

HE REPROVES THE CURLEW

O CURLEW, cry no more in the air,
Or only to the water in the West;
Because your crying brings to my mind

Passion-dimmed eyes and long heavy hair
That was shaken out over my breast:
There is enough evil in the crying of wind.

(1896)

TO HIS HEART, BIDDING IT HAVE NO FEAR

Be you still, be you still, trembling heart;
Remember the wisdom out of the old days:
Him who trembles before the flame and the flood,
And the winds that blow through the starry ways,
Let the starry winds and the flame and the flood
Cover over and hide, for he has no part
With the lonely, majestical multitude.

(1896)

THE CAP AND BELLS

The jester walked in the garden:
The garden had fallen still;
He bade his soul rise upward
And stand on her window-sill.

It rose in a straight blue garment,
When owls began to call:
It had grown wise-tongued by thinking
Of a quiet and light footfall;

But the young queen would not listen;
She rose in her pale night-gown;
She drew in the heavy casement
And pushed the latches down.

He bade his heart go to her,
When the owls called out no more;
In a red and quivering garment
It sang to her through the door.

It had grown sweet-tongued by dreaming
Of a flutter of flower-like hair;
But she took up her fan from the table
And waved it off on the air.

'I have cap and bells,' he pondered,
'I will send them to her and die';
And when the morning whitened
He left them where she went by.

She laid them upon her bosom,
Under a cloud of her hair,
And her red lips sang them a love-song
Till stars grew out of the air.

She opened her door and her window,
And the heart and the soul came through,
To her right hand came the red one,
To her left hand came the blue.

They set up a noise like crickets,
A chattering wise and sweet,
And her hair was a folded flower
And the quiet of love in her feet.

(1894)

THE VALLEY OF THE BLACK PIG

THE dews drop slowly and dreams gather: unknown spears
Suddenly hurtle before my dream-awakened eyes,
And then the clash of fallen horsemen and the cries

Of unknown perishing armies beat about my ears.
We who still labour by the cromlech on the shore,
The grey cairn on the hill, when day sinks drowned in dew,
Being weary of the world's empires, bow down to you,
Master of the still stars and of the flaming door.

(1896)

HE HEARS THE CRY OF THE SEDGE

I WANDER by the edge
Of this desolate lake
Where wind cries in the sedge:
Until the axle break
That keeps the stars in their round,
And hands hurl in the deep
The banners of East and West,
And the girdle of light is unbound,
Your breast will not lie by the breast
Of your beloved in sleep.

(1898)

THE LOVER PLEADS WITH HIS FRIENDS FOR OLD FRIENDS

THOUGH you are in your shining days,
Voices among the crowd
And new friends busy with your praise,
Be not unkind or proud,
But think about old friends the most:
Time's bitter flood will rise,
Your beauty perish and be lost
For all eyes but these eyes.

(1897)

26

HE WISHES HIS BELOVED WERE DEAD

WERE you but lying cold and dead,
And lights were paling out of the West,
You would come hither, and bend your head,
And I would lay my head on your breast;
And you would murmur tender words,
Forgiving me, because you were dead:
Nor would you rise and hasten away,
Though you have the will of the wild birds,
But know your hair was bound and wound
About the stars and moon and sun:
O would, beloved, that you lay
Under the dock-leaves in the ground,
While lights were paling one by one.

(1898)

HE WISHES FOR THE CLOTHS OF HEAVEN

HAD I the heavens' embroidered cloths,
Enwrought with golden and silver light,
The blue and the dim and the dark cloths
Of night and light and the half-light,
I would spread the cloths under your feet:
But I, being poor, have only my dreams;
I have spread my dreams under your feet;
Tread softly because you tread on my dreams.

(1899)

THE FOLLY OF BEING COMFORTED

ONE that is ever kind said yesterday:
'Your well-belovèd's hair has threads of grey,
And little shadows come about her eyes;
Time can but make it easier to be wise
Though now it seem impossible, and so
All that you need is patience.'
                                        Heart cries, 'No,
I have not a crumb of comfort, not a grain.
Time can but make her beauty over again:
Because of that great nobleness of hers
The fire that stirs about her, when she stirs,
Burns but more clearly. O she had not these ways
When all the wild summer was in her gaze.'

O heart! O heart! if she'd but turn her head,
You'd know the folly of being comforted.

(1902)

ADAM'S CURSE

WE sat together at one summer's end,
That beautiful mild woman, your close friend,
And you and I, and talked of poetry.
I said, 'A line will take us hours maybe;
Yet if it does not seem a moment's thought,

Our stitching and unstitching has been naught.
Better go down upon your marrow-bones
And scrub a kitchen pavement, or break stones
Like an old pauper, in all kinds of weather;
For to articulate sweet sounds together
Is to work harder than all these, and yet
Be thought an idler by the noisy set
Of bankers, schoolmasters, and clergymen
The martyrs call the world.'

                And thereupon
That beautiful mild woman for whose sake
There's many a one shall find out all heartache
On finding that her voice is sweet and low
Replied, 'To be born woman is to know—
Although they do not talk of it at school—
That we must labour to be beautiful.'

I said, 'It's certain there is no fine thing
Since Adam's fall but needs much labouring.
There have been lovers who thought love should be
So much compounded of high courtesy
That they would sigh and quote with learned looks
Precedents out of beautiful old books;
Yet now it seems an idle trade enough.'

We sat grown quiet at the name of love;
We saw the last embers of daylight die,
And in the trembling blue-green of the sky
A moon, worn as if it had been a shell
Washed by time's waters as they rose and fell
About the stars and broke in days and years.

I had a thought for no one's but your ears:
That you were beautiful, and that I strove
To love you in the old high way of love;
That it had all seemed happy, and yet we'd grown
As weary-hearted as that hollow moon.

(1902)

RED HANRAHAN'S SONG ABOUT IRELAND

THE old brown thorn-trees break in two high over Cummen
    Strand,
Under a bitter black wind that blows from the left hand;
Our courage breaks like an old tree in a black wind and dies,
But we have hidden in our hearts the flame out of the eyes
Of Cathleen, the daughter of Houlihan.

The wind has bundled up the clouds high over Knocknarea,
And thrown the thunder on the stones for all that Maeve can
    say.
Angers that are like noisy clouds have set our hearts abeat;
But we have all bent low and low and kissed the quiet feet
Of Cathleen, the daughter of Houlihan.

The yellow pool has overflowed high up on Clooth-na-Bare,
For the wet winds are blowing out of the clinging air;
Like heavy flooded waters our bodies and our blood;
But purer than a tall candle before the Holy Rood
Is Cathleen, the daughter of Houlihan.

(1894)

THE OLD MEN ADMIRING THEMSELVES IN THE WATER

I HEARD the old, old men say,
'Everything alters,
And one by one we drop away.'
They had hands like claws, and their knees
Were twisted like the old thorn-trees
By the waters.
I heard the old, old men say,
'All that's beautiful drifts away
Like the waters.'

(1903)

A WOMAN HOMER SUNG

IF any man drew near
When I was young,
I thought, 'He holds her dear,'
And shook with hate and fear.
But O! 'twas bitter wrong
If he could pass her by
With an indifferent eye.

Whereon I wrote and wrought,
And now, being grey,
I dream that I have brought
To such a pitch my thought
That coming time can say,
'He shadowed in a glass
What thing her body was.'

For she had fiery blood
When I was young,
And trod so sweetly proud
As 'twere upon a cloud,
A woman Homer sung,
That life and letters seem
But an heroic dream.

(1910)

WORDS

I HAD this thought a while ago,
'My darling cannot understand
What I have done, or what would do
In this blind bitter land.'

And I grew weary of the sun
Until my thoughts cleared up again,
Remembering that the best I have done
Was done to make it plain;

That every year I have cried, 'At length
My darling understands it all,
Because I have come into my strength,
And words obey my call';

That had she done so who can say
What would have shaken from the sieve?
I might have thrown poor words away
And been content to live.

(1910)

NO SECOND TROY

WHY should I blame her that she filled my days
With misery, or that she would of late
Have taught to ignorant men most violent ways,
Or hurled the little streets upon the great,
Had they but courage equal to desire?
What could have made her peaceful with a mind
That nobleness made simple as a fire,
With beauty like a tightened bow, a kind
That is not natural in an age like this,
Being high and solitary and most stern?
Why, what could she have done, being what she is?
Was there another Troy for her to burn?

(1910)

AGAINST UNWORTHY PRAISE

O HEART, be at peace, because
Nor knave nor dolt can break
What's not for their applause,
Being for a woman's sake.
Enough if the work has seemed,
So did she your strength renew,
A dream that a lion had dreamed
Till the wilderness cried aloud,
A secret between you two,
Between the proud and the proud.

What, still you would have their praise!
But here's a haughtier text,
The labyrinth of her days
That her own strangeness perplexed;
And how what her dreaming gave
Earned slander, ingratitude,
From self-same dolt and knave;
Aye, and worse wrong than these.
Yet she, singing upon her road,
Half lion, half child, is at peace.

(1910)

THE FASCINATION OF WHAT'S DIFFICULT

THE fascination of what's difficult
Has dried the sap out of my veins, and rent
Spontaneous joy and natural content
Out of my heart. There's something ails our colt
That must, as if it had not holy blood
Nor on Olympus leaped from cloud to cloud,
Shiver under the lash, strain, sweat and jolt
As though it dragged road metal. My curse on plays
That have to be set up in fifty ways,
On the day's war with every knave and dolt,

Theatre business, management of men.
I swear before the dawn comes round again
I'll find the stable and pull out the bolt.

(1910)

A DRINKING SONG

WINE comes in at the mouth
And love comes in at the eye;
That's all we shall know for truth
Before we grow old and die.
I lift the glass to my mouth,
I look at you, and I sigh.

(1910)

ON HEARING THAT THE STUDENTS OF OUR NEW UNIVERSITY HAVE JOINED THE AGITATION AGAINST IMMORAL LITERATURE

WHERE, where but here have Pride and Truth,
That long to give themselves for wage,
To shake their wicked sides at youth
Restraining reckless middle-age?

(1912)

TO A POET, WHO WOULD HAVE ME PRAISE CERTAIN BAD POETS, IMITATORS OF HIS AND MINE

YOU say, as I have often given tongue
In praise of what another's said or sung,
'Twere politic to do the like by these;
But was there ever dog that praised his fleas?

(1910)

THE MASK

'PUT off that mask of burning gold
With emerald eyes.'
'O no, my dear, you make so bold
To find if hearts be wild and wise,
And yet not cold.'

'I would but find what's there to find,
Love or deceit.'
'It was the mask engaged your mind,
And after set your heart to beat,
Not what's behind.'

'But lest you are my enemy,
I must enquire.'
'O no, my dear, let all that be;
What matter, so there is but fire
In you, in me?'

(1910)

UPON A HOUSE SHAKEN BY THE LAND AGITATION

How should the world be luckier if this house,
Where passion and precision have been one
Time out of mind, became too ruinous
To breed the lidless eye that loves the sun?
And the sweet laughing eagle thoughts that grow
Where wings have memory of wings, and all
That comes of the best knit to the best? Although
Mean roof-trees were the sturdier for its fall,
How should their luck run high enough to reach
The gifts that govern men, and after these
To gradual Time's last gift, a written speech
Wrought of high laughter, loveliness and ease?

(1910)

THESE ARE THE CLOUDS

THESE are the clouds about the fallen sun,
The majesty that shuts his burning eye:
The weak lay hand on what the strong has done,
Till that be tumbled that was lifted high
And discord follow upon unison,
And all things at one common level lie.
And therefore, friend, if your great race were run
And these things came, so much the more thereby
Have you made greatness your companion,
Although it be for children that you sigh:
These are the clouds about the fallen sun,
The majesty that shuts his burning eye.

(1910)

ALL THINGS CAN TEMPT ME

ALL things can tempt me from this craft of verse:
One time it was a woman's face, or worse—
The seeming needs of my fool-driven land;
Now nothing but comes readier to the hand
Than this accustomed toil. When I was young,
I had not given a penny for a song
Did not the poet sing it with such airs
That one believed he had a sword upstairs;
Yet would be now, could I but have my wish,
Colder and dumber and deafer than a fish.

(1909)

BROWN PENNY

I WHISPERED, 'I am too young,'
And then, 'I am old enough';
Wherefore I threw a penny

To find out if I might love.
'Go and love, go and love, young man,
If the lady be young and fair.'
Ah, penny, brown penny, brown penny,
I am looped in the loops of her hair.

O love is the crooked thing,
There is nobody wise enough
To find out all that is in it,
For he would be thinking of love
Till the stars had run away
And the shadows eaten the moon.
Ah, penny, brown penny, brown penny,
One cannot begin it too soon.

(1910)

FROM **Responsibilities**

(1914)

[PARDON, OLD FATHERS]

Pardon, old fathers, if you still remain
Somewhere in ear-shot for the story's end,
Old Dublin merchant 'free of ten and four'
Or trading out of Galway into Spain;
Old country scholar, Robert Emmet's friend,
A hundred-year-old memory to the poor;
Merchant and scholar who have left me blood
That has not passed through any huckster's loin,
Soldiers that gave, whatever die was cast:
A Butler or an Armstrong that withstood
Beside the brackish waters of the Boyne
James and his Irish when the Dutchman crossed;
Old merchant skipper that leaped overboard
After a ragged hat in Biscay Bay;
You most of all, silent and fierce old man,
Because the daily spectacle that stirred
My fancy, and set my boyish lips to say,
'Only the wasteful virtues earn the sun';
Pardon that for a barren passion's sake,
Although I have come close on forty-nine,
I have no child, I have nothing but a book,
Nothing but that to prove your blood and mine.

(1914)

SEPTEMBER 1913

WHAT need you, being come to sense,
But fumble in a greasy till

And add the halfpence to the pence
And prayer to shivering prayer, until
You have dried the marrow from the bone?
For men were born to pray and save:
Romantic Ireland's dead and gone,
It's with O'Leary in the grave.

Yet they were of a different kind,
The names that stilled your childish play,
They have gone about the world like wind,
But little time had they to pray
For whom the hangman's rope was spun,
And what, God help us, could they save?
Romantic Ireland's dead and gone,
It's with O'Leary in the grave.

Was it for this the wild geese spread
The grey wing upon every tide;
For this that all that blood was shed,
For this Edward Fitzgerald died,
And Robert Emmet and Wolfe Tone,
All that delirium of the brave?
Romantic Ireland's dead and gone,
It's with O'Leary in the grave.

Yet could we turn the years again,
And call those exiles as they were
In all their loneliness and pain,
You'd cry, 'Some woman's yellow hair
Has maddened every mother's son':
They weighed so lightly what they gave.
But let them be, they're dead and gone,
They're with O'Leary in the grave.

(1913)

TO A FRIEND WHOSE WORK HAS COME TO
NOTHING

Now all the truth is out,
Be secret and take defeat

39

From any brazen throat,
For how can you compete,
Being honour bred, with one
Who, were it proved he lies,
Were neither shamed in his own
Nor in his neighbours' eyes?
Bred to a harder thing
Than Triumph, turn away
And like a laughing string
Whereon mad fingers play
Amid a place of stone,
Be secret and exult,
Because of all things known
That is most difficult.

(1913)

PAUDEEN

INDIGNANT at the fumbling wits, the obscure spite
Of our old Paudeen in his shop, I stumbled blind
Among the stones and thorn-trees, under morning light;
Until a curlew cried and in the luminous wind
A curlew answered; and suddenly thereupon I thought
That on the lonely height where all are in God's eye,
There cannot be, confusion of our sound forgot,
A single soul that lacks a sweet crystalline cry.

(1913)

TO A SHADE

IF you have revisited the town, thin Shade,
Whether to look upon your monument
(I wonder if the builder has been paid)

Or happier-thoughted when the day is spent
To drink of that salt breath out of the sea
When grey gulls flit about instead of men,
And the gaunt houses put on majesty:
Let these content you and be gone again;
For they are at their old tricks yet.
                                    A man
Of your own passionate serving kind who had brought
In his full hands what, had they only known,
Had given their children's children loftier thought,
Sweeter emotion, working in their veins
Like gentle blood, has been driven from the place,
And insult heaped upon him for his pains,
And for his open-handedness, disgrace;
Your enemy, an old foul mouth, had set
The pack upon him.
                        Go, unquiet wanderer,
And gather the Glasnevin coverlet
About your head until the dust stops your ear,
The time for you to taste of that salt breath
And listen at the corners has not come;
You had enough of sorrow before death—
Away, away! You are safer in the tomb.

(1913)

WHEN HELEN LIVED

WE have cried in our despair
That men desert,
For some trivial affair
Or noisy, insolent sport,
Beauty that we have won
From bitterest hours;
Yet we, had we walked within
Those topless towers
Where Helen walked with her boy,

Had given but as the rest
Of the men and women of Troy,
A word and a jest.

(1914)

THE THREE HERMITS

THREE old hermits took the air
By a cold and desolate sea,
First was muttering a prayer,
Second rummaged for a flea;
On a windy stone, the third,
Giddy with his hundredth year,
Sang unnoticed like a bird:
'Though the Door of Death is near
And what waits behind the door,
Three times in a single day
I, though upright on the shore,
Fall asleep when I should pray.'
So the first, but now the second:
'We're but given what we have earned
When all thoughts and deeds are reckoned,
So it's plain to be discerned
That the shades of holy men
Who have failed, being weak of will,
Pass the Door of Birth again,
And are plagued by crowds, until
They've the passion to escape.'
Moaned the other, 'They are thrown
Into some most fearful shape.'
But the second mocked his moan:
'They are not changed to anything,
Having loved God once, but maybe
To a poet or a king
Or a witty lovely lady.'
While he'd rummaged rags and hair,
Caught and cracked his flea, the third,

Giddy with his hundredth year,
Sang unnoticed like a bird.

(1913)

BEGGAR TO BEGGAR CRIED

'TIME to put off the world and go somewhere
And find my health again in the sea air,'
Beggar to beggar cried, being frenzy-struck,
'And make my soul before my pate is bare.'

'And get a comfortable wife and house
To rid me of the devil in my shoes,'
Beggar to beggar cried, being frenzy-struck,
'And the worse devil that is between my thighs.'

'And though I'd marry with a comely lass,
She need not be too comely—let it pass,'
Beggar to beggar cried, being frenzy-struck,
'But there's a devil in a looking-glass.'

'Nor should she be too rich, because the rich
Are driven by wealth as beggars by the itch,'
Beggar to beggar cried, being frenzy-struck,
'And cannot have a humorous happy speech.'

'And there I'll grow respected at my ease,
And hear amid the garden's nightly peace,'
Beggar to beggar cried, being frenzy-struck,
'The wind-blown clamour of the barnacle-geese.'

(1914)

RUNNING TO PARADISE

As I came over Windy Gap
They threw a halfpenny into my cap,

43

For I am running to Paradise;
And all that I need do is to wish
And somebody puts his hand in the
     dish
To throw me a bit of salted fish:
And there the king is but as the beggar.

My brother Mourteen is worn out
With skelping his big brawling lout,
And I am running to Paradise;
A poor life, do what he can,
And though he keep a dog and a gun,
A serving-maid and a serving-man:
And there the king is but as the beggar.

Poor men have grown to be rich men,
And rich men grown to be poor again,
And I am running to Paradise;
And many a darling wit's grown dull
That tossed a bare heel when at
     school,
Now it has filled an old sock full:
And there the king is but as the beggar.

The wind is old and still at play
While I must hurry upon my way,
For I am running to Paradise;
Yet never have I lit on a friend
To take my fancy like the wind
That nobody can buy or bind:
And there the king is but as the beggar.

(1914)

I

THE WITCH

Toil and grow rich,
What's that but to lie

With a foul witch
And after, drained dry,
To be brought
To the chamber where
Lies one long sought
With despair?

(1914)

II
THE PEACOCK

WHAT'S riches to him
That has made a great peacock
With the pride of his eye?
The wind-beaten, stone-grey,
And desolate Three Rock
Would nourish his whim.
Live he or die
Amid wet rocks and heather,
His ghost will be gay
Adding feather to feather
For the pride of his eye.

(1914)

I
TO A CHILD DANCING IN THE WIND

DANCE there upon the shore;
What need have you to care
For wind or water's roar?
And tumble out your hair
That the salt drops have wet;
Being young you have not known
The fool's triumph, nor yet

45

Love lost as soon as won,
Nor the best labourer dead
And all the sheaves to bind.
What need have you to dread
The monstrous crying of wind?

(1912)

II

TWO YEARS LATER

HAS no one said those daring
Kind eyes should be more learn'd?
Or warned you how despairing
The moths are when they are burned?
I could have warned you; but you are young,
So we speak a different tongue.

O you will take whatever's offered
And dream that all the world's a friend,
Suffer as your mother suffered,
Be as broken in the end.
But I am old and you are young,
And I speak a barbarous tongue.

(1914)

A MEMORY OF YOUTH

THE moments passed as at a play;
I had the wisdom love brings forth;
I had my share of mother-wit,
And yet for all that I could say,
And though I had her praise for it,
A cloud blown from the cut-throat North
Suddenly hid Love's moon away.

Believing every word I said,
I praised her body and her mind
Till pride had made her eyes grow bright,
And pleasure made her cheeks grow red,
And vanity her footfall light,
Yet we, for all that praise, could find
Nothing but darkness overhead.

We sat as silent as a stone,
We knew, though she'd not said a word,
That even the best of love must die,
And had been savagely undone
Were it not that Love upon the cry
Of a most ridiculous little bird
Tore from the clouds his marvellous moon.

(1912)

FALLEN MAJESTY

ALTHOUGH crowds gathered once if she but showed her face,
And even old men's eyes grew dim, this hand alone,
Like some last courtier at a gypsy camping-place
Babbling of fallen majesty, records what's gone.

The lineaments, a heart that laughter has made sweet,
These, these remain, but I record what's gone. A crowd
Will gather, and not know it walks the very street
Whereon a thing once walked that seemed a burning cloud.

(1912)

THE COLD HEAVEN

SUDDENLY I saw the cold and rook-delighting heaven
That seemed as though ice burned and was but the more ice,

And thereupon imagination and heart were driven
So wild that every casual thought of that and this
Vanished, and left but memories, that should be out of season
With the hot blood of youth, of love crossed long ago;
And I took all the blame out of all sense and reason,
Until I cried and trembled and rocked to and fro,
Riddled with light. Ah! when the ghost begins to quicken,
Confusion of the death-bed over, is it sent
Out naked on the roads, as the books say, and stricken
By the injustice of the skies for punishment?

(1912)

THAT THE NIGHT COME

SHE lived in storm and strife,
Her soul had such desire
For what proud death may bring
That it could not endure
The common good of life,
But lived as 'twere a king
That packed his marriage day
With banneret and pennon,
Trumpet and kettledrum,
And the outrageous cannon,
To bundle time away
That the night come.

(1912)

THE MAGI

Now as at all times I can see in the mind's eye,
In their stiff, painted clothes, the pale unsatisfied ones
Appear and disappear in the blue depth of the sky
With all their ancient faces like rain-beaten stones,

48

And all their helms of silver hovering side by side,
And all their eyes still fixed, hoping to find once more,
Being by Calvary's turbulence unsatisfied,
The uncontrollable mystery on the bestial floor.

(1914)

THE DOLLS

A DOLL in the doll-maker's house
Looks at the cradle and bawls:
'That is an insult to us.'
But the oldest of all the dolls,
Who had seen, being kept for show,
Generations of his sort,
Out-screams the whole shelf: 'Although
There's not a man can report
Evil of this place,
The man and the woman bring
Hither, to our disgrace,
A noisy and filthy thing.'
Hearing him groan and stretch
The doll-maker's wife is aware
Her husband has heard the wretch,
And crouched by the arm of his chair,
She murmurs into his ear,
Head upon shoulder leant:
'My dear, my dear, O dear,
It was an accident.'

(1914)

A COAT

I MADE my song a coat
Covered with embroideries

Out of old mythologies
From heel to throat;
But the fools caught it,
Wore it in the world's eyes
As though they'd wrought it.
Song, let them take it,
For there's more enterprise
In walking naked.

(1914)

FROM **The Wild Swans at Coole**

(1919)

THE WILD SWANS AT COOLE

THE trees are in their autumn beauty,
The woodland paths are dry,
Under the October twilight the water
Mirrors a still sky;
Upon the brimming water among the stones
Are nine-and-fifty swans.

The nineteenth autumn has come upon me
Since I first made my count;
I saw, before I had well finished,
All suddenly mount
And scatter wheeling in great broken rings
Upon their clamorous wings.

I have looked upon those brilliant creatures,
And now my heart is sore.
All's changed since I, hearing at twilight,
The first time on this shore,
The bell-beat of their wings above my head,
Trod with a lighter tread.

Unwearied still, lover by lover,
They paddle in the cold
Companionable streams or climb the air;
Their hearts have not grown old;
Passion or conquest, wander where they will,
Attend upon them still.

But now they drift on the still water,
Mysterious, beautiful;
Among what rushes will they build,
By what lake's edge or pool
Delight men's eyes when I awake some day
To find they have flown away?

(1917)

IN MEMORY OF MAJOR ROBERT GREGORY

I

Now that we're almost settled in our house
I'll name the friends that cannot sup with us
Beside a fire of turf in th' ancient tower,
And having talked to some late hour
Climb up the narrow winding stair to bed:
Discoverers of forgotten truth
Or mere companions of my youth,
All, all are in my thoughts to-night being dead.

II

Always we'd have the new friend meet the old
And we are hurt if either friend seem cold,
And there is salt to lengthen out the smart
In the affections of our heart,
And quarrels are blown up upon that head;
But not a friend that I would bring
This night can set us quarrelling,
For all that come into my mind are dead.

III

Lionel Johnson comes the first to mind,
That loved his learning better than mankind,
Though courteous to the worst; much falling he
Brooded upon sanctity

Till all his Greek and Latin learning seemed
A long blast upon the horn that brought
A little nearer to his thought
A measureless consummation that he dreamed.

IV

And that enquiring man John Synge comes next,
That dying chose the living world for text
And never could have rested in the tomb
But that, long travelling, he had come
Towards nightfall upon certain set apart
In a most desolate stony place,
Towards nightfall upon a race
Passionate and simple like his heart.

V

And then I think of old George Pollexfen,
In muscular youth well known to Mayo men
For horsemanship at meets or at racecourses,
That could have shown how pure-bred horses
And solid men, for all their passion, live
But as the outrageous stars incline
By opposition, square and trine;
Having grown sluggish and contemplative.

VI

They were my close companions many a year,
A portion of my mind and life, as it were,
And now their breathless faces seem to look
Out of some old picture-book;
I am accustomed to their lack of breath,
But not that my dear friend's dear son,
Our Sidney and our perfect man,
Could share in that discourtesy of death.

VII

For all things the delighted eye now sees
Were loved by him: the old storm-broken trees

That cast their shadows upon road and bridge;
The tower set on the stream's edge;
The ford where drinking cattle make a stir
Nightly, and startled by that sound
The water-hen must change her ground;
He might have been your heartiest welcomer.

VIII

When with the Galway foxhounds he would ride
From Castle Taylor to the Roxborough side
Or Esserkelly plain, few kept his pace;
At Mooneen he had leaped a place
So perilous that half the astonished meet
Had shut their eyes; and where was it
He rode a race without a bit?
And yet his mind outran the horses' feet.

IX

We dreamed that a great painter had been born
To cold Clare rock and Galway rock and thorn,
To that stern colour and that delicate line
That are our secret discipline
Wherein the gazing heart doubles her might.
Soldier, scholar, horseman, he,
And yet he had the intensity
To have published all to be a world's delight.

X

What other could so well have counselled us
In all lovely intricacies of a house
As he that practised or that understood
All work in metal or in wood,
In moulded plaster or in carven stone?
Soldier, scholar, horseman, he,
And all he did done perfectly
As though he had but that one trade alone.

XI

Some burn damp faggots, others may consume
The entire combustible world in one small room
As though dried straw, and if we turn about
The bare chimney is gone black out
Because the work had finished in that flare.
Soldier, scholar, horseman, he,
As 'twere all life's epitome.
What made us dream that he could comb grey hair?

XII

I had thought, seeing how bitter is that wind
That shakes the shutter, to have brought to mind
All those that manhood tried, or childhood loved
Or boyish intellect approved,
With some appropriate commentary on each;
Until imagination brought
A fitter welcome; but a thought
Of that late death took all my heart for speech.

(1918)

AN IRISH AIRMAN FORESEES HIS DEATH

I know that I shall meet my fate
Somewhere among the clouds above;
Those that I fight I do not hate,
Those that I guard I do not love;
My country is Kiltartan Cross,
My countrymen Kiltartan's poor,
No likely end could bring them loss
Or leave them happier than before.
Nor law, nor duty bade me fight,
Nor public men, nor cheering crowds,
A lonely impulse of delight
Drove to this tumult in the clouds;
I balanced all, brought all to mind,

The years to come seemed waste of breath,
A waste of breath the years behind
In balance with this life, this death.

(1919)

THE COLLAR-BONE OF A HARE

Would I could cast a sail on the water
Where many a king has gone
And many a king's daughter,
And alight at the comely trees and the lawn,
The playing upon pipes and the dancing,
And learn that the best thing is
To change my loves while dancing
And pay but a kiss for a kiss.

I would find by the edge of that water
The collar-bone of a hare
Worn thin by the lapping of water,
And pierce it through with a gimlet, and stare
At the old bitter world where they marry in churches,
And laugh over the untroubled water
At all who marry in churches,
Through the white thin bone of a hare.

(1917)

SOLOMON TO SHEBA

Sang Solomon to Sheba,
And kissed her dusky face,
'All day long from mid-day
We have talked in the one place,
All day long from shadowless noon
We have gone round and round

In the narrow theme of love
Like an old horse in a pound.'

To Solomon sang Sheba,
Planted on his knees,
'If you had broached a matter
That might the learned please,
You had before the sun had thrown
Our shadows on the ground
Discovered that my thoughts, not it,
Are but a narrow pound.'

Sang Solomon to Sheba,
And kissed her Arab eyes,
'There's not a man or woman
Born under the skies
Dare match in learning with us two,
And all day long we have found
There's not a thing but love can make
The world a narrow pound.'

(1918)

TO A YOUNG BEAUTY

DEAR fellow-artist, why so free
With every sort of company,
With every Jack and Jill?
Choose your companions from the best;
Who draws a bucket with the rest
Soon topples down the hill.

You may, that mirror for a school,
Be passionate, not bountiful
As common beauties may,
Who were not born to keep in trim
With old Ezekiel's cherubim
But those of Beauvarlet.

I know what wages beauty gives,
How hard a life her servant lives,
Yet praise the winters gone:
There is not a fool can call me friend,
And I may dine at journey's end
With Landor and with Donne.

(1918)

THE SCHOLARS

BALD heads forgetful of their sins,
Old, learned, respectable bald heads
Edit and annotate the lines
That young men, tossing on their beds,
Rhymed out in love's despair
To flatter beauty's ignorant ear.

All shuffle there; all cough in ink;
All wear the carpet with their shoes;
All think what other people think;
All know the man their neighbour knows.
Lord, what would they say
Did their Catullus walk that way?

(1915)

TOM O'ROUGHLEY

'THOUGH logic-choppers rule the town,
And every man and maid and boy
Has marked a distant object down,
An aimless joy is a pure joy,'
Or so did Tom O'Roughley say
That saw the surges running by,
'And wisdom is a butterfly
And not a gloomy bird of prey.

'If little planned is little sinned
But little need the grave distress.
What's dying but a second wind?
How but in zig-zag wantonness
Could trumpeter Michael be so brave?'
Or something of that sort he said,
'And if my dearest friend were dead
I'd dance a measure on his grave.'

(1918)

LINES WRITTEN IN DEJECTION

WHEN have I last looked on
The round green eyes and the long wavering bodies
Of the dark leopards of the moon?
All the wild witches, those most noble ladies,
For all their broom-sticks and their tears,
Their angry tears, are gone.
The holy centaurs of the hills are vanished;
I have nothing but the embittered sun;
Banished heroic mother moon and vanished,
And now that I have come to fifty years
I must endure the timid sun.

(1917)

THE DAWN

I WOULD be ignorant as the dawn
That has looked down
On that old queen measuring a town
With the pin of a brooch,
Or on the withered men that saw
From their pedantic Babylon
The careless planets in their courses,

59

The stars fade out where the moon comes,
And took their tablets and did sums;
I would be ignorant as the dawn
That merely stood, rocking the glittering coach
Above the cloudy shoulders of the horses;
I would be—for no knowledge is worth a straw—
Ignorant and wanton as the dawn.

(1916)

ON WOMAN

MAY God be praised for woman
That gives up all her mind,
A man may find in no man
A friendship of her kind
That covers all he has brought
As with her flesh and bone,
Nor quarrels with a thought
Because it is not her own.

Though pedantry denies,
It's plain the Bible means
That Solomon grew wise
While talking with his queens,
Yet never could, although
They say he counted grass,
Count all the praises due
When Sheba was his lass,
When she the iron wrought, or
When from the smithy fire
It shuddered in the water:
Harshness of their desire
That made them stretch and yawn,
Pleasure that comes with sleep,
Shudder that made them one.
What else He give or keep

God grant me—no, not here,
For I am not so bold
To hope a thing so dear
Now I am growing old,
But when, if the tale's true,
The Pestle of the moon
That pounds up all anew
Brings me to birth again—
To find what once I had
And know what once I have known,
Until I am driven mad,
Sleep driven from my bed,
By tenderness and care,
Pity, an aching head,
Gnashing of teeth, despair;
And all because of some one
Perverse creature of chance,
And live like Solomon
That Sheba led a dance.

(1916)

THE FISHERMAN

ALTHOUGH I can see him still,
The freckled man who goes
To a grey place on a hill
In grey Connemara clothes
At dawn to cast his flies,
It's long since I began
To call up to the eyes
This wise and simple man.
All day I'd looked in the face
What I had hoped 'twould be
To write for my own race
And the reality;
The living men that I hate,
The dead man that I loved,

The craven man in his seat,
The insolent unreproved,
And no knave brought to book
Who has won a drunken cheer,
The witty man and his joke
Aimed at the commonest ear,
The clever man who cries
The catch-cries of the clown,
The beating down of the wise
And great Art beaten down.

Maybe a twelvemonth since
Suddenly I began,
In scorn of this audience,
Imagining a man,
And his sun-freckled face,
And grey Connemara cloth,
Climbing up to a place
Where stone is dark under froth,
And the down-turn of his wrist
When the flies drop in the stream;
A man who does not exist,
A man who is but a dream;
And cried, 'Before I am old
I shall have written him one
Poem maybe as cold
And passionate as the dawn.'

(1916)

THE HAWK

'CALL down the hawk from the air;
Let him be hooded or caged
Till the yellow eye has grown mild,
For larder and spit are bare,
The old cook enraged,
The scullion gone wild.'

'I will not be clapped in a hood,
Nor a cage, nor alight upon wrist,
Now I have learnt to be proud
Hovering over the wood
In the broken mist
Or tumbling cloud.'

'What tumbling cloud did you cleave,
Yellow-eyed hawk of the mind,
Last evening? that I, who had sat
Dumbfounded before a knave,
Should give to my friend
A pretence of wit.'

(1916)

MEMORY

ONE had a lovely face,
And two or three had charm,
But charm and face were in vain
Because the mountain grass
Cannot but keep the form
Where the mountain hare has lain.

(1916)

THE PEOPLE

'WHAT have I earned for all that work,' I said,
'For all that I have done at my own charge?
The daily spite of this unmannerly town,
Where who has served the most is most defamed,
The reputation of his lifetime lost
Between the night and morning. I might have lived,
And you know well how great the longing has been,

63

Where every day my footfall should have lit
In the green shadow of Ferrara wall;
Or climbed among the images of the past—
The unperturbed and courtly images—
Evening and morning, the steep street of Urbino
To where the Duchess and her people talked
The stately midnight through until they stood
In their great window looking at the dawn;
I might have had no friend that could not mix
Courtesy and passion into one like those
That saw the wicks grow yellow in the dawn;
I might have used the one substantial right
My trade allows: chosen my company,
And chosen what scenery had pleased me best.'
Thereon my phoenix answered in reproof,
'The drunkards, pilferers of public funds,
All the dishonest crowd I had driven away,
When my luck changed and they dared meet my face,
Crawled from obscurity, and set upon me
Those I had served and some that I had fed;
Yet never have I, now nor any time,
Complained of the people.'

                  All I could reply
Was: 'You, that have not lived in thought but deed,
Can have the purity of a natural force,
But I, whose virtues are the definitions
Of the analytic mind, can neither close
The eye of the mind nor keep my tongue from speech.'
And yet, because my heart leaped at her words,
I was abashed, and now they come to mind
After nine years, I sink my head abashed.

(1916)

A THOUGHT FROM PROPERTIUS

SHE might, so noble from head
To great shapely knees

The long flowing line,
Have walked to the altar
Through the holy images
At Pallas Athene's side,
Or been fit spoil for a centaur
Drunk with the unmixed wine.

(1917)

A DEEP-SWORN VOW

OTHERS because you did not keep
That deep-sworn vow have been friends of mine;
Yet always when I look death in the face,
When I clamber to the heights of sleep,
Or when I grow excited with wine,
Suddenly I meet your face.

(1917)

PRESENCES

THIS night has been so strange that it seemed
As if the hair stood up on my head.
From going-down of the sun I have dreamed
That women laughing, or timid or wild,
In rustle of lace or silken stuff,
Climbed up my creaking stair. They had read
All I had rhymed of that monstrous thing
Returned and yet unrequited love.
They stood in the door and stood between
My great wood lectern and the fire
Till I could hear their hearts beating:
One is a harlot, and one a child
That never looked upon man with desire,
And one, it may be, a queen.

(1917)

ON BEING ASKED FOR A WAR POEM

I THINK it better that in times like these
A poet's mouth be silent, for in truth
We have no gift to set a statesman right;
He has had enough of meddling who can please
A young girl in the indolence of her youth,
Or an old man upon a winter's night.

(1916)

Upon a Dying Lady

I

Her Courtesy

WITH the old kindness, the old distinguished grace,
She lies, her lovely piteous head amid dull red hair
Propped upon pillows, rouge on the pallor of her face.
She would not have us sad because she is lying there,
And when she meets our gaze her eyes are laughter-lit,
Her speech a wicked tale that we may vie with her,
Matching our broken-hearted wit against her wit,
Thinking of saints and of Petronius Arbiter.

II

Certain Artists Bring Her Dolls and Drawings

BRING where our Beauty lies
A new modelled doll, or drawing,
With a friend's or an enemy's
Features, or maybe showing
Her features when a tress
Of dull red hair was flowing
Over some silken dress
Cut in the Turkish fashion,
Or, it may be, like a boy's.
We have given the world our passion,
We have naught for death but toys.

She Turns the Dolls' Faces to the Wall

BECAUSE to-day is some religious festival
They had a priest say Mass, and even the Japanese,
Heel up and weight on toe, must face the wall
—Pedant in passion, learned in old courtesies,
Vehement and witty she had seemed—; the Venetian lady
Who had seemed to glide to some intrigue in her red shoes,
Her domino, her panniered skirt copied from Longhi;
The meditative critic; all are on their toes,
Even our Beauty with her Turkish trousers on.
Because the priest must have like every dog his day
Or keep us all awake with baying at the moon,
We and our dolls being but the world were best away.

IV

The End of Day

SHE is playing like a child
And penance is the play,
Fantastical and wild
Because the end of day
Shows her that some one soon
Will come from the house, and say—
Though play is but half done—
'Come in and leave the play.'

V

Her Race

SHE has not grown uncivil
As narrow natures would
And called the pleasures evil
Happier days thought good;
She knows herself a woman,
No red and white of a face,
Or rank, raised from a common
Unreckonable race;
And how should her heart fail her
Or sickness break her will

With her dead brother's valour
For an example still?

Her Courage

WHEN her soul flies to the predestined dancing-place
(I have no speech but symbol, the pagan speech I made
Amid the dreams of youth) let her come face to face,
Amid that first astonishment, with Grania's shade,
All but the terrors of the woodland flight forgot
That made her Diarmuid dear, and some old cardinal
Pacing with half-closed eyelids in a sunny spot
Who had murmured of Giorgione at his latest breath—
Aye, and Achilles, Timor, Babar, Barhaim, all
Who have lived in joy and laughed into the face of Death.

VII

Her Friends Bring Her a Christmas Tree

PARDON, great enemy,
Without an angry thought
We've carried in our tree,
And here and there have bought
Till all the boughs are gay,
And she may look from the bed
On pretty things that may
Please a fantastic head.
Give her a little grace,
What if a laughing eye
Have looked into your face?
It is about to die.

(1917)

EGO DOMINUS TUUS

Hic. On the grey sand beside the shallow stream
    Under your old wind-beaten tower, where still
    A lamp burns on beside the open book

That Michael Robartes left, you walk in the moon
And though you have passed the best of life still trace,
Enthralled by the unconquerable delusion,
Magical shapes.

Ille.   By the help of an image
  I call to my own opposite, summon all
  That I have handled least, least looked upon.

Hic. And I would find myself and not an image.

Ille. That is our modern hope and by its light
  We have lit upon the gentle, sensitive mind
  And lost the old nonchalance of the hand;
  Whether we have chosen chisel, pen or brush,
  We are but critics, or but half create,
  Timid, entangled, empty and abashed,
  Lacking the countenance of our friends.

Hic.   And yet
  The chief imagination of Christendom,
  Dante Alighieri, so utterly found himself
  That he has made that hollow face of his
  More plain to the mind's eye than any face
  But that of Christ.

Ille.   And did he find himself
  Or was the hunger that had made it hollow
  A hunger for the apple on the bough
  Most out of reach? and is that spectral image
  The man that Lapo and that Guido knew?
  I think he fashioned from his opposite
  An image that might have been a stony face
  Staring upon a Bedouin's horse-hair roof
  From doored and windowed cliff, or half upturned
  Among the coarse grass and the camel-dung.
  He set his chisel to the hardest stone.
  Being mocked by Guido for his lecherous life,
  Derided and deriding, driven out
  To climb that stair and eat that bitter bread,
  He found the unpersuadable justice, he found
  The most exalted lady loved by a man.

Hic. Yet surely there are men who have made their art
  Out of no tragic war, lovers of life,
  Impulsive men that look for happiness
  And sing when they have found it.

Ille.   No, not sing,
  For those that love the world serve it in action,
  Grow rich, popular and full of influence,
  And should they paint or write, still it is action:
  The struggle of the fly in marmalade.
  The rhetorician would deceive his neighbours,
  The sentimentalist himself; while art
  Is but a vision of reality.
  What portion in the world can the artist have
  Who has awakened from the common dream
  But dissipation and despair?

Hic.   And yet
  No one denies to Keats love of the world;
  Remember his deliberate happiness.

Ille. His art is happy, but who knows his mind?
  I see a schoolboy when I think of him,
  With face and nose pressed to a sweet-shop window,
  For certainly he sank into his grave
  His senses and his heart unsatisfied,
  And made—being poor, ailing and ignorant,
  Shut out from all the luxury of the world,
  The coarse-bred son of a livery-stable keeper—
  Luxuriant song.

Hic.   Why should you leave the lamp
  Burning alone beside an open book,
  And trace these characters upon the sands?
  A style is found by sedentary toil
  And by the imitation of great masters.

Ille. Because I seek an image, not a book.
  Those men that in their writings are most wise
  Own nothing but their blind, stupefied hearts.
  I call to the mysterious one who yet

Shall walk the wet sands by the edge of the stream
And look most like me, being indeed my double,
And prove of all imaginable things
The most unlike, being my anti-self,
And standing by these characters disclose
All that I seek; and whisper it as though
He were afraid the birds, who cry aloud
Their momentary cries before it is dawn,
Would carry it away to blasphemous men.

(1917)

THE PHASES OF THE MOON

An old man cocked his ear upon a bridge;
He and his friend, their faces to the South,
Had trod the uneven road. Their boots were soiled,
Their Connemara cloth worn out of shape;
They had kept a steady pace as though their beds,
Despite a dwindling and late risen moon,
Were distant still. An old man cocked his ear.

Aherne. What made that sound?

Robartes.   A rat or water-hen
  Splashed, or an otter slid into the stream.
  We are on the bridge; that shadow is the tower,
  And the light proves that he is reading still.
  He has found, after the manner of his kind,
  Mere images; chosen this place to live in
  Because, it may be, of the candle-light
  From the far tower where Milton's Platonist
  Sat late, or Shelley's visionary prince:
  The lonely light that Samuel Palmer engraved,
  An image of mysterious wisdom won by toil;
  And now he seeks in book or manuscript
  What he shall never find.

Aherne.   Why should not you
  Who know it all ring at his door, and speak
  Just truth enough to show that his whole life
  Will scarcely find for him a broken crust
  Of all those truths that are your daily bread;
  And when you have spoken take the roads again?

Robartes. He wrote of me in that extravagant style
  He had learnt from Pater, and to round his tale
  Said I was dead; and dead I choose to be.

Aherne. Sing me the changes of the moon once more;
  True song, though speech: 'mine author sung it me.'

Robartes. Twenty-and-eight the phases of the moon,
  The full and the moon's dark and all the crescents,
  Twenty-and-eight, and yet but six-and-twenty
  The cradles that a man must needs be rocked in;
  For there's no human life at the full or the dark.
  From the first crescent to the half, the dream
  But summons to adventure and the man
  Is always happy like a bird or a beast;
  But while the moon is rounding towards the full
  He follows whatever whim's most difficult
  Among whims not impossible, and though scarred,
  As with the cat-o'-nine-tails of the mind,
  His body moulded from within his body
  Grows comelier. Eleven pass, and then
  Athena takes Achilles by the hair,
  Hector is in the dust, Nietzsche is born,
  Because the hero's crescent is the twelfth.
  And yet, twice born, twice buried, grow he must,
  Before the full moon, helpless as a worm.
  The thirteenth moon but sets the soul at war
  In its own being, and when that war's begun
  There is no muscle in the arm; and after,
  Under the frenzy of the fourteenth moon,
  The soul begins to tremble into stillness,
  To die into the labyrinth of itself!

Aherne. Sing out the song; sing to the end, and sing
  The strange reward of all that discipline.

Robartes. All thought becomes an image and the soul
  Becomes a body: that body and that soul
  Too perfect at the full to lie in a cradle,
  Too lonely for the traffic of the world:
  Body and soul cast out and cast away
  Beyond the visible world.

Aherne.   All dreams of the soul
  End in a beautiful man's or woman's body.

Robartes. Have you not always known it?

Aherne.   The song will have it
  That those that we have loved got their long fingers
  From death, and wounds, or on Sinai's top,
  Or from some bloody whip in their own hands.
  They ran from cradle to cradle till at last
  Their beauty dropped out of the loneliness
  Of body and soul.

Robartes.   The lover's heart knows that.

Aherne. It must be that the terror in their eyes
  Is memory or foreknowledge of the hour
  When all is fed with light and heaven is bare.

Robartes. When the moon's full those creatures of the full
  Are met on the waste hills by country men
  Who shudder and hurry by: body and soul
  Estranged amid the strangeness of themselves,
  Caught up in contemplation, the mind's eye
  Fixed upon images that once were thought,
  For perfected, completed, and immovable
  Images can break the solitude
  Of lovely, satisfied, indifferent eyes.

  And thereupon with aged, high-pitched voice
  Aherne laughed, thinking of the man within,
  His sleepless candle and laborious pen.

Robartes. And after that the crumbling of the moon:
  The soul remembering its loneliness

Shudders in many cradles; all is changed.
It would be the world's servant, and as it serves,
Choosing whatever task's most difficult
Among tasks not impossible, it takes
Upon the body and upon the soul
The coarseness of the drudge.

Aherne.   Before the full
It sought itself and afterwards the world.

Robartes. Because you are forgotten, half out of life,
And never wrote a book, your thought is clear.
Reformer, merchant, statesman, learned man,
Dutiful husband, honest wife by turn,
Cradle upon cradle, and all in flight and all
Deformed, because there is no deformity
But saves us from a dream.

Aherne.   And what of those
That the last servile crescent has set free?

Robartes. Because all dark, like those that are all light,
They are cast beyond the verge, and in a cloud,
Crying to one another like the bats;
And having no desire they cannot tell
What's good or bad, or what it is to triumph
At the perfection of one's own obedience;
And yet they speak what's blown into the mind;
Deformed beyond deformity, unformed,
Insipid as the dough before it is baked,
They change their bodies at a word.

Aherne.   And then?

Robartes. When all the dough has been so kneaded up
That it can take what form cook Nature fancies,
The first thin crescent is wheeled round once more.

Aherne. But the escape; the song's not finished yet.

Robartes. Hunchback and Saint and Fool are the last cres-
cents.
The burning bow that once could shoot an arrow
Out of the up and down, the wagon-wheel

Of beauty's cruelty and wisdom's chatter—
Out of that raving tide—is drawn betwixt
Deformity of body and of mind.

Aherne. Were not our beds far off I'd ring the bell,
Stand under the rough roof-timbers of the hall
Beside the castle door, where all is stark
Austerity, a place set out for wisdom
That he will never find; I'd play a part;
He would never know me after all these years
But take me for some drunken country man;
I'd stand and mutter there until he caught
'Hunchback and Saint and Fool,' and that they came
Under the three last crescents of the moon,
And then I'd stagger out. He'd crack his wits
Day after day, yet never find the meaning.

And then he laughed to think that what seemed hard
Should be so simple—a bat rose from the hazels
And circled round him with its squeaky cry,
The light in the tower window was put out.

(1919)

THE CAT AND THE MOON

THE cat went here and there
And the moon spun round like a top,
And the nearest kin of the moon,
The creeping cat, looked up.
Black Minnaloushe stared at the moon,
For, wander and wail as he would,
The pure cold light in the sky
Troubled his animal blood.
Minnaloushe runs in the grass
Lifting his delicate feet.
Do you dance, Minnaloushe, do you dance?
When two close kindred meet,

What better than call a dance?
Maybe the moon may learn,
Tired of that courtly fashion,
A new dance turn.
Minnaloushe creeps through the grass
From moonlit place to place,
The sacred moon overhead
Has taken a new phase.
Does Minnaloushe know that his pupils
Will pass from change to change,
And that from round to crescent,
From crescent to round they range?
Minnaloushe creeps through the grass
Alone, important and wise,
And lifts to the changing moon
His changing eyes.

(1918)

THE SAINT AND THE HUNCHBACK

Hunchback. Stand up and lift your hand and bless
   A man that finds great bitterness
   In thinking of his lost renown.
   A Roman Caesar is held down
   Under this hump.

Saint.   God tries each man
   According to a different plan.
   I shall not cease to bless because
   I lay about me with the taws
   That night and morning I may thrash
   Greek Alexander from my flesh,
   Augustus Caesar, and after these
   That great rogue Alcibiades.

Hunchback. To all that in your flesh have stood
   And blessed, I give my gratitude,

Honoured by all in their degrees,
But most to Alcibiades.

(1919)

TWO SONGS OF A FOOL

I

A SPECKLED cat and a tame hare
Eat at my hearthstone
And sleep there;
And both look up to me alone
For learning and defence
As I look up to Providence.

I start out of my sleep to think
Some day I may forget
Their food and drink;
Or, the house door left unshut,
The hare may run till it's found
The horn's sweet note and the tooth of the hound.

I bear a burden that might well try
Men that do all by rule,
And what can I
That am a wandering-witted fool
But pray to God that He ease
My great responsibilities?

II

I slept on my three-legged stool by the fire,
The speckled cat slept on my knee;
We never thought to enquire
Where the brown hare might be,
And whether the door were shut.
Who knows how she drank the wind

Stretched up on two legs from the mat,
Before she had settled her mind
To drum with her heel and to leap?
Had I but awakened from sleep
And called her name, she had heard,
It may be, and had not stirred,
That now, it may be, has found
The horn's sweet note and the tooth of the hound.

(1919)

THE DOUBLE VISION OF MICHAEL ROBARTES

I

On the grey rock of Cashel the mind's eye
Has called up the cold spirits that are born
When the old moon is vanished from the sky
And the new still hides her horn.

Under blank eyes and fingers never still
The particular is pounded till it is man.
When had I my own will?
O not since life began.

Constrained, arraigned, baffled, bent and unbent
By these wire-jointed jaws and limbs of wood,
Themselves obedient,
Knowing not evil and good;

Obedient to some hidden magical breath.
They do not even feel, so abstract are they,
So dead beyond our death,
Triumph that we obey.

II

On the grey rock of Cashel I suddenly saw
A Sphinx with woman breast and lion paw,

A Buddha, hand at rest,
Hand lifted up that blest;

And right between these two a girl at play
That, it may be, had danced her life away,
For now being dead it seemed
That she of dancing dreamed.

Although I saw it all in the mind's eye
There can be nothing solider till I die;
I saw by the moon's light
Now at its fifteenth night.

One lashed her tail; her eyes lit by the moon
Gazed upon all things known, all things unknown,
In triumph of intellect
With motionless head erect.

That other's moonlit eyeballs never moved,
Being fixed on all things loved, all things unloved,
Yet little peace he had,
For those that love are sad.

O little did they care who danced between,
And little she by whom her dance was seen
So she had outdanced thought.
Body perfection brought,

For what but eye and ear silence the mind
With the minute particulars of mankind?
Mind moved yet seemed to stop
As 'twere a spinning-top.

In contemplation had those three so wrought
Upon a moment, and so stretched it out
That they, time overthrown,
Were dead yet flesh and bone.

I knew that I had seen, had seen at last
That girl my unremembering nights hold fast
Or else my dreams that fly
If I should rub an eye,

And yet in flying fling into my meat
A crazy juice that makes the pulses beat
As though I had been undone
By Homer's Paragon

Who never gave the burning town a thought;
To such a pitch of folly I am brought,
Being caught between the pull
Of the dark moon and the full,

The commonness of thought and images
That have the frenzy of our western seas.
Thereon I made my moan,
And after kissed a stone,

And after that arranged it in a song
Seeing that I, ignorant for so long,
Had been rewarded thus
In Cormac's ruined house.

(1919)

SOLOMON AND THE WITCH

AND thus declared that Arab lady:
'Last night, where under the wild moon
On grassy mattress I had laid me,
Within my arms great Solomon,
I suddenly cried out in a strange tongue
Not his, not mine.'
           Who understood
Whatever has been said, sighed, sung,
Howled, miau-d, barked, brayed, belled, yelled, cried, crowed,
Thereon replied: 'A cockerel
Crew from a blossoming apple bough
Three hundred years before the Fall,
And never crew again till now,
And would not now but that he thought,
Chance being at one with Choice at last,
All that the brigand apple brought
And this foul world were dead at last.
He that crowed out eternity
Thought to have crowed it in again.
For though love has a spider's eye
To find out some appropriate pain—
Aye, though all passion's in the glance—
For every nerve, and tests a lover
With cruelties of Choice and Chance;
And when at last that murder's over
Maybe the bride-bed brings despair,
For each an imagined image brings
And finds a real image there;
Yet the world ends when these two things,

Though several, are a single light,
When oil and wick are burned in one;
Therefore a blessed moon last night
Gave Sheba to her Solomon.'

'Yet the world stays.'
                'If that be so,
Your cockerel found us in the wrong
Although he thought it worth a crow.
Maybe an image is too strong
Or maybe is not strong enough.'

'The night has fallen; not a sound
In the forbidden sacred grove
Unless a petal hit the ground,
Nor any human sight within it
But the crushed grass where we have lain;
And the moon is wilder every minute.
O! Solomon! let us try again.'

(1921)

AN IMAGE FROM A PAST LIFE

He. Never until this night have I been stirred.
   The elaborate star-light throws a reflection
   On the dark stream,
   Till all the eddies gleam;
   And thereupon there comes that scream
   From terrified, invisible beast or bird:
   Image of poignant recollection.

She. An image of my heart that is smitten through
   Out of all likelihood, or reason,
   And when at last,
   Youth's bitterness being past,
   I had thought that all my days were cast
   Amid most lovely places; smitten as though
   It had not learned its lesson.

82

He. Why have you laid your hands upon my eyes?
   What can have suddenly alarmed you
   Whereon 'twere best
   My eyes should never rest?
   What is there but the slowly fading west,
   The river imaging the flashing skies,
   All that to this moment charmed you?

She. A sweetheart from another life floats there
   As though she had been forced to linger
   From vague distress
   Or arrogant loveliness,
   Merely to loosen out a tress
   Among the starry eddies of her hair
   Upon the paleness of a finger.

He. But why should you grow suddenly afraid
   And start—I at your shoulder—
   Imagining
   That any night could bring
   An image up, or anything
   Even to eyes that beauty had driven mad,
   But images to make me fonder?

She. Now she has thrown her arms above her head;
   Whether she threw them up to flout me,
   Or but to find,
   Now that no fingers bind,
   That her hair streams upon the wind,
   I do not know, that know I am afraid
   Of the hovering thing night brought me.

(1920)

EASTER, 1916

I HAVE met them at close of day
Coming with vivid faces
From counter or desk among grey

83

Eighteenth-century houses.
I have passed with a nod of the head
Or polite meaningless words,
Or have lingered awhile and said
Polite meaningless words,
And thought before I had done
Of a mocking tale or a gibe
To please a companion
Around the fire at the club,
Being certain that they and I
But lived where motley is worn:
All changed, changed utterly:
A terrible beauty is born.

That woman's days were spent
In ignorant good-will,
Her nights in argument
Until her voice grew shrill.
What voice more sweet than hers
When, young and beautiful,
She rode to harriers?
This man had kept a school
And rode our wingèd horse;
This other his helper and friend
Was coming into his force;
He might have won fame in the end,
So sensitive his nature seemed,
So daring and sweet his thought.
This other man I had dreamed
A drunken, vainglorious lout.
He had done most bitter wrong
To some who are near my heart,
Yet I number him in the song;
He, too, has resigned his part
In the casual comedy;
He, too, has been changed in his turn,
Transformed utterly:
A terrible beauty is born.

Hearts with one purpose alone
Through summer and winter seem

Enchanted to a stone
To trouble the living stream.
The horse that comes from the road,
The rider, the birds that range
From cloud to tumbling cloud,
Minute by minute they change;
A shadow of cloud on the stream
Changes minute by minute;
A horse-hoof slides on the brim,
And a horse plashes within it;
The long-legged moor-hens dive,
And hens to moor-cocks call;
Minute by minute they live:
The stone's in the midst of all.

Too long a sacrifice
Can make a stone of the heart.
O when may it suffice?
That is Heaven's part, our part
To murmur name upon name,
As a mother names her child
When sleep at last has come
On limbs that had run wild.
What is it but nightfall?
No, no, not night but death;
Was it needless death after all?
For England may keep faith
For all that is done and said.
We know their dream; enough
To know they dreamed and are dead;
And what if excess of love
Bewildered them till they died?
I write it out in a verse—
MacDonagh and MacBride
And Connolly and Pearse
Now and in time to be,
Wherever green is worn,
Are changed, changed utterly:
A terrible beauty is born.

(1916)

85

ON A POLITICAL PRISONER

SHE that but little patience knew,
From childhood on, had now so much
A grey gull lost its fear and flew
Down to her cell and there alit,
And there endured her fingers' touch
And from her fingers ate its bit.

Did she in touching that lone wing
Recall the years before her mind
Become a bitter, an abstract thing,
Her thought some popular enmity:
Blind and leader of the blind
Drinking the foul ditch where they lie?

When long ago I saw her ride
Under Ben Bulben to the meet,
The beauty of her country-side
With all youth's lonely wildness stirred,
She seemed to have grown clean and sweet
Like any rock-bred, sea-borne bird:

Sea-borne, or balanced on the air
When first it sprang out of the nest
Upon some lofty rock to stare
Upon the cloudy canopy,
While under its storm-beaten breast
Cried out the hollows of the sea.

(1920)

THE LEADERS OF THE CROWD

THEY must to keep their certainty accuse
All that are different of a base intent;
Pull down established honour; hawk for news
Whatever their loose fantasy invent

And murmur it with bated breath, as though
The abounding gutter had been Helicon
Or calumny a song. How can they know
Truth flourishes where the student's lamp has shone,
And there alone, that have no solitude?
So the crowd come they care not what may come.
They have loud music, hope every day renewed
And heartier loves; that lamp is from the tomb.

(1921)

TOWARDS BREAK OF DAY

Was it the double of my dream
The woman that by me lay
Dreamed, or did we halve a dream
Under the first cold gleam of day?

I thought: 'There is a waterfall
Upon Ben Bulben side
That all my childhood counted dear;
Were I to travel far and wide
I could not find a thing so dear.'
My memories had magnified
So many times childish delight.

I would have touched it like a child
But knew my finger could but have touched
Cold stone and water. I grew wild,
Even accusing Heaven because
It had set down among its laws:
Nothing that we love over-much
Is ponderable to our touch.

I dreamed towards break of day,
The cold blown spray in my nostril.
But she that beside me lay
Had watched in bitterer sleep

The marvellous stag of Arthur,
That lofty white stag, leap
From mountain steep to steep.

(1920)

DEMON AND BEAST

FOR certain minutes at the least
That crafty demon and that loud beast
That plague me day and night
Ran out of my sight;
Though I had long perned in the gyre,
Between my hatred and desire,
I saw my freedom won
And all laugh in the sun.

The glittering eyes in a death's head
Of old Luke Wadding's portrait said
Welcome, and the Ormondes all
Nodded upon the wall,
And even Strafford smiled as though
It made him happier to know
I understood his plan.
Now that the loud beast ran
There was no portrait in the Gallery
But beckoned to sweet company,
For all men's thoughts grew clear
Being dear as mine are dear.

But soon a tear-drop started up,
For aimless joy had made me stop
Beside the little lake
To watch a white gull take
A bit of bread thrown up into the air;
Now gyring down and perning there
He splashed where an absurd
Portly green-pated bird

88

Shook off the water from his back;
Being no more demoniac
A stupid happy creature
Could rouse my whole nature.

Yet I am certain as can be
That every natural victory
Belongs to beast or demon,
That never yet had freeman
Right mastery of natural things,
And that mere growing old, that brings
Chilled blood, this sweetness brought;
Yet have no dearer thought
Than that I may find out a way
To make it linger half a day.

O what a sweetness strayed
Through barren Thebaid,
Or by the Mareotic sea
When that exultant Anthony
And twice a thousand more
Starved upon the shore
And withered to a bag of bones!
What had the Caesars but their thrones?

(1920)

THE SECOND COMING

TURNING and turning in the widening gyre
The falcon cannot hear the falconer;
Things fall apart; the centre cannot hold;
Mere anarchy is loosed upon the world,
The blood-dimmed tide is loosed, and everywhere
The ceremony of innocence is drowned;
The best lack all conviction, while the worst
Are full of passionate intensity.

Surely some revelation is at hand;
Surely the Second Coming is at hand.
The Second Coming! Hardly are those words out
When a vast image out of *Spiritus Mundi*
Troubles my sight: somewhere in sands of the desert
A shape with lion body and the head of a man,
A gaze blank and pitiless as the sun,
Is moving its slow thighs, while all about it
Reel shadows of the indignant desert birds.
The darkness drops again; but now I know
That twenty centuries of stony sleep
Were vexed to nightmare by a rocking cradle,
And what rough beast, its hour come round at last,
Slouches towards Bethlehem to be born?

(1920)

A PRAYER FOR MY DAUGHTER

ONCE more the storm is howling, and half hid
Under this cradle-hood and coverlid
My child sleeps on. There is no obstacle
But Gregory's wood and one bare hill
Whereby the haystack- and roof-levelling wind,
Bred on the Atlantic, can be stayed;
And for an hour I have walked and prayed
Because of the great gloom that is in my mind.

I have walked and prayed for this young child an hour
And heard the sea-wind scream upon the tower,
And under the arches of the bridge, and scream
In the elms above the flooded stream;
Imagining in excited reverie
That the future years had come,
Dancing to a frenzied drum,
Out of the murderous innocence of the sea.

May she be granted beauty and yet not
Beauty to make a stranger's eye distraught,

Or hers before a looking-glass, for such,
Being made beautiful overmuch,
Consider beauty a sufficient end,
Lose natural kindness and maybe
The heart-revealing intimacy
That chooses right, and never find a friend.

Helen being chosen found life flat and dull
And later had much trouble from a fool,
While that great Queen, that rose out of the spray,
Being fatherless could have her way
Yet chose a bandy-leggèd smith for man.
It's certain that fine women eat
A crazy salad with their meat
Whereby the Horn of Plenty is undone.

In courtesy I'd have her chiefly learned;
Hearts are not had as a gift but hearts are earned
By those that are not entirely beautiful;
Yet many, that have played the fool
For beauty's very self, has charm made wise,
And many a poor man that has roved,
Loved and thought himself beloved,
From a glad kindness cannot take his eyes.

May she become a flourishing hidden tree
That all her thoughts may like the linnet be,
And have no business but dispensing round
Their magnanimities of sound,
Nor but in merriment begin a chase,
Nor but in merriment a quarrel.
O may she live like some green laurel
Rooted in one dear perpetual place.

My mind, because the minds that I have loved,
The sort of beauty that I have approved,
Prosper but little, has dried up of late,
Yet knows that to be choked with hate
May well be of all evil chances chief.
If there's no hatred in a mind

Assault and battery of the wind
Can never tear the linnet from the leaf.

An intellectual hatred is the worst,
So let her think opinions are accursed.
Have I not seen the loveliest woman born
Out of the mouth of Plenty's horn,
Because of her opinionated mind
Barter that horn and every good
By quiet natures understood
For an old bellows full of angry wind?

Considering that, all hatred driven hence,
The soul recovers radical innocence
And learns at last that it is self-delighting,
Self-appeasing, self-affrighting,
And that its own sweet will is Heaven's will;
She can, though every face should scowl
And every windy quarter howl
Or every bellows burst, be happy still.

And may her bridegroom bring her to a house
Where all's accustomed, ceremonious;
For arrogance and hatred are the wares
Peddled in the thoroughfares.
How but in custom and in ceremony
Are innocence and beauty born?
Ceremony's a name for the rich horn,
And custom for the spreading laurel tree.

(1919)

A MEDITATION IN TIME OF WAR

For one throb of the artery,
While on that old grey stone I sat

Under the old wind-broken tree,
I knew that One is animate,
Mankind inanimate phantasy.

(1920)

Calvary

(1921)

At the beginning of the play the First Musician comes to the front of the bare place, round three sides of which the audience are seated, with a folded cloth hanging from his joined hands. Two other Musicians come, . . . one from either side, and unfold the cloth so that it shuts out the stage, and then fold it again, singing and moving rhythmically. They do the same at the end of the play, which enables the players to leave the stage unseen.

[*Song for the folding and unfolding of the cloth*]

First Musician.

> Motionless under the moon-beam,
> Up to his feathers in the stream;
> Although fish leap, the white heron
> Shivers in a dumbfounded dream.

Second Musician.

> God has not died for the white heron.

Third Musician.

> Although half famished he'll not dare
> Dip or do anything but stare
> Upon the glittering image of a heron,
> That now is lost and now is there.

94

Second Musician.
>God has not died for the white heron.

First Musician.
>But that the full is shortly gone
>And after that is crescent moon,
>It's certain that the moon-crazed heron
>Would be but fishes' diet soon.

Second Musician.
>God has not died for the white heron.
>[*The three Musicians are now seated by the drum, flute, and zither at the back of stage.*

First Musician. The road to Calvary, and I beside it
Upon an ancient stone. Good Friday's come,
The day whereon Christ dreams His passion through.
He climbs up hither but as a dreamer climbs.
The cross that but exists because He dreams it
Shortens His breath and wears away His strength.
And now He stands amid a mocking crowd,
Heavily breathing.
>[*A player with the mask of Christ and carrying a cross has entered and now stands leaning upon the cross.*
>Those that are behind
Climb on the shoulders of the men in front
To shout their mockery: 'Work a miracle,'
Cries one, 'and save yourself'; another cries,
'Call on your father now before your bones
Have been picked bare by the great desert birds';
Another cries, 'Call out with a loud voice
And tell him that his son is cast away
Amid the mockery of his enemies.'

>[*Singing*]
>O, but the mockers' cry
>Makes my heart afraid,
>As though a flute of bone
>Taken from a heron's thigh,
>A heron crazed by the moon,
>Were cleverly, softly played.

95

[*Speaking*]
Who is this from whom the crowd has shrunk,
As though he had some look that terrified?
He has a deathly face, and yet he moves
Like a young foal that sees the hunt go by
And races in the field.
                    [*A player with the mask of Lazarus has entered.*

Lazarus.   He raised me up.
I am the man that died and was raised up;
I am called Lazarus.

Christ.   Seeing that you died,
Lay in the tomb four days and were raised up,
You will not mock at me.

Lazarus.   For four whole days
I had been dead and I was lying still
In an old comfortable mountain cavern
When you came climbing there with a great crowd
And dragged me to the light.

Christ.   I called your name:
'Lazarus, come out,' I said, and you came out
Bound up in cloths, your face bound in a cloth.

Lazarus. You took my death, give me your death instead.

Christ. I gave you life.

Lazarus.   But death is what I ask.
Alive I never could escape your love,
And when I sickened towards my death I thought,
'I'll to the desert, or chuckle in a corner,
Mere ghost, a solitary thing.' I died
And saw no more until I saw you stand
In the opening of the tomb; 'Come out!' you called;
You dragged me to the light as boys drag out
A rabbit when they have dug its hole away;
And now with all the shouting at your heels
You travel towards the death I am denied.
And that is why I have hurried to this road
And claimed your death.

Christil.   But I have conquered death,
And all the dead shall be raised up again.
Lazarus. Then what I heard is true. I thought to die
When my allotted years ran out again;
And that, being gone, you could not hinder it;
But now you will blind with light the solitude
That death has made; you will disturb that corner
Where I had thought I might lie safe for ever.

Christ. I do my Father's will.

Lazarus.   And not your own;
And I was free four days, four days being dead.
Climb up to Calvary, but turn your eyes
From Lazarus that cannot find a tomb
Although he search all height and depth: make way,
Make way for Lazarus that must go search
Among the desert places where there is nothing
But howling wind and solitary birds.   [*He goes out.*

First Musician. The crowd shrinks backward from the face that
      seems
Death-stricken and death-hungry still; and now
Martha, and those three Marys, and the rest
That live but in His love are gathered round Him.
He holds His right arm out, and on His arm
Their lips are pressed and their tears fall; and now
They cast them on the ground before His dirty
Blood-dabbled feet and clean them with their hair.

                    [*Sings*]
                    Take but His love away,
                    Their love becomes a feather
                    Of eagle, swan or gull,
                    Or a drowned heron's feather
                    Tossed hither and thither
                    Upon the bitter spray
                    And the moon at the full.

Christ. I felt their hair upon my feet a moment
And then they fled away—why have they fled?
Why has the street grown empty of a sudden
As though all fled in terror?

97

Judas [*who has just entered*].   I am Judas
  That sold you for the thirty pieces of silver.

Christ. You were beside me every day, and saw
  The dead raised up and blind men given their sight,
  And all that I have said and taught you have known,
  Yet doubt that I am God.

Judas.   I have not doubted;
  I knew it from the first moment that I saw you;
  I had no need of miracles to prove it.

Christ. And yet you have betrayed me.

Judas.   I have betrayed you
  Because you seemed all-powerful.

Christ.   My Father
  Even now, if I were but to whisper it,
  Would break the world in His miraculous fury
  To set me free.

Judas.   And is there not one man
  In the wide world that is not in your power?

Christ. My Father put all men into my hands.

Judas. That was the very thought that drove me wild.
  I could not bear to think you had but to whistle
  And I must do; but after that I thought,
  'Whatever man betrays Him will be free';
  And life grew bearable again. And now
  Is there a secret left I do not know,
  Knowing that if a man betrays a God
  He is the stronger of the two?

Christ.   But if
  'Twere the commandment of that God Himself,
  That God were still the stronger.

Judas.   When I planned it
  There was no live thing near me but a heron
  So full of itself that it seemed terrified.

Christ. But my betrayal was decreed that hour
  When the foundations of the world were laid.

Judas. It was decreed that somebody betray you—
   I'd thought of that—but not that I should do it,
   I the man Judas, born on such a day,
   In such a village, such and such his parents;
   Nor that I'd go with my old coat upon me
   To the High Priest, and chuckle to myself
   As people chuckle when alone, and do it
   For thirty pieces and no more, no less,
   And neither with a nod nor a sent message,
   But with a kiss upon your cheek. I did it,
   I, Judas, and no other man, and now
   You cannot even save me.

Christus.   Begone from me.

                  [Three Roman Soldiers have entered.

First Roman Soldier. He has been chosen to hold up the cross.
   [During what follows, Judas holds up the cross while Christ stands
   with His arms stretched out upon it.

Second Roman Soldier. We'll keep the rest away; they are too
   persistent;
   They are always wanting something.

Third Roman Soldier.   Die in peace.
   There's no one here but Judas and ourselves.

Christ. And who are you that ask your God for nothing?

Third Roman Soldier. We are the gamblers, and when you are
   dead
   We'll settle who is to have that cloak of yours
   By throwing dice.

Second Roman Soldier. Our dice were carved
   Out of an old sheep's thigh at Ephesus.

First Roman Soldier. Although but one of us can win the cloak
   That will not make us quarrel; what does it matter?
   One day one loses and the next day wins.

Second Roman Soldier. Whatever happens is the best, we say,
   So that it's unexpected.

Third Roman Soldier.   Had you sent
A crier through the world you had not found
More comfortable companions for a deathbed
Than three old gamblers that have asked for nothing.

First Roman Soldier. They say you're good and that you made
    the world,
But it's no matter.

Second Roman Soldier. Come now; let us dance
The dance of the dice-throwers, for it may be
He cannot live much longer and has not seen it.

Third Roman Soldier. If he were but the God of dice he'd know
    it,
But he is not that God.

First Roman Soldier.   One thing is plain,
To know that he has nothing that we need
Must be a comfort to him.

Second Roman Soldier.   In the dance
We quarrel for a while, but settle it
By throwing dice, and after that, being friends,
Join hand to hand and wheel about the cross.   [*They dance.*

Christ. My Father, why hast Thou forsaken Me?

        [*Song for the folding and unfolding of the cloth*]

First Musician.

            Lonely the sea-bird lies at her rest,
            Blown like a dawn-blenched parcel of spray
            Upon the wind, or follows her prey
            Under a great wave's hollowing crest.

Second Musician.

            God has not appeared to the birds.

Third Musician.

            The ger-eagle has chosen his part
            In blue deep of the upper air
            Where one-eyed day can meet his stare;
            He is content with his savage heart.

Second Musician.
> God has not appeared to the birds.

First Musician.
> But where have last year's cygnets gone?
> The lake is empty; why do they fling
> White wing out beside white wing?
> What can a swan need but a swan?

Second Musician.
> God has not appeared to the birds.

THE END ·

SAILING TO BYZANTIUM

I

THAT is no country for old men. The young
In one another's arms, birds in the trees
—Those dying generations—at their song,
The salmon-falls, the mackerel-crowded seas,
Fish, flesh, or fowl, commend all summer long
Whatever is begotten, born, and dies.
Caught in that sensual music all neglect
Monuments of unageing intellect.

II

An aged man is but a paltry thing,
A tattered coat upon a stick, unless
Soul clap its hands and sing, and louder sing
For every tatter in its mortal dress,
Nor is there singing school but studying
Monuments of its own magnificence;
And therefore I have sailed the seas and come
To the holy city of Byzantium.

III

O sages standing in God's holy fire
As in the gold mosaic of a wall,
Come from the holy fire, perne in a gyre,
And be the singing-masters of my soul.
Consume my heart away; sick with desire

And fastened to a dying animal
It knows not what it is; and gather me
Into the artifice of eternity.

IV

Once out of nature I shall never take
My bodily form from any natural thing,
But such a form as Grecian goldsmiths make
Of hammered gold and gold enamelling
To keep a drowsy Emperor awake;
Or set upon a golden bough to sing
To lords and ladies of Byzantium
Of what is past, or passing, or to come.

(1927)

THE TOWER

I

WHAT shall I do with this absurdity—
O heart, O troubled heart—this caricature,
Decrepit age that has been tied to me
As to a dog's tail?
                        Never had I more
Excited, passionate, fantastical
Imagination, nor an ear and eye
That more expected the impossible—
No, not in boyhood when with rod and fly,
Or the humbler worm, I climbed Ben Bulben's back
And had the livelong summer day to spend.
It seems that I must bid the Muse go pack,
Choose Plato and Plotinus for a friend
Until imagination, ear and eye,
Can be content with argument and deal
In abstract things; or be derided by
A sort of battered kettle at the heel.

I pace upon the battlements and stare
On the foundations of a house, or where
Tree, like a sooty finger, starts from the earth;
And send imagination forth
Under the day's declining beam, and call
Images and memories
From ruin or from ancient trees,
For I would ask a question of them all.

Beyond the ridge lived Mrs. French, and once
When every silver candlestick or sconce
Lit up the dark mahogany and the wine,
A serving-man, that could divine
That most respected lady's every wish,
Ran and with the garden shears
Clipped an insolent farmer's ears
And brought them in a little covered dish.

Some few remembered still when I was young
A peasant girl commended by a song,
Who'd lived somewhere upon that rocky place,
And praised the colour of her face,
And had the greater joy in praising her,
Remembering that, if walked she there,
Farmers jostled at the fair
So great a glory did the song confer.

And certain men, being maddened by those rhymes,
Or else by toasting her a score of times,
Rose from the table and declared it right
To test their fancy by their sight;
But they mistook the brightness of the moon
For the prosaic light of day—
Music had driven their wits astray—
And one was drowned in the great bog of Cloone.

Strange, but the man who made the song was blind;
Yet, now I have considered it, I find

That nothing strange; the tragedy began
With Homer that was a blind man,
And Helen has all living hearts betrayed.
O may the moon and sunlight seem
One inextricable beam,
For if I triumph I must make men mad.

And I myself created Hanrahan
And drove him drunk or sober through the dawn
From somewhere in the neighbouring cottages.
Caught by an old man's juggleries
He stumbled, tumbled, fumbled to and fro
And had but broken knees for hire
And horrible splendour of desire;
I thought it all out twenty years ago:

Good fellows shuffled cards in an old bawn;
And when that ancient ruffian's turn was on
He so bewitched the cards under his thumb
That all but the one card became
A pack of hounds and not a pack of cards,
And that he changed into a hare.
Hanrahan rose in a frenzy there
And followed up those baying creatures towards—

O towards I have forgotten what—enough!
I must recall a man that neither love
Nor music nor an enemy's clipped ear
Could, he was so harried, cheer;
A figure that has grown so fabulous
There's not a neighbour left to say
When he finished his dog's day:
An ancient bankrupt master of this house.

Before that ruin came, for centuries,
Rough men-at-arms, cross-gartered to the knees
Or shod in iron, climbed the narrow stairs,
And certain men-at-arms there were
Whose images, in the Great Memory stored,
Come with loud cry and panting breast

To break upon a sleeper's rest
While their great wooden dice beat on the board.

As I would question all, come all who can;
Come old, necessitous, half-mounted man;
And bring beauty's blind rambling celebrant;
The red man the juggler sent
Through God-forsaken meadows; Mrs. French,
Gifted with so fine an ear;
The man drowned in a bog's mire,
When mocking Muses chose the country wench.

Did all old men and women, rich and poor,
Who trod upon these rocks or passed this door,
Whether in public or in secret rage
As I do now against old age?
But I have found an answer in those eyes
That are impatient to be gone;
Go therefore; but leave Hanrahan,
For I need all his mighty memories.

Old lecher with a love on every wind,
Bring up out of that deep considering mind
All that you have discovered in the grave,
For it is certain that you have
Reckoned up every unforeknown, unseeing
Plunge, lured by a softening eye,
Or by a touch or a sigh,
Into the labyrinth of another's being;

Does the imagination dwell the most
Upon a woman won or woman lost?
If on the lost, admit you turned aside
From a great labyrinth out of pride,
Cowardice, some silly over-subtle thought
Or anything called conscience once;
And that if memory recur, the sun's
Under eclipse and the day blotted out.

It is time that I wrote my will;
I choose upstanding men
That climb the streams until
The fountain leap, and at dawn
Drop their cast at the side
Of dripping stone; I declare
They shall inherit my pride,
The pride of people that were
Bound neither to Cause nor to State,
Neither to slaves that were spat on,
Nor to the tyrants that spat,
The people of Burke and of Grattan
That gave, though free to refuse—
Pride, like that of the morn,
When the headlong light is loose,
Or that of the fabulous horn,
Or that of the sudden shower
When all streams are dry,
Or that of the hour
When the swan must fix his eye
Upon a fading gleam,
Float out upon a long
Last reach of glittering stream
And there sing his last song.
And I declare my faith:
I mock Plotinus' thought
And cry in Plato's teeth,
Death and life were not
Till man made up the whole,
Made lock, stock and barrel
Out of his bitter soul,
Aye, sun and moon and star, all,
And further add to that
That, being dead, we rise,
Dream and so create
Translunar Paradise.
I have prepared my peace

With learned Italian things
And the proud stones of Greece,
Poet's imaginings
And memories of love,
Memories of the words of women,
All those things whereof
Man makes a superhuman
Mirror-resembling dream.

As at the loophole there
The daws chatter and scream,
And drop twigs layer upon layer.
When they have mounted up,
The mother bird will rest
On their hollow top,
And so warm her wild nest.

I leave both faith and pride
To young upstanding men
Climbing the mountain side,
That under bursting dawn
They may drop a fly;
Being of that metal made
Till it was broken by
This sedentary trade.

Now shall I make my soul,
Compelling it to study
In a learned school
Till the wreck of body,
Slow decay of blood,
Testy delirium
Or dull decrepitude,
Or what worse evil come—
The death of friends, or death
Of every brilliant eye
That made a catch in the breath—
Seem but the clouds of the sky

When the horizon fades;
Or a bird's sleepy cry
Among the deepening shades.

(1927)

Meditations in Time of Civil War

I

Ancestral Houses

SURELY among a rich man's flowering lawns,
Amid the rustle of his planted hills,
Life overflows without ambitious pains;
And rains down life until the basin spills,
And mounts more dizzy high the more it rains
As though to choose whatever shape it wills
And never stoop to a mechanical
Or servile shape, at others' beck and call.

Mere dreams, mere dreams! Yet Homer had not sung
Had he not found it certain beyond dreams
That out of life's own self-delight had sprung
The abounding glittering jet; though now it seems
As if some marvellous empty sea-shell flung
Out of the obscure dark of the rich streams,
And not a fountain, were the symbol which
Shadows the inherited glory of the rich.

Some violent bitter man, some powerful man
Called architect and artist in, that they,
Bitter and violent men, might rear in stone
The sweetness that all longed for night and day,
The gentleness none there had ever known;
But when the master's buried mice can play,
And maybe the great-grandson of that house,
For all its bronze and marble, 's but a mouse.

O what if gardens where the peacock strays
With delicate feet upon old terraces,
Or else all Juno from an urn displays
Before the indifferent garden deities;
O what if levelled lawns and gravelled ways
Where slippered Contemplation finds his ease
And Childhood a delight for every sense,
But take our greatness with our violence?

What if the glory of escutcheoned doors,
And buildings that a haughtier age designed,
The pacing to and fro on polished floors
Amid great chambers and long galleries, lined
With famous portraits of our ancestors;
What if those things the greatest of mankind
Consider most to magnify, or to bless,
But take our greatness with our bitterness?

II

My House

AN ancient bridge, and a more ancient tower,
A farmhouse that is sheltered by its wall,
An acre of stony ground,
Where the symbolic rose can break in flower,
Old ragged elms, old thorns innumerable,
The sound of the rain or sound
Of every wind that blows;
The stilted water-hen
Crossing stream again
Scared by the splashing of a dozen cows;

A winding stair, a chamber arched with stone,
A grey stone fireplace with an open hearth,
A candle and written page.
Il Penseroso's Platonist toiled on
In some like chamber, shadowing forth
How the daemonic rage
Imagined everything.
Benighted travellers

From markets and from fairs
Have seen his midnight candle glimmering.

Two men have founded here. A man-at-arms
Gathered a score of horse and spent his days
In this tumultuous spot,
Where through long wars and sudden night alarms
His dwindling score and he seemed castaways
Forgetting and forgot;
And I, that after me
My bodily heirs may find,
To exalt a lonely mind,
Befitting emblems of adversity.

III

My Table

Two heavy trestles, and a board
Where Sato's gift, a changeless sword,
By pen and paper lies,
That it may moralise
My days out of their aimlessness.
A bit of an embroidered dress
Covers its wooden sheath.
Chaucer had not drawn breath
When it was forged. In Sato's house,
Curved like new moon, moon-luminous,
It lay five hundred years.
Yet if no change appears
No moon; only an aching heart
Conceives a changeless work of art.
Our learned men have urged
That when and where 'twas forged
A marvellous accomplishment,
In painting or in pottery, went
From father unto son
And through the centuries ran
And seemed unchanging like the sword.
Soul's beauty being most adored,
Men and their business took

The soul's unchanging look;
For the most rich inheritor,
Knowing that none could pass Heaven's door
That loved inferior art,
Had such an aching heart
That he, although a country's talk
For silken clothes and stately walk,
Had waking wits; it seemed
Juno's peacock screamed.

IV

My Descendants

HAVING inherited a vigorous mind
From my old fathers, I must nourish dreams
And leave a woman and a man behind
As vigorous of mind, and yet it seems
Life scarce can cast a fragrance on the wind,
Scarce spread a glory to the morning beams,
But the torn petals strew the garden plot;
And there's but common greenness after that.

And what if my descendants lose the flower
Through natural declension of the soul,
Through too much business with the passing hour,
Through too much play, or marriage with a fool?
May this laborious stair and this stark tower
Become a roofless ruin that the owl
May build in the cracked masonry and cry
Her desolation to the desolate sky.

The Primum Mobile that fashioned us
Has made the very owls in circles move;
And I, that count myself most prosperous,
Seeing that love and friendship are enough,
For an old neighbour's friendship chose the house
And decked and altered it for a girl's love,
And know whatever flourish and decline
These stones remain their monument and mine.

V

The Road at My Door

AN affable Irregular,
A heavily-built Falstaffian man,
Comes cracking jokes of civil war
As though to die by gunshot were
The finest play under the sun.

A brown Lieutenant and his men,
Half dressed in national uniform,
Stand at my door, and I complain
Of the foul weather, hail and rain,
A pear tree broken by the storm.

I count those feathered balls of soot
The moor-hen guides upon the stream,
To silence the envy in my thought;
And turn towards my chamber, caught
In the cold snows of a dream.

VI

The Stare's Nest by My Window

THE bees build in the crevices
Of loosening masonry, and there
The mother birds bring grubs and flies.
My wall is loosening; honey-bees,
Come build in the empty house of the stare.

We are closed in, and the key is turned
On our uncertainty; somewhere
A man is killed, or a house burned,
Yet no clear fact to be discerned:
Come build in the empty house of the stare.

A barricade of stone or of wood;
Some fourteen days of civil war;
Last night they trundled down the road

That dead young soldier in his blood:
Come build in the empty house of the stare.

We had fed the heart on fantasies,
The heart's grown brutal from the fare;
More substance in our enmities
Than in our love; O honey-bees,
Come build in the empty house of the stare.

VII

*I See Phantoms of Hatred and of the Heart's Fullness and of the
Coming Emptiness*

I CLIMB to the tower-top and lean upon broken stone,
A mist that is like blown snow is sweeping over all,
Valley, river, and elms, under the light of a moon
That seems unlike itself, that seems unchangeable,
A glittering sword out of the east. A puff of wind
And those white glimmering fragments of the mist sweep by.
Frenzies bewilder, reveries perturb the mind;
Monstrous familiar images swim to the mind's eye.

'Vengeance upon the murderers,' the cry goes up,
'Vengeance for Jacques Molay.' In cloud-pale rags, or in lace,
The rage-driven, rage-tormented, and rage-hungry troop,
Trooper belabouring trooper, biting at arm or at face,
Plunges towards nothing, arms and fingers spreading wide
For the embrace of nothing; and I, my wits astray
Because of all that senseless tumult, all but cried
For vengeance on the murderers of Jacques Molay.

Their legs long, delicate and slender, aquamarine their eyes,
Magical unicorns bear ladies on their backs.
The ladies close their musing eyes. No prophecies,
Remembered out of Babylonian almanacs,
Have closed the ladies' eyes, their minds are but a pool
Where even longing drowns under its own excess;
Nothing but stillness can remain when hearts are full
Of their own sweetness, bodies of their loveliness.

114

The cloud-pale unicorns, the eyes of aquamarine,
The quivering half-closed eyelids, the rags of cloud or of lace,
Or eyes that rage has brightened, arms it has made lean,
Give place to an indifferent multitude, give place
To brazen hawks. Nor self-delighting reverie,
Nor hate of what's to come, nor pity for what's gone,
Nothing but grip of claw, and the eye's complacency,
The innumerable clanging wings that have put out the moon.

I turn away and shut the door, and on the stair
Wonder how many times I could have proved my worth
In something that all others understand or share;
But O! ambitious heart, had such a proof drawn forth
A company of friends, a conscience set at ease,
It had but made us pine the more. The abstract joy,
The half-read wisdom of daemonic images,
Suffice the ageing man as once the growing boy.

(1923)

Nineteen Hundred and Nineteen

I

MANY ingenious lovely things are gone
That seemed sheer miracle to the multitude,
Protected from the circle of the moon
That pitches common things about. There stood
Amid the ornamental bronze and stone
An ancient image made of olive wood—
And gone are Phidias' famous ivories
And all the golden grasshoppers and bees.

We too had many pretty toys when young:
A law indifferent to blame or praise,
To bribe or threat; habits that made old wrong
Melt down, as it were wax in the sun's rays;
Public opinion ripening for so long

We thought it would outlive all future days.
O what fine thought we had because we thought
That the worst rogues and rascals had died out.

All teeth were drawn, all ancient tricks unlearned,
And a great army but a showy thing;
What matter that no cannon had been turned
Into a ploughshare? Parliament and king
Thought that unless a little powder burned
The trumpeters might burst with trumpeting
And yet it lack all glory; and perchance
The guardsmen's drowsy chargers would not prance.

Now days are dragon-ridden, the nightmare
Rides upon sleep: a drunken soldiery
Can leave the mother, murdered at her door,
To crawl in her own blood, and go scot-free;
The night can sweat with terror as before
We pieced our thoughts into philosophy,
And planned to bring the world under a rule,
Who are but weasels fighting in a hole.

He who can read the signs nor sink unmanned
Into the half-deceit of some intoxicant
From shallow wits; who knows no work can stand,
Whether health, wealth or peace of mind were spent
On master-work of intellect or hand,
No honour leave its mighty monument,
Has but one comfort left: all triumph would
But break upon his ghostly solitude.

But is there any comfort to be found?
Man is in love and loves what vanishes,
What more is there to say? That country round
None dared admit, if such a thought were his,
Incendiary or bigot could be found
To burn that stump on the Acropolis,
Or break in bits the famous ivories
Or traffic in the grasshoppers or bees.

When Loie Fuller's Chinese dancers enwound
A shining web, a floating ribbon of cloth,
It seemed that a dragon of air
Had fallen among dancers, had whirled them round
Or hurried them off on its own furious path;
So the Platonic Year
Whirls out new right and wrong,
Whirls in the old instead;
All men are dancers and their tread
Goes to the barbarous clangour of a gong.

III

Some moralist or mythological poet
Compares the solitary soul to a swan;
I am satisfied with that,
Satisfied if a troubled mirror show it,
Before that brief gleam of its life be gone,
An image of its state;
The wings half spread for flight,
The breast thrust out in pride
Whether to play, or to ride
Those winds that clamour of approaching night.

A man in his own secret meditation
Is lost amid the labyrinth that he has made
In art or politics;
Some Platonist affirms that in the station
Where we should cast off body and trade
The ancient habit sticks,
And that if our works could
But vanish with our breath
That were a lucky death,
For triumph can but mar our solitude.

The swan has leaped into the desolate heaven:
That image can bring wildness, bring a rage
To end all things, to end
What my laborious life imagined, even

The half-imagined, the half-written page;
O but we dreamed to mend
Whatever mischief seemed
To afflict mankind, but now
That winds of winter blow
Learn that we were crack-pated when we dreamed.

IV

We, who seven years ago
Talked of honour and of truth,
Shriek with pleasure if we show
The weasel's twist, the weasel's tooth.

V

Come let us mock at the great
That had such burdens on the mind
And toiled so hard and late
To leave some monument behind,
Nor thought of the levelling wind.

Come let us mock at the wise;
With all those calendars whereon
They fixed old aching eyes,
They never saw how seasons run,
And now but gape at the sun.

Come let us mock at the good
That fancied goodness might be gay,
And sick of solitude
Might proclaim a holiday:
Wind shrieked—and where are they?

Mock mockers after that
That would not lift a hand maybe
To help good, wise or great
To bar that foul storm out, for we
Traffic in mockery.

Violence upon the roads: violence of horses;
Some few have handsome riders, are garlanded
On delicate sensitive ear or tossing mane,
But wearied running round and round in their courses
All break and vanish, and evil gathers head:
Herodias' daughters have returned again,
A sudden blast of dusty wind and after
Thunder of feet, tumult of images,
Their purpose in the labyrinth of the wind;
And should some crazy hand dare touch a daughter
All turn with amorous cries, or angry cries,
According to the wind, for all are blind.
But now wind drops, dust settles; thereupon
There lurches past, his great eyes without thought
Under the shadow of stupid straw-pale locks,
That insolent fiend Robert Artisson
To whom the love-lorn Lady Kyteler brought
Bronzed peacock feathers, red combs of her cocks.

(1921)

TWO SONGS FROM A PLAY

I

I saw a staring virgin stand
Where holy Dionysus died,
And tear the heart out of his side,
And lay the heart upon her hand
And bear that beating heart away;
And then did all the Muses sing
Of Magnus Annus at the spring,
As though God's death were but a play.

Another Troy must rise and set,
Another lineage feed the crow,

Another Argo's painted prow
Drive to a flashier bauble yet.
The Roman Empire stood appalled:
It dropped the reins of peace and war
When that fierce virgin and her Star
Out of the fabulous darkness called.

II

In pity for man's darkening thought
He walked that room and issued thence
In Galilean turbulence;
The Babylonian starlight brought
A fabulous, formless darkness in;
Odour of blood when Christ was slain
Made all Platonic tolerance vain
And vain all Doric discipline.

Everything that man esteems
Endures a moment or a day.
Love's pleasure drives his love away,
The painter's brush consumes his dreams;
The herald's cry, the soldier's tread
Exhaust his glory and his might:
Whatever flames upon the night
Man's own resinous heart has fed.

(1927)

FRAGMENTS

I

Locke sank into a swoon;
The Garden died;
God took the spinning-jenny
Out of his side.

II

Where got I that truth?
Out of a medium's mouth,

Out of nothing it came,
Out of the forest loam,
Out of dark night where lay
The crowns of Nineveh.

(1931, 1933)

LEDA AND THE SWAN

A SUDDEN blow: the great wings beating still
Above the staggering girl, her thighs caressed
By the dark webs, her nape caught in his bill,
He holds her helpless breast upon his breast.

How can those terrified vague fingers push
The feathered glory from her loosening thighs?
And how can body, laid in that white rush,
But feel the strange heart beating where it lies?

A shudder in the loins engenders there
The broken wall, the burning roof and tower
And Agamemnon dead.
                              Being so caught up,
So mastered by the brute blood of the air,
Did she put on his knowledge with his power
Before the indifferent beak could let her drop?

(1924)

AMONG SCHOOL CHILDREN

I

I WALK through the long schoolroom questioning;
A kind old nun in a white hood replies;
The children learn to cipher and to sing,
To study reading-books and history,

To cut and sew, be neat in everything
In the best modern way—the children's eyes
In momentary wonder stare upon
A sixty-year-old smiling public man.

II

I dream of a Ledaean body, bent
Above a sinking fire, a tale that she
Told of a harsh reproof, or trivial event
That changed some childish day to tragedy—
Told, and it seemed that our two natures blent
Into a sphere from youthful sympathy,
Or else, to alter Plato's parable,
Into the yolk and white of the one shell.

III

And thinking of that fit of grief or rage
I look upon one child or t'other there
And wonder if she stood so at that age—
For even daughters of the swan can share
Something of every paddler's heritage—
And had that colour upon cheek or hair,
And thereupon my heart is driven wild:
She stands before me as a living child.

IV

Her present image floats into the mind—
Did Quattrocento finger fashion it
Hollow of cheek as though it drank the wind
And took a mess of shadows for its meat?
And I though never of Ledaean kind
Had pretty plumage once—enough of that,
Better to smile on all that smile, and show
There is a comfortable kind of old scarecrow.

V

What youthful mother, a shape upon her lap
Honey of generation had betrayed,

122

And that must sleep, shriek, struggle to escape
As recollection or the drug decide,
Would think her son, did she but see that shape
With sixty or more winters on its head,
A compensation for the pang of his birth,
Or the uncertainty of his setting forth?

VI

Plato thought nature but a spume that plays
Upon a ghostly paradigm of things;
Solider Aristotle played the taws
Upon the bottom of a king of kings;
World-famous golden-thighed Pythagoras
Fingered upon a fiddle-stick or strings
What a star sang and careless Muses heard:
Old clothes upon old sticks to scare a bird.

VII

Both nuns and mothers worship images,
But those the candles light are not as those
That animate a mother's reveries,
But keep a marble or a bronze repose.
And yet they too break hearts—O Presences
That passion, piety or affection knows,
And that all heavenly glory symbolise—
O self-born mockers of man's enterprise;

VIII

Labour is blossoming or dancing where
The body is not bruised to pleasure soul,
Nor beauty born out of its own despair,
Nor blear-eyed wisdom out of midnight oil.
O chestnut tree, great rooted blossomer,
Are you the leaf, the blossom or the bole?
O body swayed to music, O brightening glance,
How can we know the dancer from the dance?

(1927)

123

from A Man Young and Old

First Love

THOUGH nurtured like the sailing moon
In beauty's murderous brood,
She walked awhile and blushed awhile
And on my pathway stood
Until I thought her body bore
A heart of flesh and blood.

But since I laid a hand thereon
And found a heart of stone
I have attempted many things
And not a thing is done,
For every hand is lunatic
That travels on the moon.

She smiled and that transfigured me
And left me but a lout,
Maundering here, and maundering there,
Emptier of thought
Than the heavenly circuit of its stars
When the moon sails out.

IV

The Death of the Hare

I HAVE pointed out the yelling pack,
The hare leap to the wood,
And when I pass a compliment
Rejoice as lover should
At the drooping of an eye,
At the mantling of the blood.

Then suddenly my heart is wrung
By her distracted air
And I remember wildness lost
And after, swept from there,

Am set down standing in the wood
At the death of the hare.

The Secrets of the Old

I HAVE old women's secrets now
That had those of the young;
Madge tells me what I dared not think
When my blood was strong,
And what had drowned a lover once
Sounds like an old song.

Though Margery is stricken dumb
If thrown in Madge's way,
We three make up a solitude;
For none alive to-day
Can know the stories that we know
Or say the things we say:

How such a man pleased women most
Of all that are gone,
How such a pair loved many years
And such a pair but one,
Stories of the bed of straw
Or the bed of down.

(1927)

ALL SOULS' NIGHT

Epilogue to 'A Vision'

MIDNIGHT has come, and the great Christ Church Bell
And many a lesser bell sound through the room;
And it is All Souls' Night,
And two long glasses brimmed with muscatel

Bubble upon the table. A ghost may come;
For it is a ghost's right,
His element is so fine
Being sharpened by his death,
To drink from the wine-breath
While our gross palates drink from the whole wine,

I need some mind that, if the cannon sound
From every quarter of the world, can stay
Wound in mind's pondering
As mummies in the mummy-cloth are wound;
Because I have a marvellous thing to say,
A certain marvellous thing
None but the living mock,
Though not for sober ear;
It may be all that hear
Should laugh and weep an hour upon the clock.

Horton's the first I call. He loved strange thought
And knew that sweet extremity of pride
That's called platonic love,
And that to such a pitch of passion wrought
Nothing could bring him, when his lady died,
Anodyne for his love.
Words were but wasted breath;
One dear hope had he:
The inclemency
Of that or the next winter would be death.

Two thoughts were so mixed up I could not tell
Whether of her or God he thought the most,
But think that his mind's eye,
When upward turned, on one sole image fell;
And that a slight companionable ghost,
Wild with divinity,
Had so lit up the whole
Immense miraculous house
The Bible promised us,
It seemed a gold-fish swimming in a bowl.

On Florence Emery I call the next,
Who finding the first wrinkles on a face
Admired and beautiful,
And by foreknowledge of the future vexed;
Diminished beauty, multiplied commonplace;
Preferred to teach a school
Away from neighbour or friend,
Among dark skins, and there
Permit foul years to wear
Hidden from eyesight to the unnoticed end.

Before that end much had she ravelled out
From a discourse in figurative speech
By some learned Indian
On the soul's journey. How it is whirled about,
Wherever the orbit of the moon can reach,
Until it plunge into the sun;
And there, free and yet fast,
Being both Chance and Choice,
Forget its broken toys
And sink into its own delight at last.

I call MacGregor Mathers from his grave,
For in my first hard spring-time we were friends,
Although of late estranged.
I thought him half a lunatic, half knave,
And told him so, but friendship never ends;
And what if mind seem changed,
And it seem changed with the mind,
When thoughts rise up unbid
On generous things that he did
And I grow half contented to be blind!

He had much industry at setting out,
Much boisterous courage, before loneliness
Had driven him crazed;
For meditations upon unknown thought
Make human intercourse grow less and less;
They are neither paid nor praised.
But he'd object to the host,

The glass because my glass;
A ghost-lover he was
And may have grown more arrogant being a ghost.

But names are nothing. What matter who it be,
So that his elements have grown so fine
The fume of muscatel
Can give his sharpened palate ecstasy
No living man can drink from the whole wine.
I have mummy truths to tell
Whereat the living mock,
Though not for sober ear,
For maybe all that hear
Should laugh and weep an hour upon the clock.

Such thought—such thought have I that hold it tight
Till meditation master all its parts,
Nothing can stay my glance
Until that glance run in the world's despite
To where the damned have howled away their hearts,
And where the blessed dance;
Such thought, that in it bound
I need no other thing,
Would in mind's wandering
As mummies in the mummy-cloth are wound.

(1921)

128

(1933)

IN MEMORY OF EVA GORE-BOOTH AND CON MARKIEVICZ

THE light of evening, Lissadell,
Great windows open to the south,
Two girls in silk kimonos, both
Beautiful, one a gazelle.
But a raving autumn shears
Blossom from the summer's wreath;
The older is condemned to death,
Pardoned, drags out lonely years
Conspiring among the ignorant.
I know not what the younger dreams—
Some vague Utopia—and she seems,
When withered old and skeleton-gaunt,
An image of such politics.
Many a time I think to seek
One or the other out and speak
Of that old Georgian mansion, mix
Pictures of the mind, recall
That table and the talk of youth,
Two girls in silk kimonos, both
Beautiful, one a gazelle.

Dear shadows, now you know it all,
All the folly of a fight
With a common wrong or right.
The innocent and the beautiful

Have no enemy but time;
Arise and bid me strike a match
And strike another till time catch;
Should the conflagration climb,
Run till all the sages know.
We the great gazebo built,
They convicted us of guilt;
Bid me strike a match and blow.

(1929)

DEATH

Nor dread nor hope attend
A dying animal;
A man awaits his end
Dreading and hoping all;
Many times he died,
Many times rose again.
A great man in his pride
Confronting murderous men
Casts derision upon
Supersession of breath;
He knows death to the bone—
Man has created death.

(1929)

A DIALOGUE OF SELF AND SOUL

I

My Soul. I summon to the winding ancient stair;
Set all your mind upon the steep ascent,
Upon the broken, crumbling battlement,

Upon the breathless starlit air,
Upon the star that marks the hidden pole;
Fix every wandering thought upon
That quarter where all thought is done:
Who can distinguish darkness from the soul?

My Self. The consecrated blade upon my knees
  Is Sato's ancient blade, still as it was,
  Still razor-keen, still like a looking-glass
  Unspotted by the centuries;
  That flowering, silken, old embroidery, torn
  From some court-lady's dress and round
  The wooden scabbard bound and wound,
  Can, tattered, still protect, faded adorn.

My Soul. Why should the imagination of a man
  Long past his prime remember things that are
  Emblematical of love and war?
  Think of ancestral night that can,
  If but imagination scorn the earth
  And intellect its wandering
  To this and that and t'other thing,
  Deliver from the crime of death and birth.

My Self. Montashigi, third of his family, fashioned it
  Five hundred years ago, about it lie
  Flowers from I know not what embroidery—
  Heart's purple—and all these I set
  For emblems of the day against the tower
  Emblematical of the night,
  And claim as by a soldier's right
  A charter to commit the crime once more.

My Soul. Such fullness in that quarter overflows
  And falls into the basin of the mind
  That man is stricken deaf and dumb and blind,
  For intellect no longer knows
  Is from the *Ought*, or *Knower* from the *Known*—

That is to say, ascends to Heaven;
Only the dead can be forgiven;
But when I think of that my tongue's a stone.

II

My Self. A living man is blind and drinks his drop.
What matter if the ditches are impure?
What matter if I live it all once more?
Endure that toil of growing up;
The ignominy of boyhood; the distress
Of boyhood changing into man;
The unfinished man and his pain
Brought face to face with his own clumsiness;

The finished man among his enemies?—
How in the name of Heaven can he escape
That defiling and disfigured shape
The mirror of malicious eyes
Casts upon his eyes until at last
He thinks that shape must be his shape?
And what's the good of an escape
If honour find him in the wintry blast?

I am content to live it all again
And yet again, if it be life to pitch
Into the frog-spawn of a blind man's ditch,
A blind man battering blind men;
Or into that most fecund ditch of all,
The folly that man does
Or must suffer, if he woos
A proud woman not kindred of his soul.

I am content to follow to its source
Every event in action or in thought;
Measure the lot; forgive myself the lot!
When such as I cast out remorse
So great a sweetness flows into the breast
We must laugh and we must sing,

132

We are blest by everything,
Everything we look upon is blest.

(1929)

BLOOD AND THE MOON

I

Blessed be this place,
More blessed still this tower;
A bloody, arrogant power
Rose out of the race
Uttering, mastering it,
Rose like these walls from these
Storm-beaten cottages—
In mockery I have set
A powerful emblem up,
And sing it rhyme upon rhyme
In mockery of a time
Half dead at the top.

II

Alexandria's was a beacon tower, and Babylon's
An image of the moving heavens, a log-book of the sun's
    journey and the moon's;
And Shelley had his towers, thought's crowned powers he
    called them once.

I declare this tower is my symbol; I declare
This winding, gyring, spiring treadmill of a stair is my
    ancestral stair;
That Goldsmith and the Dean, Berkeley and Burke have
    travelled there.

Swift beating on his breast in sibylline frenzy blind
Because the heart in his blood-sodden breast had dragged him
    down into mankind,
Goldsmith deliberately sipping at the honey-pot of his mind,

133

And haughtier-headed Burke that proved the State a tree,
That this unconquerable labyrinth of the birds, century after
    century,
Cast but dead leaves to mathematical equality;

And God-appointed Berkeley that proved all things a dream,
That this pragmatical, preposterous pig of a world, its farrow
    that so solid seem,
Must vanish on the instant if the mind but change its theme;

Saeva Indignatio and the labourer's hire,
The strength that gives our blood and state magnanimity of its
    own desire;
Everything that is not God consumed with intellectual fire.

III

The purity of the unclouded moon
Has flung its arrowy shaft upon the floor.
Seven centuries have passed and it is pure;
The blood of innocence has left no stain.
There, on blood-saturated ground, have stood
Soldier, assassin, executioner,
Whether for daily pittance or in blind fear
Or out of abstract hatred, and shed blood,
But could not cast a single jet thereon.
Odour of blood on the ancestral stair!
And we that have shed none must gather there
And clamour in drunken frenzy for the moon.

IV

Upon the dusty, glittering windows cling,
And seem to cling upon the moonlit skies,
Tortoiseshell butterflies, peacock butterflies.
A couple of night-moths are on the wing.
Is every modern nation like the tower,
Half dead at the top? No matter what I said,
For wisdom is the property of the dead,
A something incompatible with life; and power,
Like everything that has the stain of blood,

134

A property of the living; but no stain
Can come upon the visage of the moon
When it has looked in glory from a cloud.

(1928)

VERONICA'S NAPKIN

The Heavenly Circuit; Berenice's Hair;
Tent-pole of Eden; the tent's drapery;
Symbolical glory of the earth and air!
The Father and His angelic hierarchy
That made the magnitude and glory there
Stood in the circuit of a needle's eye.

Some found a different pole, and where it stood
A pattern on a napkin dipped in blood.

(1932)

THE NINETEENTH CENTURY AND AFTER

Though the great song return no more
There's keen delight in what we have:
The rattle of pebbles on the shore
Under the receding wave.

(1932)

THREE MOVEMENTS

Shakespearean fish swam the sea, far away from land;
Romantic fish swam in nets coming to the hand;
What are all those fish that lie gasping on the strand?

(1932)

COOLE AND BALLYLEE, 1931

UNDER my window-ledge the waters race,
Otters below and moor-hens on the top,
Run for a mile undimmed in Heaven's face
Then darkening through 'dark' Raftery's 'cellar' drop,
Run underground, rise in a rocky place
In Coole demesne, and there to finish up
Spread to a lake and drop into a hole.
What's water but the generated soul?

Upon the border of that lake's a wood
Now all dry sticks under a wintry sun,
And in a copse of beeches there I stood,
For Nature's pulled her tragic buskin on
And all the rant's a mirror of my mood:
At sudden thunder of the mounting swan
I turned about and looked where branches break
The glittering reaches of the flooded lake.

Another emblem there! That stormy white
But seems a concentration of the sky;
And, like the soul, it sails into the sight
And in the morning's gone, no man knows why;
And is so lovely that it sets to right
What knowledge or its lack had set awry,
So arrogantly pure, a child might think
It can be murdered with a spot of ink.

Sound of a stick upon the floor, a sound
From somebody that toils from chair to chair;
Beloved books that famous hands have bound,
Old marble heads, old pictures everywhere;
Great rooms where travelled men and children found
Content or joy; a last inheritor
Where none has reigned that lacked a name and fame
Or out of folly into folly came.

A spot whereon the founders lived and died
Seemed once more dear than life; ancestral trees

Or gardens rich in memory glorified
Marriages, alliances and families,
And every bride's ambition satisfied.
Where fashion or mere fantasy decrees
We shift about—all that great glory spent—
Like some poor Arab tribesman and his tent.

We were the last romantics—chose for theme
Traditional sanctity and loveliness;
Whatever's written in what poets name
The book of the people; whatever most can bless
The mind of man or elevate a rhyme;
But all is changed, that high horse riderless,
Though mounted in that saddle Homer rode
Where the swan drifts upon a darkening flood.

(1932)

FOR ANNE GREGORY

'NEVER shall a young man,
Thrown into despair
By those great honey-coloured
Ramparts at your ear,
Love you for yourself alone
And not your yellow hair.'

'But I can get a hair-dye
And set such colour there,
Brown, or black, or carrot,
That young men in despair
May love me for myself alone
And not my yellow hair.'

'I heard an old religious man
But yesternight declare
That he had found a text to prove
That only God, my dear,

137

Could love you for yourself alone
And not your yellow hair.'

(1932)

SWIFT'S EPITAPH

SWIFT has sailed into his rest;
Savage indignation there
Cannot lacerate his breast.
Imitate him if you dare,
World-besotted traveller; he
Served human liberty.

(1931)

THE CHOICE

THE intellect of man is forced to choose
Perfection of the life, or of the work,
And if it take the second must refuse
A heavenly mansion, raging in the dark.
When all that story's finished, what's the news?
In luck or out the toil has left its mark:
That old perplexity an empty purse,
Or the day's vanity, the night's remorse.

(1932)

BYZANTIUM

THE unpurged images of day recede;
The Emperor's drunken soldiery are abed;
Night resonance recedes, night-walkers' song

After great cathedral gong;
A starlit or a moonlit dome disdains
All that man is,
All mere complexities,
The fury and the mire of human veins.

Before me floats an image, man or shade,
Shade more than man, more image than a shade;
For Hades' bobbin bound in mummy-cloth
May unwind the winding path;
A mouth that has no moisture and no breath
Breathless mouths may summon;
I hail the superhuman;
I call it death-in-life and life-in-death.

Miracle, bird or golden handiwork,
More miracle than bird or handiwork,
Planted on the starlit golden bough,
Can like the cocks of Hades crow,
Or, by the moon embittered, scorn aloud
In glory of changeless metal
Common bird or petal
And all complexities of mire or blood.

At midnight on the Emperor's pavement flit
Flames that no faggot feeds, nor steel has lit,
Nor storm disturbs, flames begotten of flame,
Where blood-begotten spirits come
And all complexities of fury leave,
Dying into a dance,
An agony of trance,
An agony of flame that cannot singe a sleeve.

Astraddle on the dolphin's mire and blood,
Spirit after spirit! The smithies break the flood,
The golden smithies of the Emperor!
Marbles of the dancing floor
Break bitter furies of complexity,
Those images that yet

Fresh images beget,
That dolphin-torn, that gong-tormented sea.

(1932)

THE MOTHER OF GOD

THE three-fold terror of love; a fallen flare
Through the hollow of an ear;
Wings beating about the room;
The terror of all terrors that I bore
The Heavens in my womb.

Had I not found content among the shows
Every common woman knows,
Chimney corner, garden walk,
Or rocky cistern where we tread the clothes
And gather all the talk?

What is this flesh I purchased with my pains,
This fallen star my milk sustains,
This love that makes my heart's blood stop
Or strikes a sudden chill into my bones
And bids my hair stand up?

(1932)

VACILLATION

I

BETWEEN extremities
Man runs his course;
A brand, or flaming breath,
Comes to destroy
All those antinomies

Of day and night;
The body calls it death,
The heart remorse.
But if these be right
What is joy?

II

A tree there is that from its topmost bough
Is half all glittering flame and half all green
Abounding foliage moistened with the dew;
And half is half and yet is all the scene;
And half and half consume what they renew,
And he that Attis' image hangs between
That staring fury and the blind lush leaf
May know not what he knows, but knows not grief.

III

Get all the gold and silver that you can,
Satisfy ambition, animate
The trivial days and ram them with the sun,
And yet upon these maxims meditate:
All women dote upon an idle man
Although their children need a rich estate;
No man has ever lived that had enough
Of children's gratitude or woman's love.

No longer in Lethean foliage caught
Begin the preparation for your death
And from the fortieth winter by that thought
Test every work of intellect or faith
And everything that your own hands have wrought,
And call those works extravagance of breath
That are not suited for such men as come
Proud, open-eyed and laughing to the tomb.

IV

My fiftieth year had come and gone,
I sat, a solitary man,

In a crowded London shop,
An open book and empty cup
On the marble table-top.

While on the shop and street I gazed
My body of a sudden blazed;
And twenty minutes more or less
It seemed, so great my happiness,
That I was blessèd and could bless.

V

Although the summer sunlight gild
Cloudy leafage of the sky,
Or wintry moonlight sink the field
In storm-scattered intricacy,
I cannot look thereon,
Responsibility so weighs me down.

Things said or done long years ago,
Or things I did not do or say
But thought that I might say or do,
Weigh me down, and not a day
But something is recalled,
My conscience or my vanity appalled.

VI

A rivery field spread out below,
An odour of the new-mown hay
In his nostrils, the great lord of Chou
Cried, casting off the mountain snow,
'Let all things pass away.'

Wheels by milk-white asses drawn
Where Babylon or Nineveh
Rose; some conqueror drew rein
And cried to battle-weary men,
'Let all things pass away.'

From man's blood-sodden heart are sprung
Those branches of the night and day

Where the gaudy moon is hung.
What's the meaning of all song?
'Let all things pass away.'

VII

The Soul. Seek out reality, leave things that seem.
The Heart. What, be a singer born and lack a theme?
The Soul. Isaiah's coal, what more can man desire?
The Heart. Struck dumb in the simplicity of fire!
The Soul. Look on that fire, salvation walks within.
The Heart. What theme had Homer but original sin?

VIII

Must we part, Von Hügel, though much alike, for we
Accept the miracles of the saints and honour sanctity?
The body of Saint Teresa lies undecayed in tomb,
Bathed in miraculous oil, sweet odours from it come,
Healing from its lettered slab. Those self-same hands
    perchance
Eternalised the body of a modern saint that once
Had scooped out Pharaoh's mummy. I—though heart might
    find relief
Did I become a Christian man and choose for my belief
What seems most welcome in the tomb—play a predestined
    part.
Homer is my example and his unchristened heart.
The lion and the honeycomb, what has Scripture said?
So get you gone, Von Hügel, though with blessings on your
    head.

(1932)

QUARREL IN OLD AGE

WHERE had her sweetness gone?
What fanatics invent
In this blind bitter town,

143

Fantasy or incident
Not worth thinking of,
Put her in a rage.
I had forgiven enough
That had forgiven old age.

All lives that has lived;
So much is certain;
Old sages were not deceived:
Somewhere beyond the curtain
Of distorting days
Lives that lonely thing
That shone before these eyes
Targeted, trod like Spring.

(1932)

REMORSE FOR INTEMPERATE SPEECH

I RANTED to the knave and fool,
But outgrew that school,
Would transform the part,
Fit audience found, but cannot rule
My fanatic[1] heart.

I sought my betters: though in each
Fine manners, liberal speech,
Turn hatred into sport,
Nothing said or done can reach
My fanatic heart.

Out of Ireland have we come.
Great hatred, little room,

[1] I pronounce 'fanatic' in what is, I suppose, the older and more Irish way, so that the last line of each stanza contains but two beats.

Maimed us at the start.
I carry from my mother's womb
A fanatic heart.

(1932)

from Words for Music Perhaps

Crazy Jane and the Bishop

BRING me to the blasted oak
That I, midnight upon the stroke,
(*All find safety in the tomb.*)
May call down curses on his head
Because of my dear Jack that's dead.
Coxcomb was the least he said:
The solid man and the coxcomb.

Nor was he Bishop when his ban
Banished Jack the Journeyman,
(*All find safety in the tomb.*)
Nor so much as parish priest,
Yet he, an old book in his fist,
Cried that we lived like beast and beast:
The solid man and the coxcomb.

The Bishop has a skin, God knows,
Wrinkled like the foot of a goose,
(*All find safety in the tomb.*)
Nor can he hide in holy black
The heron's hunch upon his back,
But a birch-tree stood my Jack:
The solid man and the coxcomb.

Jack had my virginity,
And bids me to the oak, for he

(*All find safety in the tomb.*)
Wanders out into the night
And there is shelter under it,
But should that other come, I spit:
The solid man and the coxcomb.

(1930)

II

Crazy Jane Reproved

I CARE not what the sailors say:
All those dreadful thunder-stones,
All that storm that blots the day
Can but show that Heaven yawns;
Great Europa played the fool
That changed a lover for a bull.
Fol de rol, fol de rol.

To round that shell's elaborate whorl,
Adorning every secret track
With the delicate mother-of-pearl,
Made the joints of Heaven crack:
So never hang your heart upon
A roaring, ranting journeyman.
Fol de rol, fol de rol.

(1930)

III

Crazy Jane on the Day of Judgment

'LOVE is all
Unsatisfied
That cannot take the whole
Body and soul';
And that is what Jane said.

'Take the sour
If you take me,
I can scoff and lour

146

And scold for an hour.'
'That's certainly the case,' said he.

'Naked I lay,
The grass my bed;
Naked and hidden away,
That black day';
And that is what Jane said.

'What can be shown?
What true love be?
All could be known or shown
If Time were but gone.'
'That's certainly the case,' said he.

(1932)

IV

Crazy Jane and Jack the Journeyman

I KNOW, although when looks meet
I tremble to the bone,
The more I leave the door unlatched
The sooner love is gone,
For love is but a skein unwound
Between the dark and dawn.

A lonely ghost the ghost is
That to God shall come;
I—love's skein upon the ground,
My body in the tomb—
Shall leap into the light lost
In my mother's womb.

But were I left to lie alone
In an empty bed,
The skein so bound us ghost to ghost
When he turned his head
Passing on the road that night,
Mine must walk when dead.

(1932)

V

Crazy Jane on God

THAT lover of a night
Came when he would,
Went in the dawning light
Whether I would or no;
Men come, men go,
All things remain in God.

Banners choke the sky;
Men-at-arms tread;
Armoured horses neigh
Where the great battle was
In the narrow pass:
All things remain in God.

Before their eyes a house
That from childhood stood
Uninhabited, ruinous,
Suddenly lit up
From door to top:
All things remain in God.

I had wild Jack for a lover;
Though like a road
That men pass over
My body makes no moan
But sings on:
All things remain in God.

(1932)

VI

Crazy Jane Talks with the Bishop

I MET the Bishop on the road
And much said he and I.
'Those breasts are flat and fallen now,
Those veins must soon be dry;
Live in a heavenly mansion,
Not in some foul sty.'

'Fair and foul are near of kin,
And fair needs foul,' I cried.
'My friends are gone, but that's a truth
Nor grave nor bed denied,
Learned in bodily lowliness
And in the heart's pride.

'A woman can be proud and stiff
When on love intent;
But Love has pitched his mansion in
The place of excrement;
For nothing can be sole or whole
That has not been rent.'

(1933)

VII

Crazy Jane Grown Old Looks at the Dancers

I FOUND that ivory image there
Dancing with her chosen youth,
But when he wound her coal-black hair
As though to strangle her, no scream
Or bodily movement did I dare,
Eyes under eyelids did so gleam;
Love is like the lion's tooth.

When she, and though some said she played
I said that she had danced heart's truth,
Drew a knife to strike him dead,
I could but leave him to his fate;
For no matter what is said
They had all that had their hate;
Love is like the lion's tooth.

Did he die or did she die?
Seemed to die or died they both?
God be with the times when I
Cared not a thraneen for what chanced
So that I had the limbs to try

149

Such a dance as there was danced—
Love is like the lion's tooth.

(1930)

VIII

Girl's Song

I WENT out alone
To sing a song or two,
My fancy on a man,
And you know who.

Another came in sight
That on a stick relied
To hold himself upright:
I sat and cried.

And that was all my song—
When everything is told,
Saw I an old man young
Or young man old?

(1930)

IX

Young Man's Song

'SHE will change,' I cried,
'Into a withered crone.'
The heart in my side,
That so still had lain,
In noble rage replied
And beat upon the bone:

'Uplift those eyes and throw
Those glances unafraid:
She would as bravely show
Did all the fabric fade;
No withered crone I saw
Before the world was made.'

150

Abashed by that report,
For the heart cannot lie,
I knelt in the dirt.
And all shall bend the knee
To my offended heart
Until it pardon me.

(1930)

X

Her Anxiety

EARTH in beauty dressed
Awaits returning spring.
All true love must die,
Alter at the best
Into some lesser thing.
Prove that I lie.

Such body lovers have,
Such exacting breath,
That they touch or sigh.
Every touch they give,
Love is nearer death.
Prove that I lie.

(1930)

XV

Three Things

'O CRUEL Death, give three things back,'
Sang a bone upon the shore;
'A child found all a child can lack,
Whether of pleasure or of rest,
Upon the abundance of my breast':
A bone wave-whitened and dried in the wind.

'Three dear things that women know,'
Sang a bone upon the shore;
'A man if I but held him so

When my body was alive
Found all the pleasure that life gave':
A bone wave-whitened and dried in the wind.

'The third thing that I think of yet,'
Sang a bone upon the shore;
'Is that morning when I met
Face to face my rightful man
And did after stretch and yawn':
A bone wave-whitened and dried in the wind.

(1929)

XVI

Lullaby

BELOVED, may your sleep be sound
That have found it where you fed.
What were all the world's alarms
To mighty Paris when he found
Sleep upon a golden bed
That first dawn in Helen's arms?

Sleep, beloved, such a sleep
As did that wild Tristram know
When, the potion's work being done,
Roe could run or doe could leap
Under oak and beechen bough,
Roe could leap or doe could run;

Such a sleep and sound as fell
Upon Eurotas' grassy bank
When the holy bird, that there
Accomplished his predestined will,
From the limbs of Leda sank
But not from her protecting care.

(1931)

XVII

After Long Silence

SPEECH after long silence; it is right,
All other lovers being estranged or dead,
Unfriendly lamplight hid under its shade,
The curtains drawn upon unfriendly night,
That we descant and yet again descant
Upon the supreme theme of Art and Song:
Bodily decrepitude is wisdom; young
We loved each other and were ignorant.

(1932)

XX

'I Am of Ireland'

'I am of Ireland,
And the Holy Land of Ireland,
And time runs on,' cried she.
'Come out of charity,
Come dance with me in Ireland.'

One man, one man alone
In that outlandish gear,
One solitary man
Of all that rambled there
Had turned his stately head.
'That is a long way off,
And time runs on,' he said,
'And the night grows rough.'

'I am of Ireland,
And the Holy Land of Ireland,
And time runs on,' cried she.
'Come out of charity,
And dance with me in Ireland.'

'The fiddlers are all thumbs,
Or the fiddle-string accursed,

The drums and the kettledrums
And the trumpets all are burst,
And the trombone,' cried he,
'The trumpet and trombone,'
And cocked a malicious eye,
'But time runs on, runs on.'

'I am of Ireland,
And the Holy Land of Ireland,
And time runs on,' cried she.
'Come out of charity,
And dance with me in Ireland.'

(1932)

XXII

Tom the Lunatic

SANG old Tom the lunatic
That sleeps under the canopy:
'What change has put my thoughts astray
And eyes that had so keen a sight?
What has turned to smoking wick
Nature's pure unchanging light?

'Huddon and Duddon and Daniel O'Leary,
Holy Joe, the beggar-man,
Wenching, drinking, still remain
Or sing a penance on the road;
Something made these eyeballs weary
That blinked and saw them in a shroud.

'Whatever stands in field or flood,
Bird, beast, fish or man,
Mare or stallion, cock or hen,
Stands in God's unchanging eye
In all the vigour of its blood;
In that faith I live or die.'

(1932)

The Delphic Oracle upon Plotinus

BEHOLD that great Plotinus swim
Buffeted by such seas;
Bland Rhadamanthus beckons him,
But the Golden Race looks dim,
Salt blood blocks his eyes.

Scattered on the level grass
Or winding through the grove
Plato there and Minos pass,
There stately Pythagoras
And all the choir of Love.

(1932)

from A Woman Young and Old

III

A First Confession

I ADMIT the briar
Entangled in my hair
Did not injure me;
My blenching and trembling
Nothing but dissembling,
Nothing but coquetry.

I long for truth, and yet
I cannot stay from that
My better self disowns,
For a man's attention
Brings such satisfaction
To the craving in my bones.

Brightness that I pull back
From the Zodiac,

Why those questioning eyes
That are fixed upon me?
What can they do but shun me
If empty night replies?

(1929)

VI

Chosen

THE lot of love is chosen. I learnt that much
Struggling for an image on the track
Of the whirling Zodiac.
Scarce did he my body touch,
Scarce sank he from the west
Or found a subterranean rest
On the maternal midnight of my breast
Before I had marked him on his northern way,
And seemed to stand although in bed I lay.

I struggled with the horror of daybreak,
I chose it for my lot! If questioned on
My utmost pleasure with a man
By some new-married bride, I take
That stillness for a theme
Where his heart my heart did seem
And both adrift on the miraculous stream
Where—wrote a learned astrologer—
The Zodiac is changed into a sphere.

(1929)

IX

A Last Confession

WHAT lively lad most pleasured me
Of all that with me lay?
I answered that I gave my soul
And loved in misery,
But had great pleasure with a lad
That I loved bodily.

156

Flinging from his arms I laughed
To think his passion such
He fancied that I gave a soul
Did but our bodies touch,
And laughed upon his breast to think
Beast gave beast as much.

I gave what other women gave
That stepped out of their clothes,
But when this soul, its body off,
Naked to naked goes,
He it has found shall find therein
What none other knows,

And give his own and take his own
And rule in his own right;
And though it loved in misery
Close and cling so tight,
There's not a bird of day that dare
Extinguish that delight.

(1929)

157

The Words Upon the Window-Pane

(1934)

PERSONS IN THE PLAY

Dr. Trench	Cornelius Patterson
Miss Mackenna	Abraham Johnson
John Corbet	Mrs. Mallet

Mrs. Henderson

A lodging-house room, an armchair, a little table in front of it, chairs on either side. A fireplace and window. A kettle on the hob and some tea-things on a dresser. A door to back and towards the right. Through the door one can see an entrance hall. The sound of a knocker. Miss Mackenna passes through and then she re-enters hall together with John Corbet, a man of twenty-two or twenty-three, and Dr. Trench, a man of between sixty and seventy.

Dr. Trench [*in hall*]. May I introduce John Corbet, one of the Corbets of Ballymoney, but at present a Cambridge student? This is Miss Mackenna, our energetic secretary.

        [*They come into room, take off their coats.*

Miss Mackenna. I thought it better to let you in myself. This country is still sufficiently medieval to make spiritualism an undesirable theme for gossip. Give me your coats and hats, I will put them in my own room. It is just across the hall. Better sit down; your watches must be fast. Mrs. Henderson is lying down, as she always does before a séance. We won't begin for ten minutes yet.

        [*She goes out with hats and coats.*

Dr. Trench. Miss Mackenna does all the real work of the Dublin Spiritualists' Association. She did all the correspondence with Mrs. Henderson, and persuaded the landlady to let her this big room and a small room upstairs. We are a poor society and could not guarantee anything in advance. Mrs. Henderson has come from London at her own risk. She was born in Dublin and wants to spread the movement here. She lives very economically and does not expect a great deal. We all

158

give what we can. A poor woman with the soul of an apostle.

John Corbet. Have there been many séances?

Dr. Trench. Only three so far.

John Corbet. I hope she will not mind my scepticism. I have looked into Myers' *Human Personality* and a wild book by Conan Doyle, but am unconvinced.

Dr. Trench. We all have to find the truth for ourselves. Lord Dunraven, then Lord Adare, introduced my father to the famous David Home. My father often told me that he saw David Home floating in the air in broad daylight, but I did not believe a word of it. I had to investigate for myself, and I was very hard to convince. Mrs. Piper, an American trance medium, not unlike Mrs. Henderson, convinced me.

John Corbet. A state of somnambulism and voices coming through her lips that purport to be those of dead persons?

Dr. Trench. Exactly: quite the best kind of mediumship if you want to establish the identity of a spirit. But do not expect too much. There has been a hostile influence.

John Corbet. You mean an evil spirit?

Dr. Trench. The poet Blake said that he never knew a bad man that had not something very good about him. I say a hostile influence, an influence that disturbed the last séance very seriously. I cannot tell you what happened, for I have not been at any of Mrs. Henderson's séances. Trance mediumship has nothing new to show me—I told the young people when they made me their President that I would probably stay at home, that I could get more out of Emanuel Swedenborg than out of any séance. [*A knock*] That is probably old Cornelius Patterson; he thinks they race horses and whippets in the other world, and is, so they tell me, so anxious to find out if he is right that he is always punctual. Miss Mackenna will keep him to herself for some minutes. He gives her tips for Harold's Cross.

[*Miss Mackenna crosses to hall door and admits Cornelius Patterson. She brings him to her room across the hall.*

John Corbet [*who has been wandering about*]. This is a wonderful room for a lodging-house.

Dr. Trench. It was a private house until about fifty years ago. It was not so near the town in those days, and there are large stables at the back. Quite a number of notable people lived here. Grattan was born upstairs; no, not Grattan, Curran perhaps—I forget—but I do know that this house in the early part of the eighteenth century belonged to friends of Jonathan Swift, or rather of Stella. Swift chaffed her in the *Journal to Stella* because of certain small sums of money she lost at cards probably in this very room. That was before Vanessa appeared upon the scene. It was a country-house in those days, surrounded by trees and gardens. Somebody cut some lines from a poem of hers upon the window-pane—tradition says Stella herself. [*A knock*] Here they are, but you will hardly make them out in this light.

    [*They stand in the window. Corbet stoops down to see better. Miss Mackenna and Abraham Johnson enter and stand near door.*

Abraham Johnson. Where is Mrs. Henderson?

Miss Mackenna. She is upstairs; she always rests before a séance.

Abraham Johnson. I must see her before the séance. I know exactly what to do to get rid of this evil influence.

Miss Mackenna. If you go up to see her there will be no séance at all. She says it is dangerous even to think, much less to speak, of an evil influence.

Abraham Johnson. Then I shall speak to the President.

Miss Mackenna. Better talk the whole thing over first in my room. Mrs. Henderson says that there must be perfect harmony.

Abraham Johnson. Something must be done. The last séance was completely spoiled.   [*A knock.*

Miss Mackenna. That may be Mrs. Mallet; she is a very experienced spiritualist. Come to my room, old Patterson and some others are there already.

    [*She brings him to the other room and later crosses to hall door to admit Mrs. Mallet.*

John Corbet. I know those lines well—they are part of a poem Stella wrote for Swift's fifty-fourth birthday. Only three poems of hers—and some lines she added to a poem of Swift's—have come down to us, but they are enough to prove her a better poet than Swift. Even those few words on the window make me think of a seventeenth-century poet, Donne or Crashaw. [*He quotes.*]

       'You taught how I might youth prolong
       By knowing what is right and wrong,
       How from my heart to bring supplies
       Of lustre to my fading eyes.'

How strange that a celibate scholar, well on in life, should keep the love of two such women! He met Vanessa in London at the height of his political power. She followed him to Dublin. She loved him for nine years, perhaps died of love, but Stella loved him all her life.

Dr. Trench. I have shown that writing to several persons, and you are the first who has recognized the lines.

John Corbet. I am writing an essay on Swift and Stella for my doctorate at Cambridge. I hope to prove that in Swift's day men of intellect reached the height of their power—the greatest position they ever attained in society and the State, that everything great in Ireland and in our character, in what remains of our architecture, comes from that day; that we have kept its seal longer than England.

Dr. Trench. A tragic life: Bolingbroke, Harley, Ormonde, all those great Ministers that were his friends, banished and broken.

John Corbet. I do not think you can explain him in that way— his tragedy had deeper foundations. His ideal order was the Roman Senate, his ideal men Brutus and Cato. Such an order and such men had seemed possible once more, but the movement passed and he foresaw the ruin to come. Democracy, Rousseau, the French Revolution; that is why he hated the common run of men,—'I hate lawyers, I hate doctors,' he said, 'though I love Dr. So-and-so and Judge So-and-so'—that is why he wrote *Gulliver,* that is why he wore out his brain, that is why he felt *saeva indignatio,* that is why he sleeps under the greatest epitaph in history. You remember how it goes? It is almost finer in English than in Latin: 'He has gone where fierce indignation can lacerate his heart no more.'

    [*Abraham Johnson comes in, followed by Mrs. Mallet and Cornelius Patterson.*

Abraham Johnson. Something must be done, Dr. Trench, to drive away the influence that has destroyed our séances. I have come here week after week at considerable expense. I am from Belfast. I am by profession a minister of the Gospel, I do a great deal of work among the poor and ignorant. I produce considerable effect by singing and preaching, but I know that my effect should be much greater than it is. My hope is that I shall be able to communicate with the great Evangelist Moody. I want to ask him to stand invisible beside me when I speak or sing, and lay his hands upon my head and give me such a portion of his power that my work may be blessed as the work of Moody and Sankey was blessed.

Mrs. Mallet. What Mr. Johnson says about the hostile influence is quite true. The last two séances were completely spoilt. I am thinking of starting a tea-shop in Folkestone. I followed Mrs. Henderson to Dublin to get my husband's advice, but two spirits kept talking and would not let any other spirit say a word.

Dr. Trench. Did the spirits say the same thing and go through the same drama at both séances?

Mrs. Mallet. Yes—just as if they were characters in some kind of horrible play.

Dr. Trench. That is what I was afraid of.

Mrs. Mallet. My husband was drowned at sea ten years ago, but constantly speaks to me through Mrs. Henderson as if he were still alive. He advises me about everything I do, and I am utterly lost if I cannot question him.

Cornelius Patterson. I never did like the Heaven they talk about in churches: but when somebody told me that Mrs. Mallet's husband ate and drank and went about with his favourite dog, I said to myself, 'That is the place for Corney Patterson.' I came here to find out if it was true, and I declare to God I have not heard one word about it.

Abraham Johnson. I ask you, Dr. Trench, as President of the Dublin Spiritualists' Association, to permit me to read the ritual of exorcism appointed for such occasions. After the last séance I copied it out of an old book in the library of Belfast University. I have it here.

[*He takes paper out of his pocket.*

Dr. Trench. The spirits are people like ourselves, we treat them as our guests and protect them from discourtesy and violence, and every exorcism is a curse or a threatened curse. We do not admit that there are evil spirits. Some spirits are earth-bound—they think they are still living and go over and over some action of their past lives, just as we go over and over some painful thought, except that where they are thought is reality. For instance, when a spirit which has died a violent death comes to a medium for the first time, it re-lives all the pains of death.

Mrs. Mallet. When my husband came for the first time the medium gasped and struggled as if she was drowning. It was terrible to watch.

Dr. Trench. Sometimes a spirit re-lives not the pain of death but some passionate or tragic moment of life. Swedenborg describes this and gives the reason for it. There is an incident of the kind in the *Odyssey*, and many in Eastern literature; the murderer repeats his murder, the robber his robbery, the lover his serenade, the soldier hears the trumpet once again. If I were a Catholic I would say that such spirits were in Purgatory. In vain do we write *requiescat in pace* upon the tomb, for they must suffer, and we in our turn must suffer until God gives peace. Such spirits do not often come to séances unless those séances are held in houses where those spirits lived, or where the event took place. This spirit which speaks those incomprehensible words and does not answer when spoken to is of such a nature. The more patient we are, the more quickly will it pass out of its passion and its remorse.

Abraham Johnson. I am still convinced that the spirit which disturbed the last séance is evil. If I may not exorcise it I will certainly pray for protection.

Dr. Trench. Mrs. Henderson's control, Lulu, is able and experienced and can protect both medium and sitters, but it may help Lulu if you pray that the spirit find rest.

[*Abraham Johnson sits down and prays silently, moving his lips. Mrs. Henderson comes in with Miss Mackenna and others. Miss Mackenna shuts the door.*

Dr. Trench. Mrs. Henderson, may I introduce to you Mr. Corbet, a young man from Cambridge and a sceptic, who hopes that you will be able to convince him?

Mrs. Henderson. We were all sceptics once. He must not expect too much from a first séance. He must persevere.

[*She sits in the armchair, and the others begin to seat themselves. Miss Mackenna goes to John Corbet and they remain standing.*

Miss Mackenna. I am glad that you are a sceptic.

John Corbet. I thought you were a spiritualist.

Miss Mackenna. I have seen a good many séances, and sometimes think it is all coincidence and thought-transference. [*She says this in a low voice.*] Then at other times I think as Dr. Trench does, and then I feel like Job—you know the quotation—the hair of my head stands up. A spirit passes before my face.

Mrs. Mallet. Turn the key, Dr. Trench, we don't want anybody blundering in here. [*Dr. Trench locks door.*] Come and sit here, Miss Mackenna.

Miss Mackenna. No, I am going to sit beside Mr. Corbet.

[*Corbet and Miss Mackenna sit down.*

John Corbet. You feel like Job to-night?

Miss Mackenna. I feel that something is going to happen, that is why I am glad that you are a sceptic.

John Corbet. You feel safer?

Miss Mackenna. Yes, safer.

Mrs. Henderson. I am glad to meet all my dear friends again and to welcome Mr. Corbet amongst us. As he is a stranger I must explain that we do not call up spirits, we make the right conditions and they come. I do not know who is going to come; sometimes there are a great many and the guides choose between them. The guides try to send somebody for everybody but do not always succeed. If you want to speak to some dear friend who has passed over, do not be discouraged. If your friend cannot come this time, maybe he can next time. My control is a dear little girl called Lulu who died when she was five or six years old. She describes the spirits present and tells us what spirit wants to speak. Miss Mackenna, a verse of a hymn, please, the same we had last time, and will everyone join in the singing.

[*They sing the following lines from Hymn 564, Irish Church Hymnal.*

'Sun of my soul, Thou Saviour dear,
It is not night if Thou be near:
O may no earth-born cloud arise
To hide Thee from Thy servant's eyes.'

[*Mrs. Henderson is leaning back in her chair asleep.*

Miss Mackenna [to John Corbet]. She always snores like that when she is going off.

Mrs. Henderson [*in a child's voice*]. Lulu so glad to see all her friends.

Mrs. Mallet. And we are glad you have come, Lulu.

Mrs. Henderson [*in a child's voice*]. Lulu glad to see new friend.

Miss Mackenna [to John Corbet]. She is speaking to you.

John Corbet. Thank you, Lulu.

Mrs. Henderson [*in a child's voice*]. You mustn't laugh at the way I talk.

John Corbet. I am not laughing, Lulu.

Mrs. Henderson [*in a child's voice*]. Nobody must laugh. Lulu does her best but can't say big long words. Lulu sees a tall man here, lots of hair on face [*Mrs. Henderson passes her hands over her cheeks and chin*], not much on the top of his head [*Mrs. Henderson passes her hand over the top of her head*], red necktie, and such a funny sort of pin.

Mrs. Mallet. Yes. . . . Yes. . . .

Mrs. Henderson [*in a child's voice*]. Pin like a horseshoe.

Mrs. Mallet. It's my husband.

Mrs. Henderson [*in a child's voice*]. He has a message.

Mrs. Mallet. Yes.

Mrs Henderson [*in a child's voice*]. Lulu cannot hear. He is too far off. He has come near. Lulu can hear now. He says . . . he says, 'Drive that man away!' He is pointing to somebody in the corner, that corner over there. He says it is the bad man who spoilt everything last time. If they won't drive him away, Lulu will scream.

Miss Mackenna. That horrible spirit again.

Abraham Johnson. Last time he monopolised the séance.

Mrs. Mallet. He would not let anybody speak but himself.

Mrs. Henderson [*in a child's voice*]. They have driven that bad man away. Lulu sees a young lady.

Mrs. Mallet. Is not my husband here?

Mrs. Henderson [*in a child's voice*]. Man with funny pin gone away. Young lady here—Lulu thinks she must be at a fancy dress party, such funny clothes, hair all in curls—all bent down on floor near that old man with glasses.

Dr. Trench. No, I do not recognize her.

Mrs. Henderson [*in a child's voice*]. That bad man, that bad old man in the corner, they have let him come back. Lulu is going to scream. O. . . . O. . . . [*In a man's voice*]. How dare you write to her? How dare you ask if we were married? How dare you question her?

Dr Trench. A soul in its agony—it cannot see us or hear us.

Mrs. Henderson [*upright and rigid, only her lips moving, and still in a man's voice*]. You sit crouching there. Did you not hear what I said? How dare you question her? I found you an ignorant little girl without intellect, without moral ambition. How-many times did I not stay away from great men's houses, how many times forsake the Lord Treasurer, how many times neglect the business of the State that we might read Plutarch together!

> [*Abraham Johnson half rises. Dr. Trench motions him to remain seated.*

Dr. Trench. Silence!

Abraham Johnson. But, Dr. Trench . . .

Dr. Trench. Hush—we can do nothing.

Mrs. Henderson [*speaking as before*]. I taught you to think in every situation of life not as Hester Vanhomrigh would think in that situation, but as Cato or Brutus would, and now you behave like some common slut with her ear against the keyhole.

John Corbet [*to Miss Mackenna*]. It is Swift, Jonathan Swift, talking to the woman he called Vanessa. She was christened Hester Vanhomrigh.

Mrs. Henderson [*in Vanessa's voice*]. I questioned her, Jonathan, because I love. Why have you let me spend hours in your company if you did not want me to love you? [*In Swift's voice.*] When I rebuilt Rome in your mind it was as though I walked its streets. [*In Vanessa's voice.*] Was that all, Jonathan? Was I nothing but a painter's canvas? [*In Swift's voice.*] My God, do you think it was easy? I was a man of strong passions and I had sworn never to marry. [*In Vanessa's voice.*] If you and she are not married, why should we not marry like other men and women? I loved you from the first moment when you came to my mother's house and began to teach me. I thought it would be enough to look at you, to speak to you, to hear you speak. I followed you to Ireland five years ago and I can bear it no longer. It is not enough to look, to speak, to hear. Jonathan, Jonathan, I am a woman, the women Brutus and Cato loved were not different. [*In Swift's voice.*] I have something in my blood that no child must inherit. I have constant attacks of dizziness; I pretend they come from a surfeit of fruit when I was a child. I had them in London. . . . There was a great doctor there, Dr. Arbuthnot; I told him of those attacks of dizziness, I told him of worse things. It was he who explained. There is a line of Dryden's. . . . [*In Vanessa's voice.*] O, I know—'Great wits are sure to madness near allied.' If you had children, Jonathan, my blood would make them healthy. I will take your hand, I will lay it upon my heart—upon the Vanhomrigh

166

blood that has been healthy for generations. [*Mrs. Henderson slowly raises her left hand.*] That is the first time you have touched my body, Jonathan. [*Mrs. Henderson stands up and remains rigid. In Swift's voice.*] What do I care if it be healthy? What do I care if it could make mine healthy? Am I to add another to the healthy rascaldom and knavery of the world? [*In Vanessa's voice.*] Look at me, Jonathan. Your arrogant intellect separates us. Give me both your hands. I will put them upon my breast. [*Mrs. Henderson raises her right hand to the level of her left and then raises both to her breast.*] O, it is white—white as the gambler's dice—white ivory dice. Think of the uncertainty. Perhaps a mad child—perhaps a rascal—perhaps a knave—perhaps not, Jonathan. The dice of the intellect are loaded, but I am the common ivory dice. [*Her hands are stretched out as though drawing somebody towards her.*] It is not my hands that draw you back. My hands are weak, they could not draw you back if you did not love as I love. You said that you have strong passions; that is true, Jonathan—no man in Ireland is so passionate. That is why you need me, that is why you need children, nobody has greater need. You are growing old. An old man without children is very solitary. Even his friends, men as old as he, turn away, they turn towards the young, their children or their children's children. They cannot endure an old man like themselves. [*Mrs. Henderson moves away from the chair, her movements gradually growing convulsive.*] You are not too old for the dice, Jonathan, but a few years if you turn away will make you an old miserable childless man. [*In Swift's voice.*] O God, hear the prayer of Jonathan Swift, that afflicted man, and grant that he may leave to posterity nothing but his intellect that came to him from Heaven. [*In Vanessa's voice.*] Can you face solitude with that mind, Jonathan? [*Mrs. Henderson goes to the door, finds that it is closed.*] Dice, white ivory dice. [*In Swift's voice.*] My God, I am left alone with my enemy. Who locked the door, who locked me in with my enemy? [*Mrs. Henderson beats upon the door, sinks to the floor and then speaks as Lulu.*] Bad old man! Do not let him come back. Bad old man does not know he is dead. Lulu cannot find fathers, mothers, sons that have passed over. Power almost gone. [*Mrs. Mallet leads Mrs. Henderson, who seems very exhausted, back to her chair. She is still asleep. She speaks again as Lulu.*] Another verse of hymn. Everybody sing. Hymn will bring good influence.

[*They sing*]
'If some poor wandering child of Thine
Have spurned to-day the voice divine,
Now, Lord, the gracious work begin;
Let him no more lie down in sin.'

[*During the hymn Mrs. Henderson has been murmuring 'Stella,'
but the singing has almost drowned her voice. The singers draw one
another's attention to the fact that she is speaking. The singing
stops.*

Dr. Trench. I thought she was speaking.
Mrs. Mallet. I saw her lips move.
Dr. Trench. She would be more comfortable with a cushion, but
we might wake her.
Mrs. Mallet. Nothing can wake her out of a trance like that until
she wakes up herself.
[*She brings a cushion and she and Dr. Trench put Mrs. Hen-
derson into a more comfortable position.*
Mrs. Henderson [*in Swift's voice*]. Stella.
Miss Mackenna [*to John Corbet*]. Did you hear that? She said
'Stella.'
John Corbet. Vanessa has gone, Stella has taken her place.
Miss Mackenna. Did you notice the change while we were sing-
ing? The new influence in the room?
John Corbet. I thought I did, but it must have been fancy.
Mrs. Mallet. Hush!
Mrs. Henderson [*in Swift's voice*]. Have I wronged you, beloved
Stella? Are you unhappy? You have no children, you have no
lover, you have no husband. A cross and ageing man for friend—
nothing but that. But no, do not answer—you have answered
already in that poem you wrote for my last birthday. With what
scorn you speak of the common lot of women 'with no endow-
ments but a face—'

'Before the thirtieth year of life
A maid forlorn or hated wife.'

It is the thought of the great Chrysostom who wrote in a famous
passage that women loved according to the soul, loved as saints
can love, keep their beauty longer, have greater happiness than

women loved according to the flesh. That thought has comforted me, but it is a terrible thing to be responsible for another's happiness. There are moments when I doubt, when I think Chrysostom may have been wrong. But now I have your poem to drive doubt away. You have addressed me in these noble words:

> 'You taught how I might youth prolong
> By knowing what is right and wrong;
> How from my heart to bring supplies
> Of lustre to my fading eyes;
> How soon a beauteous mind repairs
> The loss of chang'd or falling hairs;
> How wit and virtue from within
> Can spread a smoothness o'er the skin.'

John Corbet. The words upon the window-pane!

Mrs. Henderson [*in Swift's voice*]. Then, because you understand that I am afraid of solitude, afraid of outliving my friends—and myself—you comfort me in that last verse—you overpraise my moral nature when you attribute to it a rich mantle, but O how touching those words which describe your love:

> 'Late dying may you cast a shred
> Of that rich mantle o'er my head;
> To bear with dignity my sorrow,
> One day alone, then die to-morrow.'

Yes, you will close my eyes, Stella. O, you will live long after me, dear Stella, for you are still a young woman, but you will close my eyes. [*Mrs. Henderson sinks back in chair and speaks as Lulu.*] Bad old man gone. Power all used up. Lulu can do no more. Good-bye, friends. [*Mrs. Henderson, speaking in her own voice.*] Go away, go away! [*She wakes.*] I saw him a moment ago, has he spoilt the séance again?

Mrs. Mallet. Yes, Mrs. Henderson, my husband came, but he was driven away.

Dr. Trench. Mrs. Henderson is very tired. We must leave her to rest. [*To Mrs. Henderson.*] You did your best and nobody can do more than that. [*He takes out money.*

Mrs. Henderson. No. . . . No. . . . I cannot take any money, not after a séance like that.

Dr. Trench. Of course you must take it, Mrs. Henderson.

[*He puts money on table, and Mrs. Henderson gives a furtive glance to see how much it is. She does the same as each sitter lays down his or her money.*

Mrs. Mallet. A bad séance is just as exhausting as a good séance, and you must be paid.

Mrs. Henderson. No. . . . No. . . . Please don't. It is very wrong to take money for such a failure. [*Mrs. Mallet lays down money.*

Cornelius Patterson. A jockey is paid whether he wins or not.

[*He lays down money.*

Miss Mackenna. That spirit rather thrilled me.

[*She lays down money.*

Mrs. Henderson. If you insist, I must take it.

Abraham Johnson. I shall pray for you to-night. I shall ask God to bless and protect your séances.

[*He lays down money. All go out except John Corbet and Mrs. Henderson.*

John Corbet. I know you are tired, Mrs. Henderson, but I must speak to you. I have been deeply moved by what I have heard. This is my contribution to prove that I am satisfied, completely satisfied. [*He puts a note on the table.*

Mrs. Henderson. A pound note—nobody ever gives me more than ten shillings, and yet the séance was a failure.

John Corbet [*sitting down near Mrs. Henderson*]. When I say I am satisfied I do not mean that I am convinced it was the work of spirits. I prefer to think that you created it all, that you are an accomplished actress and scholar. In my essay for my Cambridge doctorate I examine all the explanations of Swift's celibacy offered by his biographers and prove that the explanation you selected was the only plausible one. But there is something I must ask you. Swift was the chief representative of the intellect of his epoch, that arrogant intellect free at last from superstition. He foresaw its collapse. He foresaw Democracy, he must have dreaded the future. Did he refuse to beget children because of that dread? Was Swift mad? Or was it the intellect itself that was mad?

Mrs. Henderson. Who are you talking of, sir?

John Corbet. Swift, of course.

Mrs. Henderson. Swift? I do not know anybody called Swift.

John Corbet. Jonathan Swift, whose spirit seemed to be present tonight.

Mrs. Henderson. What? That dirty old man?

John Corbet. He was neither old nor dirty when Stella and Vanessa loved him

Mrs. Henderson. I saw him very clearly just as I woke up. His clothes were dirty, his face covered with boils. Some disease had made one of his eyes swell up, it stood out from his face like a hen's egg.

John Corbet. He looked like that in his old age. Stella had been dead a long time. His brain had gone, his friends had deserted him. The man appointed to take care of him beat him to keep him quiet.

Mrs. Henderson. Now they are old, now they are young. They change all in a moment as their thought changes. It is sometimes a terrible thing to be out of the body, God help us all.

Dr. Trench [at doorway]. Come along, Corbet, Mrs. Henderson is tired out.

John Corbet. Good-bye, Mrs. Henderson.

[*He goes out with Dr. Trench. All the sitters except Miss Mackenna, who has returned to her room, pass along the passage on their way to the front door. Mrs. Henderson counts the money, finds her purse, which is in a vase on the mantelpiece, and puts the money in it.*]

Mrs. Henderson. How tired I am! I'd be the better of a cup of tea. [*She finds the teapot and puts kettle on fire, and then as she crouches down by the hearth suddenly lifts up her hands and counts her fingers, speaking in Swift's voice.*] Five great Ministers that were my friends are gone, ten great Ministers that were my friends are gone. I have not fingers enough to count the great Ministers that were my friends and that are gone. [*She wakes with a start and speaks in her own voice.*] Where did I put that tea-caddy? Ah! there it is. And there should be a cup and saucer. [*She finds the saucer.*] But where's the cup? [*She moves aimlessly about the stage and then, letting the saucer fall and break, speaks in Swift's voice.*] Perish the day on which I was born!

THE END

171

FROM A Full Moon in March: "Parnell's Funeral" and Other Poems

(1935)

PARNELL'S FUNERAL

I

UNDER the Great Comedian's tomb the crowd.
A bundle of tempestuous cloud is blown
About the sky; where that is clear of cloud
Brightness remains; a brighter star shoots down;
What shudders run through all that animal blood?
What is this sacrifice? Can someone there
Recall the Cretan barb that pierced a star?

Rich foliage that the starlight glittered through,
A frenzied crowd, and where the branches sprang
A beautiful seated boy; a sacred bow;
A woman, and an arrow on a string;
A pierced boy, image of a star laid low.
That woman, the Great Mother imaging,
Cut out his heart. Some master of design
Stamped boy and tree upon Sicilian coin.

An age is the reversal of an age:
When strangers murdered Emmet, Fitzgerald, Tone,
We lived like men that watched a painted stage.
What matter for the scene, the scene once gone:
It had not touched our lives. But popular rage,
Hysterica passio dragged this quarry down.
None shared our guilt; nor did we play a part
Upon a painted stage when we devoured his heart.

Come, fix upon me that accusing eye.
I thirst for accusation. All that was sung,
All that was said in Ireland is a lie
Bred out of the contagion of the throng,
Saving the rhyme rats hear before they die.
Leave nothing but the nothings that belong
To this bare soul, let all men judge that can
Whether it be an animal or a man.

II

The rest I pass, one sentence I unsay.
Had de Valéra eaten Parnell's heart
No loose-lipped demagogue had won the day,
No civil rancour torn the land apart.

Had Cosgrave eaten Parnell's heart, the land's
Imagination had been satisfied,
Or lacking that, government in such hands,
O'Higgins its sole statesman had not died.

Had even O'Duffy—but I name no more—
Their school a crowd, his master solitude;
Through Jonathan Swift's dark grove he passed, and there
Plucked bitter wisdom that enriched his blood.

(1934)

CHURCH AND STATE

HERE is fresh matter, poet,
Matter for old age meet;
Might of the Church and the State,
Their mobs put under their feet.
O but heart's wine shall run pure,
Mind's bread grow sweet.

That were a cowardly song,
Wander in dreams no more;
What if the Church and the State
Are the mob that howls at the door!
Wine shall run thick to the end,
Bread taste sour.

(1934)

from Supernatural Songs

I

Ribh at the Tomb of Baile and Aillinn

BECAUSE you have found me in the pitch-dark night
With open book you ask me what I do.
Mark and digest my tale, carry it afar
To those that never saw this tonsured head
Nor heard this voice that ninety years have cracked.
Of Baile and Aillinn you need not speak,
All know their tale, all know what leaf and twig,
What juncture of the apple and the yew,
Surmount their bones; but speak what none have heard.

The miracle that gave them such a death
Transfigured to pure substance what had once
Been bone and sinew; when such bodies join
There is no touching here, nor touching there,
Nor straining joy, but whole is joined to whole;
For the intercourse of angels is a light
Where for its moment both seem lost, consumed.

Here in the pitch-dark atmosphere above
The trembling of the apple and the yew,
Here on the anniversary of their death,
The anniversary of their first embrace,
Those lovers, purified by tragedy,

Hurry into each other's arms; these eyes,
By water, herb and solitary prayer
Made aquiline, are open to that light.
Though somewhat broken by the leaves, that light
Lies in a circle on the grass; therein
I turn the pages of my holy book.

(1934)

III

Ribh in Ecstasy

WHAT matter that you understood no word!
Doubtless I spoke or sang what I had heard
In broken sentences. My soul had found
All happiness in its own cause or ground.
Godhead on Godhead in sexual spasm begot
Godhead. Some shadow fell. My soul forgot
Those amorous cries that out of quiet come
And must the common round of day resume.

(1935)

IV

There

THERE all the barrel-hoops are knit,
There all the serpent-tails are bit,
There all the gyres converge in one,
There all the planets drop in the Sun.

(1935)

VI

He and She

As the moon sidles up
Must she sidle up,
As trips the scared moon
Away must she trip:
'His light had struck me blind
Dared I stop.'

175

She sings as the moon sings:
'I am I, am I;
The greater grows my light
The further that I fly.'
All creation shivers
With that sweet cry.

(1934)

VIII

Whence Had They Come?

ETERNITY is passion, girl or boy
Cry at the onset of their sexual joy
'For ever and for ever'; then awake
Ignorant what Dramatis Personae spake;
A passion-driven exultant man sings out
Sentences that he has never thought;
The Flagellant lashes those submissive loins
Ignorant what that dramatist enjoins,
What master made the lash. Whence had they come,
The hand and lash that beat down frigid Rome?
What sacred drama through her body heaved
When world-transforming Charlemagne was conceived?

(1935)

IX

The Four Ages of Man

HE with body waged a fight,
But body won; it walks upright.

Then he struggled with the heart;
Innocence and peace depart.

Then he struggled with the mind;
His proud heart he left behind.

Now his wars on God begin;
At stroke of midnight God shall win.

(1934)

Meru

CIVILISATION is hooped together, brought
Under a rule, under the semblance of peace
By manifold illusion; but man's life is thought,
And he, despite his terror, cannot cease
Ravening through century after century,
Ravening, raging, and uprooting that he may come
Into the desolation of reality:
Egypt and Greece good-bye, and good-bye, Rome!
Hermits upon Mount Meru or Everest,
Caverned in night under the drifted snow,
Or where that snow and winter's dreadful blast
Beat down upon their naked bodies, know
That day brings round the night, that before dawn
His glory and his monuments are gone.

(1934)

THE GYRES

THE GYRES! the gyres! Old Rocky Face, look forth;
Things thought too long can be no longer thought
For beauty dies of beauty, worth of worth,
And ancient lineaments are blotted out.
Irrational streams of blood are staining earth;
Empedocles has thrown all things about;
Hector is dead and there's a light in Troy;
We that look on but laugh in tragic joy.

What matter though numb nightmare ride on top
And blood and mire the sensitive body stain?
What matter? Heave no sigh, let no tear drop,
A greater, a more gracious time has gone;
For painted forms or boxes of make-up
In ancient tombs I sighed, but not again;
What matter? Out of Cavern comes a voice
And all it knows is that one word 'Rejoice.'

Conduct and work grow coarse, and coarse the soul,
What matter? Those that Rocky Face holds dear,
Lovers of horses and of women, shall
From marble of a broken sepulchre
Or dark betwixt the polecat and the owl,
Or any rich, dark nothing disinter
The workman, noble and saint, and all things run
On that unfashionable gyre again.

(1938)

LAPIS LAZULI

(*For Harry Clifton*)

I HAVE heard that hysterical women say
They are sick of the palette and fiddle-bow,
Of poets that are always gay,
For everybody knows or else should know
That if nothing drastic is done
Aeroplane and Zeppelin will come out,
Pitch like King Billy bomb-balls in
Until the town lie beaten flat.

All perform their tragic play,
There struts Hamlet, there is Lear,
That's Ophelia, that Cordelia;
Yet they, should the last scene be there,
The great stage curtain about to drop,
If worthy their prominent part in the play,
Do not break up their lines to weep.
They know that Hamlet and Lear are gay;
Gaiety transfiguring all that dread.
All men have aimed at, found and lost;
Black out; Heaven blazing into the head:
Tragedy wrought to its uttermost.
Though Hamlet rambles and Lear rages,
And all the drop-scenes drop at once
Upon a hundred thousand stages,
It cannot grow by an inch or an ounce.

On their own feet they came, or on shipboard,
Camel-back, horse-back, ass-back, mule-back,
Old civilisations put to the sword.
Then they and their wisdom went to rack:
No handiwork of Callimachus,
Who handled marble as if it were bronze,
Made draperies that seemed to rise
When sea-wind swept the corner, stands;
His long lamp chimney shaped like the stem

Of a slender palm, stood but a day;
All things fall and are built again
And those that build them again are gay.

Two Chinamen, behind them a third,
Are carved in Lapis Lazuli,
Over them flies a long-legged bird,
A symbol of longevity;
The third, doubtless a serving-man,
Carries a musical instrument.

Every discoloration of the stone,
Every accidental crack or dent,
Seems a water-course or an avalanche,
Or lofty slope where it still snows
Though doubtless plum or cherry-branch
Sweetens the little half-way house
Those Chinamen climb towards, and I
Delight to imagine them seated there;
There, on the mountain and the sky,
On all the tragic scene they stare.
One asks for mournful melodies;
Accomplished fingers begin to play.
Their eyes mid many wrinkles, their eyes,
Their ancient, glittering eyes, are gay.

(1938)

THE THREE BUSHES

(An incident from the 'Historia mei Temporis' of the Abbé Michel
de Bourdeille)

SAID lady once to lover,
'None can rely upon
A love that lacks its proper food;
And if your love were gone

180

How could you sing those songs of love?
I should be blamed, young man.
                    O my dear, O my dear.

'Have no lit candles in your room,'
That lovely lady said,
'That I at midnight by the clock
May creep into your bed,
For if I saw myself creep in
I think I should drop dead.'
                    O my dear, O my dear.

'I love a man in secret,
Dear chambermaid,' said she.
'I know that I must drop down dead
If he stop loving me,
Yet what could I but drop down dead
If I lost my chastity?
                    O my dear, O my dear.

'So you must lie beside him
And let him think me there,
And maybe we are all the same
Where no candles are,
And maybe we are all the same
That strip the body bare.'
                    O my dear, O my dear.

But no dogs barked and midnights chimed,
And through the chime she'd say,
'That was a lucky thought of mine,
My lover looked so gay';
But heaved a sigh if the chambermaid
Looked half asleep all day.
                    O my dear, O my dear.

'No, not another song,' said he,
'Because my lady came
A year ago for the first time

At midnight to my room,
And I must lie between the sheets
When the clock begins to chime.'
                    O my dear, O my dear.

'A laughing, crying, sacred song,
A leching song,' they said.
Did ever men hear such a song?
No, but that day they did.
Did ever man ride such a race?
No, not until he rode.
                    O my dear, O my dear.

But when his horse had put its hoof
Into a rabbit-hole
He dropped upon his head and died.
His lady saw it all
And dropped and died thereon, for she
Loved him with her soul.
                    O my dear, O my dear.

The chambermaid lived long, and took
Their graves into her charge,
And there two bushes planted
That when they had grown large
Seemed sprung from but a single root
So did their roses merge.
                    O my dear, O my dear.

When she was old and dying,
The priest came where she was;
She made a full confession.
Long looked he in her face,
And O he was a good man
And understood her case.
                    O my dear, O my dear.

He bade them take and bury her
Beside her lady's man,
And set a rose-tree on her grave.

And now none living can
When they have plucked a rose there
Know where its roots began.
             O my dear, O my dear.

(1937)

THE LADY'S FIRST SONG

I TURN round
Like a dumb beast in a show,
Neither know what I am
Nor where I go,
My language beaten
Into one name;
I am in love
And that is my shame.
What hurts the soul
My soul adores,
No better than a beast
Upon all fours.

(1938)

THE LADY'S SECOND SONG

WHAT sort of man is coming
To lie between your feet?
What matter, we are but women.
Wash; make your body sweet;
I have cupboards of dried fragrance,
I can strew the sheet.
             The Lord have mercy upon us.

He shall love my soul as though
Body were not at all,

183

He shall love your body
Untroubled by the soul,
Love cram love's two divisions
Yet keep his substance whole.
                The Lord have mercy upon us.

Soul must learn a love that is
Proper to my breast,
Limbs a love in common
With every noble beast.
If soul may look and body touch
Which is the more blest?
                The Lord have mercy upon us.

(1938)

THE LADY'S THIRD SONG

WHEN you and my true lover meet
And he plays tunes between your feet,
Speak no evil of the soul,
Nor think that body is the whole
For I that am his daylight lady
Know worse evil of the body;
But in honour split his love
Till either neither have enough,
That I may hear if we should kiss
A contrapuntal serpent hiss,
You, should hand explore a thigh,
All the labouring heavens sigh.

(1938)

THE LOVER'S SONG

BIRD sighs for the air,
Thought for I know not where,

For the womb the seed sighs.
Now sinks the same rest
On mind, on nest,
On straining thighs.

(1938)

THE CHAMBERMAID'S FIRST SONG

How came this ranger
Now sunk in rest,
Stranger with stranger,
On my cold breast?
What's left to sigh for?
Strange night has come;
God's love has hidden him
Out of all harm,
Pleasure has made him
Weak as a worm.

(1938)

THE CHAMBERMAID'S SECOND SONG

FROM pleasure of the bed,
Dull as a worm,
His rod and its butting head
Limp as a worm,
His spirit that has fled
Blind as a worm.

(1938)

AN ACRE OF GRASS

PICTURE and book remain,
An acre of green grass

For air and exercise,
Now strength of body goes;
Midnight, an old house
Where nothing stirs but a mouse.

My temptation is quiet.
Here at life's end
Neither loose imagination,
Nor the mill of the mind
Consuming its rag and bone,
Can make the truth known.

Grant me an old man's frenzy.
Myself must I remake
Till I am Timon and Lear
Or that William Blake
Who beat upon the wall
Till Truth obeyed his call;

A mind Michael Angelo knew
That can pierce the clouds
Or inspired by frenzy
Shake the dead in their shrouds;
Forgotten else by mankind
An old man's eagle mind.

(1938)

WHAT THEN?

His chosen comrades thought at school
He must grow a famous man;
He thought the same and lived by rule,
All his twenties crammed with toil;
'What then?' sang Plato's ghost, 'what then?'

Everything he wrote was read,
After certain years he won

Sufficient money for his need,
Friends that have been friends indeed;
'What then?' sang Plato's ghost, 'what then?'

All his happier dreams came true—
A small old house, wife, daughter, son,
Grounds where plum and cabbage grew,
Poets and Wits about him drew;
'What then?' sang Plato's ghost, 'what then?'

'The work is done,' grown old he thought,
'According to my boyish plan;
Let the fools rage, I swerved in nought,
Something to perfection brought';
But louder sang that ghost, 'What then?'

(1937)

BEAUTIFUL LOFTY THINGS

BEAUTIFUL lofty things: O'Leary's noble head;
My father upon the Abbey stage, before him a raging crowd:
'This Land of Saints,' and then as the applause died out,
'Of plaster Saints'; his beautiful mischievous head thrown
  back.
Standish O'Grady supporting himself between the tables
Speaking to a drunken audience high nonsensical words;
Augusta Gregory seated at her great ormolu table,
Her eightieth winter approaching: 'Yesterday he threatened my
  life;
I told him that nightly from six to seven I sat at this table,
The blinds drawn up'; Maud Gonne at Howth station waiting
  a train,
Pallas Athena in that straight back and arrogant head:
All the Olympians; a thing never known again.

(1938)

COME GATHER ROUND ME, PARNELLITES

Come gather round me, Parnellites,
And praise our chosen man,
Stand upright on your legs awhile,
Stand upright while you can,
For soon we lie where he is laid
And he is underground;
Come fill up all those glasses
And pass the bottle round.

And here's a cogent reason
And I have many more,
He fought the might of England
And saved the Irish poor,
Whatever good a farmer's got
He brought it all to pass;
And here's another reason,
That Parnell loved a lass.

And here's a final reason,
He was of such a kind
Every man that sings a song
Keeps Parnell in his mind
For Parnell was a proud man,
No prouder trod the ground,
And a proud man's a lovely man
So pass the bottle round.

The Bishops and the Party
That tragic story made,
A husband that had sold his wife
And after that betrayed;
But stories that live longest
Are sung above the glass,
And Parnell loved his country
And Parnell loved his lass.

(1937)

THE WILD OLD WICKED MAN

'BECAUSE I am mad about women
I am mad about the hills,'
Said that wild old wicked man
Who travels where God wills.
'Not to die on the straw at home,
Those hands to close these eyes,
That is all I ask, my dear,
From the old man in the skies.'
              Daybreak and a candle-end.

'Kind are all your words, my dear,
Do not the rest withhold.
Who can know the year, my dear,
When an old man's blood grows cold?
I have what no young man can have
Because he loves too much.
Words I have that can pierce the heart,
But what can he do but touch?'
              Daybreak and a candle-end.

Then said she to that wild old man,
His stout stick under his hand,
'Love to give or to withhold
Is not at my command.
I gave it all to an older man:
That old man in the skies.
Hands that are busy with His beads
Can never close those eyes.'
              Daybreak and a candle-end.

'Go your ways, O go your ways,
I choose another mark,
Girls down on the seashore
Who understand the dark;
Bawdy talk for the fishermen;
A dance for the fisher-lads;
When dark hangs upon the water
They turn down their beds.'
              Daybreak and a candle-end.

'A young man in the dark am I
But a wild old man in the light
That can make a cat laugh, or
Can touch by mother wit
Things hid in their marrow bones
From time long passed away,
Hid from all those warty lads
That by their bodies lay.'
Daybreak and a candle-end.

'All men live in suffering
I know as few can know,
Whether they take the upper road
Or stay content on the low,
Rower bent in his row-boat
Or weaver bent at his loom,
Horseman erect upon horseback
Or child hid in the womb.'
Daybreak and a candle-end.

'That some stream of lightning
From the old man in the skies
Can burn out that suffering
No right taught man denies.
But a coarse old man am I,
I choose the second-best,
I forget it all awhile
Upon a woman's breast.'
Daybreak and a candle-end.

(1938)

THE GREAT DAY

HURRAH for revolution and more cannon-shot!
A beggar upon horseback lashes a beggar on foot.
Hurrah for revolution and cannon come again!
The beggars have changed places but the lash goes on.

(1938)

PARNELL

PARNELL came down the road, he said to a cheering man:
'Ireland shall get her freedom and you still break stone.'

(1938)

THE SPUR

You think it horrible that lust and rage
Should dance attention upon my old age;
They were not such a plague when I was young;
What else have I to spur me into song?

(1938)

A MODEL FOR THE LAUREATE

On thrones from China to Peru
All sorts of kings have sat
That men and women of all sorts
Proclaimed both good and great;
And what's the odds if such as these
For reason of the State
Should keep their lovers waiting,
    Keep their lovers waiting?

Some boast of beggar-kings and kings
Of rascals black and white
That rule because a strong right arm
Puts all men in a fright,
And drunk or sober live at ease
Where none gainsay their right,
And keep their lovers waiting,
    Keep their lovers waiting.

The Muse is mute when public men
Applaud a modern throne:
Those cheers that can be bought or sold,
That office fools have run,
That waxen seal, that signature.
For things like these what decent man
Would keep his lover waiting,
    Keep his lover waiting?

(1938)

THE OLD STONE CROSS

A STATESMAN is an easy man,
He tells his lies by rote;
A journalist makes up his lies
And takes you by the throat;
So stay at home and drink your beer
And let the neighbours vote,
        Said the man in the golden breastplate
        Under the old stone Cross.

Because this age and the next age
Engender in the ditch,
No man can know a happy man
From any passing wretch;
If Folly link with Elegance
No man knows which is which,
        Said the man in the golden breastplate
        Under the old stone Cross.

But actors lacking music
Do most excite my spleen,
They say it is more human
To shuffle, grunt and groan,

Not knowing what unearthly stuff
Rounds a mighty scene,
  Said the man in the golden breastplate
  Under the old stone Cross.

(1938)

THOSE IMAGES

WHAT if I bade you leave
The cavern of the mind?
There's better exercise
In the sunlight and wind.

I never bade you go
To Moscow or to Rome.
Renounce that drudgery,
Call the Muses home.

Seek those images
That constitute the wild,
The lion and the virgin,
The harlot and the child.

Find in middle air
An eagle on the wing,
Recognise the five
That make the Muses sing.

(1938)

THE MUNICIPAL GALLERY REVISITED

I

AROUND me the images of thirty years:
An ambush; pilgrims at the water-side;
Casement upon trial, half hidden by the bars,

Guarded; Griffith staring in hysterical pride;
Kevin O'Higgins' countenance that wears
A gentle questioning look that cannot hide
A soul incapable of remorse or rest;
A revolutionary soldier kneeling to be blessed;

II

An Abbot or Archbishop with an upraised hand
Blessing the Tricolour. 'This is not,' I say,
'The dead Ireland of my youth, but an Ireland
The poets have imagined, terrible and gay.'
Before a woman's portrait suddenly I stand,
Beautiful and gentle in her Venetian way.
I met her all but fifty years ago
For twenty minutes in some studio.

III

Heart-smitten with emotion I sink down,
My heart recovering with covered eyes;
Wherever I had looked I had looked upon
My permanent or impermanent images:
Augusta Gregory's son; her sister's son,
Hugh Lane, 'onlie begetter' of all these;
Hazel Lavery living and dying, that tale
As though some ballad-singer had sung it all;

IV

Mancini's portrait of Augusta Gregory,
'Greatest since Rembrandt,' according to John Synge;
A great ebullient portrait certainly;
But where is the brush that could show anything
Of all that pride and that humility?
And I am in despair that time may bring
Approved patterns of women or of men
But not that selfsame excellence again.

V

My mediaeval knees lack health until they bend,
But in that woman, in that household where

Honour had lived so long, all lacking found.
Childless I thought, 'My children may find here
Deep-rooted things,' but never foresaw its end,
And now that end has come I have not wept;
No fox can foul the lair the badger swept—

VI

(An image out of Spenser and the common tongue).
John Synge, I and Augusta Gregory, thought
All that we did, all that we said or sang
Must come from contact with the soil, from that
Contact everything Antaeus-like grew strong.
We three alone in modern times had brought
Everything down to that sole test again,
Dream of the noble and the beggarman.

VII

And here's John Synge himself, that rooted man
'Forgetting human words,' a grave deep face.
You that would judge me, do not judge alone
This book or that, come to this hallowed place
Where my friends' portraits hang and look thereon;
Ireland's history in their lineaments trace;
Think where man's glory most begins and ends
And say my glory was I had such friends.

(1937)

WHY SHOULD NOT OLD MEN BE MAD?

WHY should not old men be mad?
Some have known a likely lad
That had a sound fly fisher's wrist
Turn to a drunken journalist;
A girl that knew all Dante once
Live to bear children to a dunce;
A Helen of social welfare dream
Climb on a wagonette to scream.
Some think it matter of course that chance
Should starve good men and bad advance,
That if their neighbours figured plain,
As though upon a lighted screen,
No single story would they find
Of an unbroken happy mind,
A finish worthy of the start.
Young men know nothing of this sort,
Observant old men know it well;
And when they know what old books tell
And that no better can be had
Know why an old man should be mad.

(1939)

CRAZY JANE ON THE MOUNTAIN

I AM tired of cursing the Bishop,
(Said Crazy Jane)

Nine books or nine hats
Would not make him a man.
I have found something worse
To meditate on.
A King had some beautiful cousins,
But where are they gone?
Battered to death in a cellar,
And he stuck to his throne.
Last night I lay on the mountain,
(Said Crazy Jane)
There in a two-horsed carriage
That on two wheels ran
Great-bladdered Emer sat,
Her violent man
Cuchulain sat at her side;
Thereupon,
Propped upon my two knees,
I kissed a stone;
I lay stretched out in the dirt
And I cried tears down.

(1939)

A STATESMAN'S HOLIDAY

I LIVED among great houses,
Riches drove out rank,
Base drove out the better blood,
And mind and body shrank.
No Oscar ruled the table,
But I'd a troop of friends
That knowing better talk had gone
Talked of odds and ends.
Some knew what ailed the world
But never said a thing,
So I have picked a better trade
And night and morning sing:
Tall dames go walking in grass-green Avalon.

Am I a great Lord Chancellor
That slept upon the Sack?
Commanding officer that tore
The khaki from his back?
Or am I De Valéra,
Or the King of Greece,
Or the man that made the motors?
Ach, call me what you please!
Here's a Montenegrin lute,
And its old sole string
Makes me sweet music
And I delight to sing:
Tall dames go walking in grass-green Avalon.

With boys and girls about him,
With any sort of clothes,
With a hat out of fashion,
With old patched shoes,
With a ragged bandit cloak,
With an eye like a hawk,
With a stiff straight back,
With a strutting turkey walk,
With a bag full of pennies,
With a monkey on a chain,
With a great cock's feather,
With an old foul tune.
Tall dames go walking in grass-green Avalon.

(1939)

FROM Last Poems and Two Plays

(1939)

UNDER BEN BULBEN

I

SWEAR by what the Sages spoke
Round the Mareotic Lake
That the Witch of Atlas knew,
Spoke and set the cocks a-crow.

Swear by those horsemen, by those women
Complexion and form prove superhuman,
That pale, long-visaged company
That air in immortality
Completeness of their passions won;
Now they ride the wintry dawn
When Ben Bulben sets the scene.

Here's the gist of what they mean.

II

Many times man lives and dies
Between his two eternities,
That of race and that of soul,
And ancient Ireland knew it all.
Whether man dies in his bed
Or the rifle knocks him dead,
A brief parting from those dear
Is the worst man has to fear.
Though grave-diggers' toil is long,
Sharp their spades, their muscles strong,
They but thrust their buried men
Back in the human mind again.

You that Mitchel's prayer have heard,
'Send war in our time, O Lord!'
Know that when all words are said
And a man is fighting mad,
Something drops from eyes long blind,
He completes his partial mind,
For an instant stands at ease,
Laughs aloud, his heart at peace.
Even the wisest man grows tense
With some sort of violence
Before he can accomplish fate,
Know his work or choose his mate.

IV

Poet and sculptor, do the work,
Nor let the modish painter shirk
What his great forefathers did,
Bring the soul of man to God,
Make him fill the cradles right.

Measurement began our might:
Forms a stark Egyptian thought,
Forms that gentler Phidias wrought.
Michael Angelo left a proof
On the Sistine Chapel roof,
Where but half-awakened Adam
Can disturb globe-trotting Madam
Till her bowels are in heat,
Proof that there's a purpose set
Before the secret working mind:
Profane perfection of mankind.

Quattrocento put in paint
On backgrounds for a God or Saint
Gardens where a soul's at ease;
Where everything that meets the eye,
Flowers and grass and cloudless sky,
Resemble forms that are or seem

When sleepers wake and yet still dream,
And when it's vanished still declare,
With only bed and bedstead there,
That heavens had opened.

                                    Gyres run on;
When that greater dream had gone
Calvert and Wilson, Blake and Claude,
Prepared a rest for the people of God,
Palmer's phrase, but after that
Confusion fell upon our thought.

                    V

Irish poets, learn your trade,
Sing whatever is well made,
Scorn the sort now growing up
All out of shape from toe to top,
Their unremembering hearts and heads
Base-born products of base beds.
Sing the peasantry, and then
Hard-riding country gentlemen,
The holiness of monks, and after
Porter-drinkers' randy laughter;
Sing the lords and ladies gay
That were beaten into the clay
Through seven heroic centuries;
Cast your mind on other days
That we in coming days may be
Still the indomitable Irishry.

                    VI

Under bare Ben Bulben's head
In Drumcliff churchyard Yeats is laid.
An ancestor was rector there
Long years ago, a church stands near,
By the road an ancient cross.
No marble, no conventional phrase;
On limestone quarried near the spot

By his command these words are cut:

> Cast a cold eye
> On life, on death.
> Horseman, pass by!

(1939)

THE BLACK TOWER

SAY that the men of the old black tower
Though they but feed as the goatherd feeds,
Their money spent, their wine gone sour,
Lack nothing that a soldier needs,
That all are oath-bound men;
Those banners come not in.

There in the tomb stand the dead upright,
But winds come up from the shore:
They shake when the winds roar,
Old bones upon the mountain shake.

Those banners come to bribe or threaten
Or whisper that a man's a fool
Who, when his own right king's forgotten,
Cares what king set up his rule.
If he died long ago
Why do you dread us so?

There in the tomb drops the faint moonlight
But wind comes up from the shore.
They shake when the winds roar,
Old bones upon the mountain shake.

The tower's old cook that must climb and clamber
Catching small birds in the dew of the morn
When we hale men lie stretched in slumber
Swears that he hears the king's great horn.
But he's a lying hound;
Stand we on guard oath-bound!

There in the tomb the dark grows blacker,
But wind comes up from the shore.
They shake when the winds roar,
Old bones upon the mountain shake.

(1939)

CUCHULAIN COMFORTED

A MAN that had six mortal wounds, a man
Violent and famous, strode among the dead;
Eyes stared out of the branches and were gone.

Then certain Shrouds that muttered head to head
Came and were gone. He leant upon a tree
As though to meditate on wounds and blood.

A Shroud that seemed to have authority
Among those bird-like things came, and let fall
A bundle of linen. Shrouds by two and three

Came creeping up because the man was still.
And thereupon that linen-carrier said:
'Your life can grow much sweeter if you will

'Obey our ancient rule and make a shroud;
Mainly because of what we only know
The rattle of those arms makes us afraid.

'We thread the needles' eyes, and all we do
All must together do.' That done, the man
Took up the nearest and began to sew.

'Now we shall sing and sing the best we can
But first you must be told our character:
Convicted cowards all by kindred slain

'Or driven from home and left to die in fear.'
They sang, but had nor human notes nor words,
Though all was done in common as before;

They had changed their throats and had the throats of birds.

(1939)

from THREE MARCHING SONGS

I

REMEMBER all those renowned generations,
They left their bodies to fatten the wolves,
They left their homesteads to fatten the foxes,
Fled to far countries, or sheltered themselves
In cavern, crevice, or hole,
Defending Ireland's soul.

Be still, be still, what can be said?
My father sang that song,
But time amends old wrong,
All that is finished, let it fade.

Remember all those renowned generations,
Remember all that have sunk in their blood,
Remember all that have died on the scaffold,
Remember all that have fled, that have stood,
Stood, took death like a tune
On an old tambourine.

Be still, be still, what can be said?
My father sang that song,
But time amends old wrong,
And all that's finished, let it fade.

Fail, and that history turns into rubbish,
All that great past to a trouble of fools;
Those that come after shall mock at O'Donnell,
Mock at the memory of both O'Neills,
Mock Emmet, mock Parnell,
All the renown that fell.

Be still, be still, what can be said?
My father sang that song,
But time amends old wrong,
And all that's finished, let it fade.

(1939)

THE STATUES

PYTHAGORAS planned it. Why did the people stare?
His numbers, though they moved or seemed to move
In marble or in bronze, lacked character.
But boys and girls pale from the imagined love
Of solitary beds knew what they were,
That passion could bring character enough;
And pressed at midnight in some public place
Live lips upon a plummet-measured face.

No; greater than Pythagoras, for the men
That with a mallet or a chisel modelled these
Calculations that look but casual flesh, put down
All Asiatic vague immensities,
And not the banks of oars that swam upon
The many-headed foam at Salamis.
Europe put off that foam when Phidias
Gave women dreams and dreams their looking-glass.

One image crossed the many-headed, sat
Under the tropic shade, grew round and slow,
No Hamlet thin from eating flies, a fat

Dreamer of the Middle Ages. Empty eyeballs knew
That knowledge increases unreality, that
Mirror on mirror mirrored is all the show.
When gong and conch declare the hour to bless
Grimalkin crawls to Buddha's emptiness.

When Pearse summoned Cuchulain to his side,
What stalked through the Post Office? What intellect,
What calculation, number, measurement, replied?
We Irish, born into that ancient sect
But thrown upon this filthy modern tide
And by its formless spawning fury wrecked,
Climb to our proper dark, that we may trace
The lineaments of a plummet-measured face.

(1939)

NEWS FOR THE DELPHIC ORACLE

I

THERE all the golden codgers lay,
There the silver dew,
And the great water sighed for love
And the wind sighed too.
Man-picker Niamh leant and sighed
By Oisin on the grass;
There sighed amid his choir of love
Tall Pythagoras.
Plotinus came and looked about,
The salt-flakes on his breast,
And having stretched and yawned awhile
Lay sighing like the rest.

II

Straddling each a dolphin's back
And steadied by a fin,
Those Innocents re-live their death,

Their wounds open again.
The ecstatic waters laugh because
Their cries are sweet and strange,
Through their ancestral patterns dance,
And the brute dolphins plunge
Until in some cliff-sheltered bay
Where wades the choir of love
Proferring its sacred laurel crowns,
They pitch their burdens off.

III

Slim adolescence that a nymph has stripped,
Peleus on Thetis stares.
Her limbs are delicate as an eyelid,
Love has blinded him with tears;
But Thetis' belly listens.
Down the mountain walls
From where Pan's cavern is
Intolerable music falls.
Foul goat-head, brutal arm appear,
Belly, shoulder, bum,
Flash fishlike; nymphs and satyrs
Copulate in the foam.

(1939)

LONG-LEGGED FLY

THAT civilisation may not sink,
Its great battle lost,
Quiet the dog, tether the pony
To a distant post;
Our master Caesar is in the tent
Where the maps are spread,
His eyes fixed upon nothing,
A hand under his head.

Like a long-legged fly upon the stream
His mind moves upon silence.

That the topless towers be burnt
And men recall that face,
Move most gently if move you must
In this lonely place.
She thinks, part woman, three parts a child,
That nobody looks; her feet
Practise a tinker shuffle
Picked up on the street.

Like a long-legged fly upon the stream
Her mind moves upon silence.

That girls at puberty may find
The first Adam in their thought,
Shut the door of the Pope's chapel,
Keep those children out.
There on that scaffolding reclines
Michael Angelo.
With no more sound than the mice make
His hand moves to and fro.

Like a long-legged fly upon the stream
His mind moves upon silence.

(1939)

JOHN KINSELLA'S LAMENT FOR MRS. MARY MOORE

A BLOODY and a sudden end,
    Gunshot or a noose,
For Death who takes what man would keep,
    Leaves what man would lose.
He might have had my sister,
    My cousins by the score,
But nothing satisfied the fool
    But my dear Mary Moore,

None other knows what pleasures man
    At table or in bed.
What shall I do for pretty girls
    Now my old bawd is dead?

Though stiff to strike a bargain,
    Like an old Jew man,
Her bargain struck we laughed and talked
    And emptied many a can;
And O! but she had stories,
    Though not for the priest's ear,
To keep the soul of man alive,
    Banish age and care,
And being old she put a skin
    On everything she said.
What shall I do for pretty girls
    Now my old bawd is dead?

The priests have got a book that says
    But for Adam's sin
Eden's Garden would be there
    And I there within.
No expectation fails there,
    No pleasing habit ends,
No man grows old, no girl grows cold,
    But friends walk by friends.
Who quarrels over halfpennies
    That plucks the trees for bread?
What shall I do for pretty girls
    Now my old bawd is dead?

(1938)

THE APPARITIONS

Because there is safety in derision
I talked about an apparition,
I took no trouble to convince,

209

Or seem plausible to a man of sense,
Distrustful of that popular eye
Whether it be bold or sly.
Fifteen apparitions have I seen;
The worst a coat upon a coat-hanger.

I have found nothing half so good
As my long-planned half solitude,
Where I can sit up half the night
With some friend that has the wit
Not to allow his looks to tell
When I am unintelligible.
Fifteen apparitions have I seen;
The worst a coat upon a coat-hanger.

When a man grows old his joy
Grows more deep day after day,
His empty heart is full at length
But he has need of all that strength
Because of the increasing Night
That opens her mystery and fright.
Fifteen apparitions have I seen;
The worst a coat upon a coat-hanger.

(1938)

MAN AND THE ECHO

Man

In a cleft that's christened Alt
Under broken stone I halt
At the bottom of a pit
That broad noon has never lit,
And shout a secret to the stone.
All that I have said and done,
Now that I am old and ill,

Turns into a question till
I lie awake night after night
And never get the answers right.
Did that play of mine send out
Certain men the English shot?
Did words of mine put too great strain
On that woman's reeling brain?
Could my spoken words have checked
That whereby a house lay wrecked?
And all seems evil until I
Sleepless would lie down and die.

Echo

Lie down and die.

Man

         That were to shirk
The spiritual intellect's great work
And shirk it in vain. There is no release
In a bodkin or disease,
Nor can there be a work so great
As that which cleans man's dirty slate.
While man can still his body keep
Wine or love drug him to sleep,
Waking he thanks the Lord that he
Has body and its stupidity,
But body gone he sleeps no more
And till his intellect grows sure
That all's arranged in one clear view
Pursues the thoughts that I pursue,
Then stands in judgment on his soul,
And, all work done, dismisses all
Out of intellect and sight
And sinks at last into the night.

Echo

Into the night.

Man

O rocky voice,
Shall we in that great night rejoice?
What do we know but that we face
One another in this place?
But hush, for I have lost the theme,
Its joy or night seem but a dream;
Up there some hawk or owl has struck
Dropping out of sky or rock,
A stricken rabbit is crying out
And its cry distracts my thought.

(1939)

THE CIRCUS ANIMALS' DESERTION

I

I SOUGHT a theme and sought for it in vain,
I sought it daily for six weeks or so.
Maybe at last, being but a broken man,
I must be satisfied with my heart, although
Winter and summer till old age began
My circus animals were all on show,
Those stilted boys, that burnished chariot,
Lion and woman and the Lord knows what.

II

What can I but enumerate old themes?
First that sea-rider Oisin led by the nose
Through three enchanted islands, allegorical dreams,
Vain gaiety, vain battle, vain repose,
Themes of the embittered heart, or so it seems,
That might adorn old songs or courtly shows;
But what cared I that set him on to ride,
I, starved for the bosom of his faery bride?

And then a counter-truth filled out its play,
The Countess Cathleen was the name I gave it;
She, pity-crazed, had given her soul away
But masterful Heaven had intervened to save it.
I thought my dear must her own soul destroy,
So did fanaticism and hate enslave it,
And this brought forth a dream and soon enough
This dream itself had all my thought and love.

And when the Fool and Blind Man stole the bread
Cuchulain fought the ungovernable sea;
Heart-mysteries there, and yet when all is said
It was the dream itself enchanted me:
Character isolated by a deed
To engross the present and dominate memory.
Players and painted stage took all my love
And not those things that they were emblems of.

III

Those masterful images because complete
Grew in pure mind but out of what began?
A mound of refuse or the sweepings of a street,
Old kettles, old bottles, and a broken can,
Old iron, old bones, old rags, that raving slut
Who keeps the till. Now that my ladder's gone
I must lie down where all the ladders start
In the foul rag and bone shop of the heart.

(1939)

POLITICS

*'In our time the destiny of man presents its meanings
in political terms.'*—THOMAS MANN

How can I, that girl standing there,
My attention fix

On Roman or on Russian
Or on Spanish politics?
Yet here's a travelled man that knows
What he talks about,
And there's a politician
That has both read and thought,
And maybe what they say is true
Of war and war's alarms,
But O that I were young again
And held her in my arms.

(1939)

The Death of Cuchulain

(1939)

PERSONS IN THE PLAY

Cuchulain	An Old Man
Eithne Inguba	A Blind Man
Aoife	A Servant
Emer	A Singer, a Piper, and
The Morrigu, *Goddess of War*	a Drummer

Scene.—A bare stage of any period. A very old man looking like something out of mythology.

Old Man. I have been asked to produce a play called *The Death of Cuchulain.* It is the last of a series of plays which has for theme his life and death. I have been selected because I am out of fashion and out of date like the antiquated romantic stuff the thing is made of. I am so old that I have forgotten the name of my father and mother, unless indeed I am, as I affirm, the son of Talma, and he was so old that his friends and acquaintances still read Virgil and Homer. When they told me that I could have my own way I wrote certain guiding principles on a bit of newspaper. I wanted an audience of fifty or a hundred, and if there are more I beg them not to shuffle their feet or talk when the actors are speaking. I am sure that as I am producing a play for people I like it is not probable in this vile age that they will be more in number than those who listened to the first performance of Milton's *Comus.* On the present occasion they must know the old epics and Mr. Yeats' plays about them. Such people however poor have libraries of their own. If there are more than a hundred I won't be able to escape people who are educating themselves out of the book societies, book clubs and the like, sciolists all, pickpockets and opinionated bitches. Why pickpockets? I will explain that, I will make it all quite clear.

[*Drum and pipe behind the scene, then silence.*

That's from the musicians; I asked them to do that if I was
getting excited. If you were as old you would find it easy to
get excited. Before the night ends you will meet the music.
There is a singer, a piper and a drummer. I have picked them
up here and there about the streets, and I will teach them,
if I live, the music of the beggarman, Homer's music. I prom-
ise a dance. I wanted a dance because where there are no
words there is less to spoil. Emer must dance, there must be
severed heads—I am old, I belong to mythology—severed heads
for her to dance before. I had thought to have had those
heads carved, but no, if the dancer can dance properly no
wood-carving can look as well as a parallelogram of painted
wood. But I was at my wit's end to find a good dancer; I
could have got such a dancer once, but she has gone; the
tragi-comedian dancer, the tragic dancer, upon the same neck
love and loathing, life and death. I spit three times. I spit
upon the dancers painted by Degas. I spit upon their short
bodices, their stiff stays, their toes whereon they spin like
peg-tops, above all upon that chambermaid face. They might
have looked timeless, Rameses the Great, but not the cham-
bermaid, that old maid history. I spit! I spit! I spit!

[*The stage is darkened, the curtain falls. Pipe and drum begin
and continue until the curtain rises again on a bare stage
half a minute later. Eithne Inguba enters.*

Eithne. Cuchulain! Cuchulain!

[*Cuchulain enters from back.*

             I am Emer's messenger,
I am your wife's messenger, she has bid me say
You must not linger here in sloth, for Maeve
With all those Connacht ruffians at her back
Burns barns and houses up at Emain Macha:
Your house at Muirthemne already burns.
No matter what's the odds, no matter though
Your death may come of it, ride out and fight.
The scene is set and you must out and fight.

Cuchulain. You have told me nothing. I am already armed,
I have sent a messenger to gather men,
And wait for his return. What have you there?

Eithne. I have nothing.

Cuchulain.   There is something in your hand.

Eithne. No.

Cuchulain.　Have you not a letter in your hand?

Eithne. I do not know how it got into my hand.
　I am straight from Emer. We were in some place.
　She spoke. She saw.

Cuchulain.　　　　This letter is from Emer.
　It tells a different story. I am not to move
　Until tomorrow morning, for, if now,
　I must face odds no man can face and live.
　Tomorrow morning Conal Caernach comes
　With a great host.

Eithne.　　　　I do not understand.
　Who can have put that letter in my hand?

Cuchulain. And there is something more to make it certain
　I shall not stir till morning: you are sent
　To be my bedfellow, but have no fear,
　All that is written but I much prefer
　Your own unwritten words. I am for the fight,
　I and my handful are set upon the fight;
　We have faced great odds before, a straw decided.

　　　[*The Morrigu enters and stands between them.*

Eithne. I know that somebody or something is there
　Yet nobody that I can see.

Cuchulain.　　　　　There is nobody.

Eithne. Who among the gods of the air and the upper air
　Has a bird's head?

Cuchulain.　　　　Morrigu is headed like a crow.

Eithne [*dazed*]. Morrigu, war goddess, stands between.
　Her black wing touched me upon the shoulder, and now
　All is intelligible.　　　　　[*The Morrigu goes out.*
　　　　　Maeve put me in a trance.
　Though when Cuchulain slept with her as a boy
　She seemed as pretty as a bird, she has changed,
　She has an eye in the middle of her forehead.

Cuchulain. A woman that has an eye in the middle of her
　　forehead!
　A woman that is headed like a crow!
　But she that put those words into your mouth
　Had nothing monstrous; you put them there yourself.

217

You need a younger man, a friendlier man,
But fearing what my violence might do
Thought out those words to send me to my death,
And were in such excitement you forgot
The letter in your hand.
Eithne.   Now that I wake
   I say that Maeve did nothing out of error;
   What mouth could you believe if not my mouth?
Cuchulain. When I went mad at my son's death and drew
   My sword against the sea it was my wife
   That brought me back.
Eithne.   Better women than I
   Have served you well but 'twas to me you turned.
Cuchulain. You thought that if you changed I'd kill you for it
   When everything sublunary must change
   And if I have not changed that goes to prove
   That I am monstrous.
Eithne.   You're not the man I loved,
   That violent man forgave no treachery.
   If thinking what you think you can forgive
   It is because you are about to die.
Cuchulain. Spoken too loudly and too near the door;
   Speak low if you would speak about my death
   Or not in that strange voice exulting in it.
   Who knows what ears listen behind the door?
Eithne. Some that would not forgive a traitor, some
   That have the passion necessary to life,
   Some not about to die. When you are gone
   I shall denounce myself to all your cooks,
   Scullions, armourers, bed-makers and messengers,
   Until they hammer me with a ladle, cut me with a knife,
   Impale me upon a spit, put me to death
   By what foul way best please their fancy,
   So that my shade can stand among the shades
   And greet your shade and prove it is no traitor.
Cuchulain. Women have spoken so plotting a man's death.
                         [Enter a servant.
Servant. Your great horse is bitted. All wait the word.
Cuchulain. I come to give it, but must ask a question.
   This woman, wild with grief, declares that she

218

Out of pure treachery has told me lies
That should have brought my death. What can I do?
How can I save her from her own wild words?
Servant. Is her confession true?
Cuchulain.   I make the truth,
  I say she brings a message from my wife.
Servant. What if I make her swallow poppy juice?
Cuchulain. What herbs seem suitable but protect her life
  As if it were your own and should I not return
  Give her to Conal Caernach because the women
  Have called him a good lover.
Eithne.   I might have peace that know
  The Morrigu, the woman like a crow,
  Stands to my defence and cannot lie
  But that Cuchulain is about to die.

> [Pipe and drum. The stage grows dark for a moment. When it
> lights up again it is empty. Cuchulain enters wounded. He
> tries to fasten himself to a pillar-stone with his belt. Aoife,
> an erect white-haired woman, enters.

Aoife. Am I recognised, Cuchulain?
Cuchulain.   You fought with a sword,
  It seemed that we should kill each other; then
  Your body wearied and I took your sword.
Aoife. But look again, Cuchulain! Look again!
Cuchulain. Your hair is white.
Aoife.   That time was long ago
  And now it is my time. I have come to kill you.
Cuchulain. Where am I? Why am I here?
Aoife.   You asked their leave
  When certain that you had six mortal wounds
  To drink out of the pool.
Cuchulain.   I have put my belt
  About this stone and want to fasten it
  And die upon my feet, but am too weak.
  Fasten this belt.   [She helps him to do so.
                        And now I know your name,
  Aoife the mother of my son. We met
  At the Hawk's Well under the withered trees.
  I killed him upon Baile's Strand, that is why

219

Maeve parted ranks that she might let you through.
You have a right to kill me.
Aoife.   Though I have
Her army did not part to let me through.
The grey of Macha, that great horse of yours
Killed in the battle, came out of the pool
As though it were alive, and went three times
In a great circle round you and that stone,
Then leaped into the pool and not a man
Of all that terrified army dare approach,
But I approach.
Cuchulain.   Because you have the right.
Aoife. But I am an old woman now and that
Your strength may not start up when the time comes
I wind my veil about this ancient stone
And fasten down your hands.
Cuchulain.   But do not spoil your veil.
Your veils are beautiful, some with threads of gold.
Aoife. I am too old to care for such things now.
                              [She has wound the veil about him.
Cuchulain. There was no reason so to spoil your veil:
I am weak from loss of blood.
Aoife.   I was afraid,
But now that I have wound you in the veil
I am not afraid. Our son—how did he fight?
Cuchulain. Age makes more skilful but not better men.
Aoife. I have been told you did not know his name,
And wanted, because he had a look of me,
To be his friend, but Conchubar forbade it.
Cuchulain. Forbade it and commanded me to fight;
That very day I had sworn to do his will,
Yet I refused him and spoke about a look,
But somebody spoke of witchcraft and I said
Witchcraft had made the look and fought and killed him.
Then I went mad, I fought against the sea.
Aoife. I seemed invulnerable; you took my sword,
You threw me on the ground and left me there.
I searched the mountain for your sleeping place
And laid my virgin body at your side,

And yet because you had left me hated you
And thought that I would kill you in your sleep
And yet begot a son that night between
Two black thorn trees.
Cuchulain.   I cannot understand.
Aoife. Because about to die.
                             Somebody comes,
Some countryman, and when he finds you there
And none to protect him, will be terrified.
I will keep out of his sight, for I have things
That I must ask questions on before I kill you.
   [She goes. The Blind Man of "On Baile's Strand" comes in.
      He moves his stick about until he finds the standing stone;
      he lays his stick down, stoops and touches Cuchulain's feet.
      He feels the legs.
Blind Man. Ah! Ah!
Cuchulain.   I think you are a blind old man.
Blind Man. A blind old beggar man. What is your name?
Cuchulain. Cuchulain.
Blind Man.   They say that you are weak with wounds.
   I stood between a Fool and the sea at Baile's Strand
When you went mad. What's bound about your hands
So that they cannot move? Some womanish stuff.
I have been fumbling with my stick since the dawn
And then heard many voices. I began to beg.
Somebody said that I was in Maeve's tent,
And somebody else, a big man by his voice,
That if I brought Cuchulain's head in a bag
I would be given twelve pennies; I had the bag
To carry what I get at kitchen doors,
Somebody told me how to find the place;
I thought it would have taken till the night
But this has been my lucky day.
Cuchulain.   Twelve pennies!
Blind Man. I would not promise anything until the woman,
   The great Queen Maeve herself, repeated the words.
Cuchulain. Twelve pennies. What better reason for killing a
   man?
   You have a knife, but have you sharpened it?

Blind Man. I keep it sharp because it cuts my food.
> *[He lays bag on ground and begins feeling Cuchulain's body,*
> *his hands mounting upward.*

Cuchulain. I think that you know everything, Blind Man,
My mother or my nurse said that the blind
Know everything.

Blind Man.　　　　　No, but they have good sense.
How could I have got twelve pennies for your head
If I had not good sense?

Cuchulain.　　　　　There floats out there
The shape that I shall take when I am dead,
My soul's first shape, a soft feathery shape,
And is not that a strange shape for a soul
Of a great fighting man?

Blind Man.　　　　　Your shoulder is there,
This is your neck. Ah! Ah! Are you ready, Cuchulain?

Cuchulain. I say it is about to sing.

> *[The stage darkens.*

Blind Man.　　　　　Ah! Ah!

> *[Music of pipe and drum, the curtain falls. The music ceases*
> *as the curtain rises upon a bare stage. There is nobody upon*
> *the stage except a woman with a crow's head. She is the*
> *Morrigu. She stands towards the back. She holds a black*
> *parallelogram, the size of a man's head. There are six other*
> *parallelograms near the back cloth.*

The Morrigu. The dead can hear me and to the dead I speak.
This head is great Cuchulain's, those other six
Gave him six mortal wounds; this man came first,
Youth lingered though the years ran on, that season
A woman loves the best, Maeve's latest lover;
This man had given him the second wound,
He had possessed her once; these were her sons,
Two valiant men that gave the third and fourth;
These other men were men of no account,
They saw that he was weakening and crept in;
One gave him the sixth wound and one the fifth;
Conal avenged him. I arranged the dance.

> *[Emer enters. The Morrigu places the head of Cuchulain upon*
> *the ground and goes out. Emer runs in and begins to dance.*
> *She so moves that she seems to rage against the heads of*

those that had wounded Cuchulain, perhaps makes move-
ments as though to strike them, going three times round the
circle of the heads. She then moves towards the head of Cu-
chulain; it may, if need be, be raised above the others on a
pedestal. She moves as if in adoration or triumph. She is
about to prostrate herself before it, perhaps does so, then
rises looking up as if listening; she seems to hesitate between
the head and what she hears. Then she stands motionless.
There is silence and in the silence a few faint bird notes.
The stage darkens slowly. Then comes loud music but now
it's quite different. It is the music of some Irish fair of our
day. The stage brightens. Emer and the head are gone. There
is none there but the three Musicians. They are in ragged
street singers' clothes; two of them play pipe and drum. They
cease. The Street Singer begins to sing.

Singer.

    The harlot sang to the beggar man.
    I meet them face to face,
    Conal, Cuchulain, Usna's boys,
    All that most ancient race;
    Maeve had three in an hour, they say;
    I adore those clever eyes,
    Those muscular bodies, but can get
    No grip upon their thighs.
    I meet those long pale faces,
    Hear their great horses, then
    Recall what centuries have passed
    Since they were living men,
    That there are still some living
    That do my limbs unclothe,
    But that the flesh my flesh has gripped
    I both adore and loathe.

                       [Pipe and drum music.

    Are those things that men adore and loathe
    Their sole reality?
    What stood in the Post Office
    With Pearse and Connolly?
    What comes out of the mountain
    Where men first shed their blood?

Who thought Cuchulain till it seemed
He stood where they had stood?

No body like his body
Has modern woman borne,
But an old man looking back on life
Imagines it in scorn.
A statue's there to mark the place
By Oliver Sheppard done.
So ends the tale that the harlot
Sang to the beggar man.

[*Music from pipe and drum.*

THE CURTAIN FALLS

Purgatory

(1939)

PERSONS IN THE PLAY

A Boy   An Old Man

Scene.—A ruined house and a bare tree in the background.

Boy. Half door, hall door,
　　Hither and thither day and night,
　　Hill or hollow, shouldering this pack,
　　Hearing you talk.

Old Man.　　　　　　Study that house.
　　I think about its jokes and stories;
　　I try to remember what the butler
　　Said to a drunken gamekeeper
　　In mid-October, but I cannot.
　　If I cannot, none living can.
　　Where are the jokes and stories of a house,
　　Its threshold gone to patch a pig-sty?

Boy. So you have come this path before?

Old Man. The moonlight falls upon the path,
　　The shadow of a cloud upon the house
　　And that's symbolical; study that tree,
　　What is it like?

Boy.　　　　　　A silly old man.

Old Man. It's like—no matter what it's like.
　　I saw it a year ago stripped bare as now,
　　I saw it fifty years ago
　　Before the thunderbolt had riven it,
　　Green leaves, ripe leaves, leaves thick as butter,

Fat, greasy life. Stand there and look,
Because there is somebody in that house.
            [*The Boy puts down pack and stands in the doorway.*

Boy. There's nobody here.

Old Man.   There's somebody there.

Boy. The floor is gone, the windows gone,
    And where there should be roof there's sky,
    And here's a bit of an egg-shell thrown
    Out of a jackdaw's nest.

Old Man.   But there are some
    That do not care what's gone, what's left,
    The souls in Purgatory that come back
    To habitations and familiar spots.

Boy. Your wits are out again.

Old Man.   Re-live
    Their transgressions, and that not once
    But many times; they know at last
    The consequence of those transgressions
    Whether upon others or upon themselves;
    Upon others, others may bring help
    For when the consequence is at an end
    The dream must end; upon themselves
    There is no help but in themselves
    And in the mercy of God.

Boy.   I have had enough!
    Talk to the jackdaws, if talk you must.

Old Man. Stop! Sit there upon that stone.
    That is the house where I was born.

Boy. The big old house that was burnt down?

Old Man. My mother that was your grand-dam owned it,
    This scenery and this countryside,
    Kennel and stable, horse and hound—
    She had a horse at the Curragh, and there met

My father, a groom in a training stable;
Looked at him and married him.
Her mother never spoke to her again,
And she did right.

Boy.   What's right and wrong?
My grand-dad got the girl and the money.

Old Man. Looked at him and married him,
And he squandered everything she had.
She never knew the worst, because
She died in giving birth to me,
But now she knows it all, being dead.
Great people lived and died in this house;
Magistrates, colonels, members of Parliament,
Captains and governors, and long ago
Men that had fought at Aughrim and the Boyne.
Some that had gone on government work
To London or to India came home to die,
Or came from London every spring
To look at the may-blossom in the park.
They had loved the trees that he cut down
To pay what he had lost at cards
Or spent on horses, drink and women;
Had loved the house, had loved all
The intricate passages of the house,
But he killed the house; to kill a house
Where great men grew up, married, died,
I here declare a capital offence.

Boy. My God, but you had luck. Grand clothes,
And maybe a grand horse to ride.

Old Man. That he might keep me upon his level
He never sent me to school, but some
Half-loved me for my half of her,
A gamekeeper's wife taught me to read,
A Catholic curate taught me Latin.
There were old books and books made fine
By eighteenth century French binding, books
Modern and ancient, books by the ton.

Boy. What education have you given me?

Old Man. I gave the education that befits
  A bastard that a pedlar got
  Upon a tinker's daughter in a ditch.
  When I had come to sixteen years old
  My father burned down the house when drunk.

Boy. But that is my age, sixteen years old.
  At the Puck Fair.

Old Man.   And everything was burnt;
  Books, library, all were burnt.

Boy. Is what I have heard upon the road the truth,
  That you killed him in the burning house?

Old Man. There's nobody here but our two selves?

Boy. Nobody, Father.

Old Man.   I stuck him with a knife,
  That knife that cuts my dinner now,
  And after that I left him in the fire;
  They dragged him out, somebody saw
  The knife-wound but could not be certain
  Because the body was all black and charred.
  Then some that were his drunken friends
  Swore they would put me upon trial,
  Spoke of quarrels, a threat I had made.
  The gamekeeper gave me some old clothes,
  I ran away, worked here and there
  Till I became a pedlar on the roads,
  No good trade, but good enough
  Because I am my father's son,
  Because of what I did or may do.
  Listen to the hoof-beats! Listen, listen!

Boy. I cannot hear a sound.

Old Man.   Beat! Beat!
  This night is the anniversary
  Of my mother's wedding night,

Or of the night wherein I was begotten.
My father is riding from the public-house,
A whiskey bottle under his arm.
                    [*A window is lit showing a young girl.*
Look at the window; she stands there
Listening, the servants are all in bed,
She is alone, he has stayed late
Bragging and drinking in the public house.

Boy. There's nothing but an empty gap in the wall.
You have made it up. No, you are mad!
You are getting madder every day.

Old Man. It's louder now because he rides
Upon a gravelled avenue
All grass to-day. The hoof beat stops,
He has gone to the other side of the house,
Gone to the stable, put the horse up.
She has gone down to open the door.
This night she is no better than her man
And does not mind that he is half drunk,
She is mad about him. They mount the stairs,
She brings him into her own chamber.
And that is the marriage chamber now.
The window is dimly lit again.
Do not let him touch you! It is not true
That drunken men cannot beget
And if he touch he must beget
And you must bear his murderer.
Deaf! Both deaf! If I should throw
A stick or a stone they would not hear;
And that's a proof my wits are out.
But there's a problem: she must live
Through everything in exact detail,
Driven to it by remorse, and yet
Can she renew the sexual act
And find no pleasure in it, and if not,
If pleasure and remorse must both be there
Which is the greater?
                    I lack schooling.
Go fetch Tertullian; he and I

Will ravel all that problem out
While those two lie upon the mattress
Begetting me.
                    Come back! Come back!
And so you thought to slip away,
My bag of money between your fingers,
And that I could not talk and see!
You have been rummaging in the pack.
                    [*The light in the window has faded out.*

Boy. You never gave me my right share.

Old Man. And had I given it, young as you are
You would have spent it upon drink.

Boy. What if I did? I had a right
To get it and spend it as I chose.

Old Man. Give me that bag and no more words.

Boy. I will not.

Old Man.   I will break your fingers.
    [*They struggle for the bag. In the struggle it drops, scattering the
        money. The Old Man staggers but does not fall. They stand
        looking at each other.*

Boy. What if I killed you? You killed my grand-dad
Because you were young and he was old.
Now I am young and you are old.
    [*Window is lit up. A man is seen pouring whiskey into a glass.*

Old Man [*staring at window*]. Better looking, those sixteen years—

Boy. What are you muttering?

Old Man.   Younger—and yet
She should have known he was not her kind.

Boy. What are you saying? Out with it!
                    [*Old Man points to window.*
My God! The window is lit up
And somebody stands there, although
The floorboards are all burnt away.

230

Old Man. The window is lit up because my father
  Has come to find a glass for his whiskey.
  He leans there like some tired beast.

Boy. A dead, living, murdered man.

Old Man. 'Then the bride-sleep fell upon Adam':
  Where did I read those words?
                          And yet
  There's nothing leaning in the window
  But the impression upon my mother's mind,
  Being dead she is alone in her remorse.

Boy. A body that was a bundle of old bones
  Before I was born. Horrible! Horrible!   [He covers his eyes.

Old Man. That beast there would know nothing, being
                nothing,
  If I should kill a man under the window.
  He would not even turn his head.   [He stabs the Boy.
  My father and my son on the same jack-knife!
  That finishes—there—there—there—
                [He stabs again and again. The window grows dark.
  'Hush-a-bye baby, thy father's a knight,
  Thy mother a lady, lovely and bright.'
  No, that is something that I read in a book
  And if I sing it must be to my mother,
  And I lack rhyme.
    [The stage has grown dark except where the tree stands in white
    light.
                        Study that tree.
  It stands there like a purified soul,
  All cold, sweet, glistening light.
  Dear mother, the window is dark again
  But you are in the light because
  I finished all that consequence.
  I killed that lad because had he grown up
  He would have struck a woman's fancy,
  Begot, and passed pollution on.
  I am a wretched foul old man
  And therefore harmless. When I have stuck

This old jack-knife into a sod
And pulled it out all bright again,
And picked up all the money that he dropped
I'll to a distant place, and there
Tell my old jokes among new men.
                    [*He cleans the knife and begins to pick up money.*
Hoof beats! Dear God,
How quickly it returns—beat—beat—
Her mind cannot hold up that dream.
Twice a murderer and all for nothing,
And she must animate that dead night
Not once but many times!
                    O God!
Release my mother's soul from its dream!
Mankind can do no more. Appease
The misery of the living and the remorse of the dead.

THE END

Notes[1]

CROSSWAYS (1889), pp. 1 ff.

In these early poems Yeats experiments with dialogue, with an extended refrain (*The Stolen Child*, p. 2), and with simple forms from Irish folk song and themes from Irish folklore.—The places named in *The Stolen Child* are "round about Sligo."

THE ROSE (1893), pp. 6 ff.

Yeats gives us various symbolic meanings for the Rose. It "has been for many centuries a symbol of spiritual love and supreme beauty" and has been called "a symbol of the sun,—itself a principal symbol of the divine nature, and the symbolic heart of things." It is "the flower sacred to the Virgin Mary," the "western Flower of Life," and therefore "I have imagined it growing upon the Tree of Life." Among the Irish poets it has been used "as a religious symbol" and "a symbol of woman's beauty." Perhaps the ancient Celts "associated the Rose with Eire, or Fotla, or Banba—goddesses who gave their names to Ireland." Thus it carries connotations of an idealized feminine principle as well. Finally, "the quality symbolized by the Rose differs from the Intellectual Beauty of Shelley and of Spenser in that I have imagined it as suffering with man and not as something pursued and seen from afar."

This last idea, that what is idealized involves quite as much human suffering as does ordinary life, is a unique aspect of Yeats's romanticism which obtains throughout his career.

To the Rose upon the Rood of Time (p. 6).—The title suggests the combining of Rose and Cross in Rosicrucianism. Its literal meaning might be: "To the sacred visions crucified by time."

Fergus and the Druid (p. 7) and *Who Goes with Fergus?* (p. 15).—See comment on pp. xxiii ff.

Cuchulain's Fight with the Sea (p. 8).—*one sweet-throated like a bird:* Eithne Inguba, Cuchulain's young concubine. (See *The Death of Cuchulain*, pp. 215 ff.)

The Man Who Dreamed of Faeryland (p. 15).—The word *had* in this poem is used in its subjunctive sense of *would have* or *might have*. The places named in this poem are, like those in *The Stolen Child*, "round about Sligo."

The Two Trees (p. 17).—The contrast between the "holy tree" with its "ignorant leafy" ways and the "fatal image" of a tree with broken branches through which move the "ravens of unresting thought" seems related to that between the two trees of the Bible: the tree of life and the tree of the knowledge of good and evil. It has cabalistic parallels also. However, Yeats's con-

---

[1] Unless otherwise attributed, comments in quotation marks are Yeats's own, from notes collated in the *Variorum Editions* of his poems and plays.

trast between the objective and subjective aspects of the Beloved, or between her inward self and her opposite, fearful image, provides a good example of the way he reoriented traditional symbols for his own artistic purposes.

The Wind Among the Reeds (1899), pp. 20 ff.

The Hosting of the Sidhe (p. 20).—"The gods of ancient Ireland, the Tuatha de Danaan, or the Tribes of the goddess Dana, or the Sidhe, from Aes Sidhe, or Sluagh Sidhe, the people of the Faery Hills, as these words are usually explained, still ride the country as of old. Sidhe is also Gaelic for wind. . . . They journey in whirling wind, the winds that were called the dance of the daughters of Herodias in the Middle Ages, Herodias doubtless taking the place of some old goddess." Thus the Sidhe are more than mere faeries in the ordinary sense; they are supernatural beings of a more exalted character. Yeats sometimes thinks of them as including all mythical heroes, and at other times makes them quite sinister. To be touched by them is to be set apart from other mortals, an ambivalent condition common to all who succumb to enchantment.

The Unappeasable Host (p. 21).—*Danaan children:* children of the Sidhe, whose intense joy and beauty are irresistible yet a threat to human love and security.

He Bids His Beloved Be at Peace (p. 23).—*Shadowy Horses:* "November, the old beginning of winter, or of the victory of the Fomor, or powers of death, and dismay, and cold, and darkness, is associated by the Irish people with the horse-shaped Púcas. . . ."—*The North,* etc.: "I follow much Irish and other mythology, and the magical tradition, in associating the North with night and sleep, and the East . . . with hope, and the South . . . with passion and desire, and the West . . . with fading and dreaming things."

The Cap and Bells (p. 24).—Yeats's note includes a caveat useful for many of his poems: "The poem has always meant a great deal to me, though, as is the way with symbolic poems, it has not always meant the same thing."

The Valley of the Black Pig (p. 25).—"All over Ireland there are prophecies of the coming rout of the enemies of Ireland, in a certain Valley of the Black Pig, and these prophecies are, no doubt, now, as they were in the Fenian days, a political force. . . . If one reads Rhys' *Celtic Heathendom* by the light of Frazer's *Golden Bough* . . . one sees that the Battle is mythological, and that the Pig it is named from must be a type of cold and winter doing battle with the summer, or of death battling with life."

He Hears the Cry of the Sedge (p. 26).—*the axle:* "the pole of the heavens," with the constellations that move about it, "the ancient Tree of Life in many countries."

In the Seven Woods (1904), pp. 28 ff.

Adam's Curse, p. 28.—See comment, pp. xxxv ff.

The Green Helmet and Other Poems (1910), pp. 31 ff.

Many of Yeats's poems have been traced to his relationship with Maud Gonne, but the four which begin this section, and a number of the later pieces included in this volume, perhaps call more explicitly for this identification.

To a Poet etc. (p. 34).—The poet is George Russell (AE).

Upon a House Shaken by the Land Agitation (p. 35).—The "house" is that of the Gregorys at Coole (though it might be any such house), "shaken" by the movement to break up the great landed estates. Lady Gregory's husband, Governor of Ceylon, had had "the gifts that govern men" here attributed to the Irish aristocracy, and the final lines refer in particular to Lady Gregory's literary style. It is characteristic of Yeats that in the midst of this eloquent defense of aristocratic values he makes the telling concession of line 8.

These Are the Clouds (p. 36).—The "friend" being praised and consoled here is Lady Gregory.

RESPONSIBILITIES (1914), pp. 38 ff.

[Pardon, Old Fathers] (p. 38).—*Old Dublin merchant 'free of ten and four'*: Jervis Yeats (d. 1712), a linen merchant. " 'Free of ten and four' is an error I cannot now correct, without more rewriting than I have a mind for. Some merchant in Villon . . . was 'free of the ten and four.' Irish merchants exempted from certain duties by the Irish Parliament were, unless memory deceives me again, for I am writing away from books, 'free of the eight and six.' "—*Old country scholar*: the poet's great-grandfather, John Yeats (1774–1847).—*Old merchant skipper*: the poet's maternal grandfather, William Pollexfen.—*Huckster's loin*: In this poem Yeats implies a distinction between his "merchant" ancestors and a more vulgar sort of modern businessman; this usage is inconsistent in his poetry, but the important point is that from an early age he keenly desired to identify himself as within the aristocratic Anglo-Irish tradition.—*a barren passion*: for Maud Gonne.

This prefatory poem prepares us for the four somewhat polemical poems that follow. It presents Yeats as a spokesman for the disinterested integrity which he finds in the best Irish traditions. "Three public disputes," he wrote in 1914, "have stirred my imagination. The first was the Parnell controversy. There were reasons to justify a man's joining either party, but there were none to justify, on one side or on the other, lying accusations forgetful of past service, a frenzy of detraction. And another was the dispute over *The Playboy*" (John Synge's *The Playboy of the Western World*, attacked for supposedly presenting Irish characters and Irish life in a bad light). "There could not, wrote Yeats, have been any justification "for the lies, for the unscrupulous rhetoric spread against it in Ireland, and from Ireland to America." The third dispute was occasioned by "the Corporation's refusal of a building for Sir Hugh Lane's famous collection of pictures" in Dublin. "Religious Ireland . . . thinks of divine things as a round of duties separated from life . . . , while political Ireland sees the good citizen but as a man who holds to certain opinions. . . . Against all this we have but a few educated men and the remnants of an old traditional culture among the poor."

September 1913 (p. 38).—The poem contrasts the paltry, commercial spirit of the new ruling class in Ireland with the selflessness of her revolutionary martyrs and of the "Wild Geese," men of great families who served under foreign standards after 1691 because of the penal laws against Catholics. Yeats was reacting specifically against a lockout of strikers by employers in Dublin. The leading employer involved was William Martin Murphy (1844–1919), publisher of the *Irish Independent*, who had been actively opposed to Parnell and, later, to Hugh Lane's proposals for presenting his art collection to Ireland.

To a Friend etc. (p. 39).—The friend is Lady Gregory, whose work has "come to nothing" in the sense that her contribution to Irish culture was not popularly appreciated and was sometimes attacked by her fellow countrymen. The treatment of Hugh Lane (her nephew) was particularly discouraging to her, and she suffered other personal disappointments.

To a Shade (p. 40).—The "Shade" is Parnell; his "monument" is on O'Connell Street in Dublin.—*A man:* Hugh Lane.—*Your enemy:* presumably Murphy.

Running to Paradise (p. 43).—It seems likely that the use of roman type for "is" in the refrain is an imitation of biblical usage; in the Authorized version of the Old Testament copulative verbs are italicized because not employed in the original text. Thus Yeats gives a "sacred" coloration to his own text, whose speaker is beggar, fool, and prophet all at once.

To a Child Dancing in the Wind (p. 45) and *Two Years Later* (p. 46).—The child is Iseult, Maud Gonne's daughter (by Lucien Millevoye). Their relationship was a complex one; later Yeats proposed both to Maud Gonne and to Iseult in the summer of 1917, shortly before his betrothal and marriage to George Hyde-Lees.—*your mother:* Maud Gonne, who is also the subject of the two poems that follow, and of *That the Night Come* (p. 48).

The Magi (p. 48) and *The Dolls* (p. 49).—Of the latter poem, Yeats writes: "I had noticed . . . how all thought among us is frozen into 'something other than human life.' After I had made the poem, I looked up one day into the blue of the sky, and suddenly imagined, as if lost in the blue of the sky, stiff figures in procession. I remembered that they were the habitual image suggested by blue sky, and looking for a second fable called them 'The Magi,' complementary forms of those enraged dolls." It is interesting that despite the order in which he describes them in this note, Yeats placed *The Magi* first and *The Dolls* second in his *Collected Poems*. The reason may be that the second elucidates the first. In *A Vision*, Yeats remarks that there are crucial times in an individual's (or, by implication, a civilization's) development when "the old realization of an objective moral law is changed into a subconscious turbulent instinct" and, as he says (quoting from *The Magi*), "the world of rigid law and custom is broken up by 'the uncontrollable mystery upon the bestial floor.' " The Magi of the poem suggest not only the figures of the New Testament but all projections of the human imagination whether in myth, religion, theory, or art; the images in which these projections are embodied return to their human source to rediscover their meanings and perhaps discover new forms. The dolls, too, represent human constructs— the "world of rigid law and custom" by which men torment their own consciences until they realize they themselves are its source. (The apologetic wife has not reached this realization, but the poet's revulsion against the screaming of the ancient doll-moralist is clear.) These poems carry the motif of hostility to repressive, petty-minded "morality"—that of Parnell's and Synge's critics, etc.—to a new plane.

THE WILD SWANS AT COOLE (1919), pp. 51 ff.

The Wild Swans at Coole (p. 51).—*The nineteenth autumn:* 1916.

In Memory of Major Robert Gregory (p. 52).—*our house:* Thoor Ballylee, which Major Gregory had encouraged the Yeatses to buy and about whose rebuilding he had advised them.—*much falling:* an allusion both to Johnson's dissipation and to his physical falls from stools, etc.—*stony place:* the Aran Islands, which John Synge studied and wrote about.

An Irish Airman etc. (p. 55).—The airman was Major Robert Gregory.

Lines Written in Dejection (p. 59).—The "heroic" and "holy" world of the moon is that of the true poetic imagination. The poet feels he has been out of touch with its primal inspiration and is too much of the objective world, timidly calculating and embroiled in the bitterness of external conflicts, symbolized by the sun.

The Dawn (p. 59).—*that old queen:* Emain, who measured out the site of her palace in Armagh with a pin. Yeats implies that this mythical event in Celtic tradition is no more absurd than the achievements of scientific measurement and that it may be paralleled, in Grecian mythology, with Phaeton's pathetic attempt to master the horses of the sun. All these signs of human ambition are alike meaningless to indifferent nature, as personified by the "ignorant and wanton" dawn that looked down uncomprehending on Emain and on the Babylonian astronomers and that rocked Phaeton in the chariot without caring what his fate might be. The poet, whose passions have presumably been too engaged by life, wishes to take on pure nature's own disengagement.

The People (p. 63).—*my phoenix:* Maud Gonne. On one occasion she was hissed in the Abbey Theatre because of her divorce action in 1905.

Upon a Dying Lady (p. 66).—The lady was the actress Mrs. Mabel Wright, sister of Aubrey Beardsley and wife of the actor George Bealby Wright.

The Phases of the Moon (p. 71).—The following note was intended to accompany not only this poem but also *The Double Vision of Michael Robartes* (p. 78); it has an obvious bearing as well on *Ego Dominus Tuus* (p. 68): "Years ago I wrote three stories in which occur the names of Michael Robartes and Owen Aherne. I now consider that I used the actual names of two friends, and that one of these friends, Michael Robartes, has but lately returned from Mesopotamia, where he has partly found and partly thought out much philosophy. I consider that Aherne and Robartes, men to whose namesakes I had attributed a turbulent life or death, have quarrelled with me. They take their place in a phantasmagoria in which I endeavour to explain my philosophy of life and death. To some extent I wrote these poems as a text for exposition." *The Phases of the Moon* forms part of the prefatory matter of *A Vision.* See comment on pp. xxxviii ff.—*the tower:* Thoor Ballylee, where Yeats sits reading.—*Milton's Platonist:* see *Il Penseroso.*—*Shelley's visionary prince:* see *Prince Athanase.*—*Pater:* Walter Pater (1839–1894), whose style affected Yeats's writing of the nineties.—*Twenty-and-eight the phases of the moon*, etc.: From this point on, Robartes presents a concentrated and dramatic picture of the soul's progress through succeeding phases as described in the section of *A Vision* (pp. 105–184) called "The Twenty-Eight Incarnations." The soul begins out of primal darkness in a state of natural innocence like "a bird or a beast" and grows into the intense intellectual subjectivity of "The Obsessed Man." The latter phase, the fourteenth, corresponds to the full moon; it is prefigured by the triumph of Athena's wisdom over Achilles' brute power and heralded by the birth of Nietzsche. Personality is now extinguished, through its very triumph in imposing itself on external reality and, as it were, remaking and thus identifying itself with it. ("All dreams of the soul," says Aherne, "end in a beautiful . . . body.") After this achievement, objective reality slowly regains its primacy until, in the twenty-sixth phase, the soul loses its distinguishing personality and becomes "deformed" through the outside world's manifold pull upon it; hence Yeats calls the man of this phase "The Hunchback." In the twenty-seventh phase, the soul renounces the insistence on its lost personality that distorted The Hunchback, who still dreams of being a great conqueror or lover; this new phase is that of "The Saint," joyously and purposefully reducing himself to nothing "to permit the total life . . . to flow in upon him and to express itself through his acts and thoughts." (See the poem *The Saint and the Hunchback*, p. 76.) The twenty-eighth phase is that of "The Fool," "a straw blown by the wind, with no mind but the wind and no act but a nameless drifting and turning, and sometimes called 'The Child of God.' " (See *Two Songs of a Fool*, p. 77.)

The Cat and the Moon (p. 75). See preceding note and page xxxviii.

The Saint and the Hunchback (p. 76) and *Two Songs of a Fool* (p. 77). See note to *The Phases of the Moon*.

The Double Vision of Michael Robartes (p. 78). See note to *The Phases of the Moon*.—Here Michael Robartes is Yeats's own spokesman. His "double vision" brings into a single focus the two extreme conditions, or phases, of man: *I*. the dark of the moon, when the human is obliterated and the self seems moved by coldly mechanical, "dead" forces, and *II*. the full of the moon, when the triumph of the human is bodied forth in the Grecian image of the female Sphinx (physical and intellectual powers combined, with the latter ascendant), in the Oriental image of Buddha (universal love, with the physical kept tranquil), and in the universal image of the girl dancing beyond death (the aesthetic, transcending yet uniting the traditional and religious implications of the other two images). In this opposition of *I* and *II* we can see a principle resembling that of early poems like *Who Goes with Fergus?* That is, each of the opposites colors and is moving toward the condition of the other. Despite the automatism of the spirits in *I*, they are ultimately obedient to "some hidden magical breath"; and despite the triumph of the human in *II*, the images still suggest the sadness of mortality. In *III* we return to the human being whose "mind's eye" has conjured up all these symbols and who is grateful to have been vouchsafed the vision of that dancing girl which has brought him the nearest man can come to a triumph over mortality.—*Cormac's ruined house*: the site of the vision is a vivid reminder of death and mutability.

MICHAEL ROBARTES AND THE DANCER (1921), pp. 81 ff.

An Image from a Past Life (p. 82).—It is hard to avoid reading this poem, the first Yeats wrote at Thoor Ballylee (in 1919), in the light of the poet's love for Maud Gonne and its relationship to his marriage to another woman in 1917. Yeats, however, went to great pains to explain it differently. "No lover, no husband has ever met in dreams the true image of wife or mistress. She who has perhaps filled his whole life with joy or disquiet cannot enter there." The images that do enter dreams are from *Spiritus Mundi* ("a general storehouse of images which have ceased to be a property of any personality or spirit") or "from the state immediately preceding our birth." When they are images of beloved people, they are the forms of those the dreamer "has loved in some past earthly life, chosen from *Spiritus Mundi* by the subconscious will, and through them . . . the dead at whiles outface a living rival." Notice that in the poem it is the woman who sees the image most clearly; the "scream" and "image of poignant recollection" stir the man, but it is she who discerns their specific character. "In moments of excitement images pass from one mind to another with extraordinary ease."

Easter, 1916 (p. 83).—See comment on p. xxx. The poem concerns the abortive Easter Rebellion and its transforming effect on the Irish people. It names or alludes to some of its leaders who were (except for Countess Markievicz, who was imprisoned) court-martialed and shot.—*That woman:* Countess Constance Markievicz, née Gore-Booth.—*This man:* Patrick Pearse.—*England may keep faith:* An allusion to the promise of Home Rule, voted by Parliament but delayed by the outbreak of the world war, and to the possible good intentions of England generally (a characteristic Yeatsian concession which greatly deepens this poem).

On a Political Prisoner (p. 86).—Countess Markievicz, in Holloway Gaol. See preceding note.

Towards Break of Day (p. 87).—The poem is said to record actual simultaneous dreams by Yeats and his wife. The dreams seem to image forth the unattainability of perfection, partly because they suggest the limits life imposes on romantic and sexual love—neither the "over-much" loved water nor the "marvellous" stag is ultimately "ponderable to our touch"—and partly because they hark back to the irrecoverable past, whether literal or mythical.—*The marvellous stag of Arthur:* perhaps the white stag killed by Arthur in the *Mabinogion,* or the one that appeared at his wedding feast in *Morte d'Arthur.* Its use in this poem, though, is primarily as an image of frustration to match that of the husband's dream.

Demon and Beast (p. 88).—The pictures mentioned in the second stanza were in the National Gallery, Dublin. In the third stanza the poet is in St. Stephen's Green, nearby. The poet feels that his aging, his "chilled blood," has given him momentary freedom from the demoniac and bestial powers that rule nature, as though he had gone beyond life. Thus he has learned what the ecstasy of the ascetic followers of St. Anthony must have been like.

The Second Coming (p. 89).—The title suggests a new manifestation of God to man. The Christian era draws to its close, now that its "great year" of two thousand years is ending. We do not know what the new shape of things will be, but it must be terror-filled for us by virtue of the simple fact that it will entail so revolutionary a change. Already we have seen the break-down of the old assumptions in the Great War and in civil wars and the rise of mob tyrannies; the dark forces of the pre-Christian age will come into their own again.—*Spiritus mundi*: the storehouse of archetypal symbols out of which the Sphinx-image of the poem has been drawn. Its source of this particular image is in ancient Egypt, which is felt to be impervious to the humanitarian, individualistic tendency of Christianity. The "rocking cradle" of a new age, whose specific form is not yet revealed to us, has "vexed to nightmare" the sleep of the barbaric past and brought into the poet's mind this prophetic image.

A Prayer for My Daughter (p. 90).—Anne Butler Yeats, born in 1919. —*that great Queen . . . a bandy leggèd smith*: Aphrodite and Hephaestus.

CALVARY (1921), pp. 94 ff.

God has not died for the white heron: Yeats uses birds as "symbols of subjec-tive life," beings "who have served neither God nor Caesar, and await for none or for a different Saviour." Christ was for "objective men," those "never alone in their thought" but always relating it to the thoughts of others and seeking "the welfare of some cause or institution." The bird symbolism, Yeats says, is intended "to increase the objective loneliness of Christ," for "He died in vain" for all beings, human or not, whose subjective loneliness is self-sufficient or who—like Lazarus, Judas, and the Roman soldiers—resent His domination or are indifferent to Him. The soul's ultimate solitude is impen-etrable at either extreme. (See p. xlii.)

THE TOWER (1928), pp. 102 ff.

Sailing to Byzantium (p. 102).—"Byzantium" in Yeats's poetry refers spe-cifically to the capital of the Byzantine empire, in the fifth and sixth centu-ries, when there was "substituted for formal Roman magnificence, with its glorification of physical power, an architecture that suggests the Sacred City in the Apocalypse of St. John. I think if I could be given a month of Antiq-uity . . . I would spend it in Byzantium a little before Justinian opened St. Sophia and closed the Academy of Plato. I think I could find in some little wine-shop some philosophical worker in mosaic who could answer all my questions, the supernatural descending nearer to him than to Plotinus even. . . . I think that in early Byzantium, maybe never before or since in recorded history, religious, aesthetic and practical life were one. . . . The painter, the mosaic worker, the worker in gold and silver, the illuminator of sacred books, were almost impersonal, almost perhaps without the consciousness of individ-ual design. . . ." (*A Vision*, pp. 270–280). Thus, Byzantium, in addition to its exotic Eastern connotations of a romantic nature, and of a stylized art and orientalized Christianity, represents a perfection of aesthetic and spiritual imagination toward which the old man who is the protagonist of Yeats's poem wishes to turn.—*That . . . country*: the country of animal sensuality.—*perne in a gyre*: swoop down in a whirling movement.—*such a form . . . make*: "I have read somewhere that in the Emperor's palace at Byzantium was a tree made of gold and silver, and artificial birds that sang."

The Tower (p. 103).—The Tower, literally, is Thoor Ballylee. In various poems it takes on many symbolic connotations—for instance, the isolation of the poet, his difficult climb (up the "winding stair," whose "gyres" take on related connotations) toward vision and toward reconciliation with death, the limitations of both the body and modern society as "crumbling battlements," the constructs of art, the tradition that goes into the making of a civilization (and specifically, the Irish tradition). The context in any particular poem provides the sense of the symbol. See *Blood and the Moon*, p. 133.—"The persons mentioned are associated by legend, story and tradition with the neighbourhood of Thoor Ballylee or Ballylee Castle, where the poem was written. Mrs. French lived at Peterswell in the eighteenth century. . . . The peasant beauty and the blind poet are Mary Hynes and Raftery, and the incident of the man drowned in Cloone Bog is recorded in my *Celtic Twilight*. . . . When I wrote the lines about Plato and Plotinus I forgot that it is something in our own eyes that makes us see them as all transcendence. Has not Plotinus written: 'Let every soul recall, then, at the outset the truth that soul is the author of all . . . things . . . '?"—*Old lecher*: Hanrahan.

Meditations in Time of Civil War (p. 109).—"These poems were written in Thoor Ballylee in 1922, during the civil war. . . ."—*IV. My Descendants: an old neighbour . . . a girl*: Lady Gregory and Mrs. Yeats.—*V. The Road at My Door: Irregular*: member of Irish Republican Army, which opposed any alliance with English power and started Civil War.—*brown Lieutenant*: member of National Army of provisional "Free State" government, which accepted Dominion status.—*VI. The Stare's Nest* etc.: *stare*: starling.—*We are closed in*: an allusion to the lack of communication, blowing up of bridges (even the "ancient bridge" of poem *II*), etc., in the Civil War.—*VII. I See Phantoms* etc.: *'Vengeance upon the murderers'*: "A cry for vengeance because of the murder of the Grand Master of the Templars seems to me fit symbol of those who labour from hatred, and so for sterility in various kinds. . . ."

Nineteen Hundred and Nineteen (p. 115).—*I. Now days are dragon-ridden*: This stanza is the clue to the mood of the whole of this six-part poem; it alludes to the atrocities perpetrated by the Auxiliaries and the Black and Tans in the course of the British efforts to subdue the Irish Republican Army. —*VI.* "The country-people see at times certain apparitions whom they name now 'fallen angels,' now 'ancient inhabitants of the country,' and describe as riding at whiles 'with flowers upon the heads of the horses.' I have assumed . . . that these horsemen, now that the times worsen, give way to worse. My last symbol, Robert Artisson, was an evil spirit much run after in Kilkenny at the start of the fourteenth century."—*Herodias' daughters*: malevolent spirits, or witches. See note to *The Hosting of the Sidhe*, p. 220.

Two Songs from a Play (p. 119).—The play is *The Resurrection*.—*a staring virgin*: Athene. Yeats parallels the death and rebirth of Dionysus (whose heart was swallowed by Zeus so that he might be reborn) with those of Jesus, alluded to in the closing lines ("that fierce virgin and her Star," etc.) of the first of these "songs."—*Another Troy*, etc.: This stanza echoes Virgil's fourth *Eclogue*, lines 31–36, which foretells a golden age; and a famous chorus in Shelley's *Hellas*, which does so also, though with misgivings. But Yeats's lines seem a refutation of Shelley, for they put forth the idea that "God's death"

241

and indeed all history are "but a play" with no significance beyond its cyclical character, except what man reads into it. As the death and rebirth of Dionysus ushered in the Grecian age, so those of Christ heralded an irrational age.—The closing stanza of the second "song" resolves the problem back to man's own self-consuming imagination.

Fragments (p. 120).—John Locke's philosophy is here associated with the triumph of the machine and the death of mystical faith in modern religion.

Leda and the Swan (p. 121).—In the Greek myth, Leda was ravished by Zeus in the form of a swan. From that act were born two sets of twins: Helen and Pollux, and Clytemnestra and Castor. Yeats's sonnet recalls the Trojan War that ensued from Helen's beauty, and the murder of Agamemnon by his wife, Clytemnestra, upon his return from that war. These and related events became the subject matter of much literature and thought and in a sense created a civilization. The poet asks whether the impregnation of Leda was accompanied by any divine illumination of her understanding; in the context of Yeats's other poetry, the question is one to be asked about every miraculous conception reported in myth and religion. Ultimately perhaps the poem asks what is the relationship between man's fate and his will or knowledge.

Among School Children (p. 121).—*public man*: Yeats was appointed to the Irish Senate in 1922.—*Ledaean body*: a body like Leda's. Presumably the allusion is to Maud Gonne when both were younger.—*Plato's parable*: Aristophanes' account, in Plato's *Symposium*, of the origin of the sexes. (At one time male and female were the two halves of a single body, which was then cut in half like a hard-cooked egg divided with a thread.) The Ledaean allusion drew Yeats into developing the egg figure, which in addition has an ancient cosmogonic significance. Both Aristophanes, in Plato's account, and Yeats combine humor with a deeper seriousness.—*daughters of the swan*: this phrase suggests that "Ledaean body" is meant to refer to Helen, who shared her mother's beauty. By using "Ledaean," Yeats was enabled to bring in the figures of egg and swan more easily.—*Quattrocento finger*: artist of fifteenth-century Italy, perhaps Leonardo.

THE WINDING STAIR AND OTHER POEMS (1933), pp. 129 ff.

In Memory of Eva Gore-Booth and Con Markievicz (p. 129).—The poem commemorates two sisters, who died in 1926 and 1927 respectively. In addition to their mystical and artistic pursuits, both were politically committed. Constance Markievicz was a leader in the 1916 Rising, sentenced to death afterwards but then given a prison term instead; after her release she returned to a militant political career.—*Lissadell*: the richly appointed Gore-Booth estate in Sligo.—*gazebo*: literally, a high-windowed balcony or turret, or a summer house designed for gazing outward at scenery. Here the word suggests an idealistic or visionary construct that has gone down in ruins during one of history's irresistible cyclical changes ("conflagrations").

Blood and the Moon (p. 133).—"Part of the symbolism . . . was suggested by the fact that Thoor Ballylee has a waste room at the top and that butterflies come in through the loopholes and die against the window-panes."—*Saeva Indignatio*: savage indignation; the phrase is used in Swift's epitaph, which is virtually translated in Yeats's poem on p. 138.—"I think that I was roused to write *Death* (p. 130) and *Blood and the Moon* by the assassination of Kevin O'Higgins, the finest intellect in Irish public life. . . ."

Coole and Ballylee, 1931 (pp. 136 ff).—*Somebody that toils*, etc.: Lady Gregory.

Byzantium (p. 138).—See note on *Sailing to Byzantium*, p. 226.—*cathedral: Sancta Sophia.*—The first three stanzas give three images of the relation between the superhuman and the human: first, the dome of the cathedral rises above human complexities, "disdaining" them through transcendence; second, there is the ghostly image linking the living speaker to life beyond death; third, there is the golden bird on the golden bough, similar to the figure of the last stanza of *Sailing to Byzantium*. The fourth stanza pictures symbolically the midnight moment of aesthetic transformation, and the fifth reminds us of the endless life of the body and the emotions out of which the transcendent images of art are begotten. While the language of the poem suggests an aesthetic emphasis, every kind of spiritual and intellectual transcendence is implied at the same time.—*Astraddle on the dolphin:* traditionally, the dolphin carries the dead to the Isles of the Blest. Here the dolphin is also associated with the "mire and blood" of the "disdained" physical world; the picture is related to Yeats's sexual and aesthetic-centered picture of the Earthly Paradise in *News for the Delphic Oracle* (p. 192) and to the argument of *Crazy Jane Talks with the Bishop* (p. 148).

The Mother of God (p. 140).—*a fallen flare . . . ear:* "I had in my memory Byzantine mosaic pictures of the Annunciation, which show a line drawn from a star to the ear of the Virgin. She received the Word through the ear, a star fell and a star was born."

Vacillation (p. 140).—This sequence of poems balances against one another two possible approaches to joy, in the face of death and of the endless pull on man of extreme opposites of value. Poem *I* presents the issue whether or not joy is possible. Poem *II* puts forward the ascetic approach, in the image of those worshipers of Attis who castrated themselves at his annual festival. Thus they met the challenge of life, symbolized in the tree, half of which is lushly natural and half blazing in a perfection beyond life, through renunciation alone. They achieved a partial joy only, not that transcendence which can only begin (as in *A Dialogue of Self and Soul*, p. 130) with self-acceptance. Poem *III* suggests a practical program such as Yeats himself might have wished to follow, which involves renunciation of all that will not make for true artistic success; but poem *IV*, with its picture of the solitary man in the midst of ordinary life, shows a kind of joy not hard-won but simply, suddenly, blazing up. Despite the moods of remorse and fatalism of poems *V* and *VI*, the final two return to the theme of taking the main chance in the midst of life, of following the pagan and half-secular way of myth and art rather than the ascetic path of orthodox Christianity.

Crazy Jane and Jack the Journeyman (p. 147).—*Mine must walk when dead:* Richard J. Finneran (*Editing Yeats's Poems*, pp. 19–22) argues thoughtfully, on both bibliographical and interpretive grounds, for the reading: "Mine would walk being dead." The editorial problem—given the unresolved question of which set of proofs (among those available) has priority—is typical of many presented by Yeats's materials. Under the circumstances, I have chosen Yeats's poetically more emphatic, and equally suggestive, alternative.

'I Am of Ireland' (p. 153).—The words of the refrain, except for the third line, are virtually the same as those of the fourteenth-century lyric from which it is taken.

The Delphic Oracle upon Plotinus (p. 155).—In Porphyry's Life of Plotinus, the Delphic oracle explains where the philosopher Plotinus' soul has gone after death. This poem, a condensed version, shows the dying man "swimming" through difficult waters of transformation toward the Happy Isles. There, noble figures like Plato and himself join the "Choir of Love" forever. They have been selected by Rhadamanthus and Minos, sons of Zeus and thus members of "the Golden Race," who are judges in the realm of the dead, selecting the most worthy for this place in it.

THE WORDS UPON THE WINDOW-PANE (1934), pp. 158 ff.

The best account of the motives underlying this play appears in Yeats's *Wheels and Butterflies* (1934) as " 'The Words Upon the Window-Pane,' Introduction" and in *The Variorum Edition of the Plays of W. B. Yeats* (1966) as "Notes." It is a brilliant essay on Swift and his world ("Swift haunts me; he is always just around the next corner") and at the same time an essential presentation of Yeats's political theories grounded in eighteenth-century Irish thinking and of his attitudes toward séances and spiritualism. Much of what John Corbet says in the play is repeated in the essay, which, however, has a wider range. It ponders Swift's puzzling relationship to "Stella" and "Vanessa" (Esther Johnson and Hester Vanhomrigh, intimate friends of Swift—perhaps lovers, perhaps platonic loves). Yeats speculates that Swift's reluctance to marry was due to fear of his coming madness and its possibly hereditary character, and tries to connect his pathology to his dread of the disastrous direction he thought Western civilization was taking.

Ballymony: one of two possible localities in Ireland.—Human Personality: book by F. W. H. Meyers [not "Myers"] (1903).—David Hume: Actually, Daniel Horne, Scottish spiritualist and medium.—Harold's Cross: a dog-racing track. Grattan: See Glossary.—saeva indignatio: savage indignation (See the poem "Swift's Epitaph," p. 138.)—Perish the day on which I was born!: See Job, 3:3.

I am indebted to Professor Mary Margaret FitzGerald for information about the text.

A FULL MOON IN MARCH (1935), pp. 172 ff.

Parnell's Funeral (p. 172).—The Great Comedian: Daniel O'Connell (1775–1847), sometimes jocular, sometimes bitterly witty leader of the successful movement for Catholic Emancipation and opponent of violence. "As we discussed and argued, the national character changed. O'Connell, the great comedian, left the scene and the tragedian Parnell took his place."—a brighter star: one of the strange sights reported by people attending Parnell's funeral.—A beautiful seated boy etc.: Yeats refers us to a note in his Autobiography (p. 382) concerning the woman who shot the arrow: "She was, it seems, the Mother-Goddess whose representative priestess shot the arrow at the child whose sacrificial death symbolized the death and resurrection of the Tree-Spirit, or Apollo." The note to the poem says: "I ask if the fall of the star may not, upon occasion, symbolise an accepted sacrifice." Thus Yeats seeks to put the death of Parnell on the same plane as that of one of the great mythical figures of Frazer's *The Golden Bough*. The removal and devouring of the heart suggests a profane sacrament deifying Parnell as if he were Dionysus or even Jesus. (See *Two Songs from a Play*, p. 119.) Unlike other Irish martyrs, he has been dragged down by his own people, the poet among them. As yet no rebirth has taken place. The leaders that have followed him might have purified and strengthened themselves and thus brought him into being again by "eating his heart" in another sense: that is, by taking on his steadfast will and intense purpose. But theirs is the opposite sin to the viciousness of the mob. It is the sin of omission, a failure of passionate, idealistic conviction.— The third stanza was published by itself over two years before the poem in its complete form appeared.

Supernatural Songs (p. 174).—"I would consider [that old hermit] Ribh, were it not for his ideas about the Trinity, an orthodox man." (Irony aside, the viewpoint is similar to that of the last section of *Vacillation*, p. 143.)

New Poems (1938), pp. 178 ff.

The Gyres (p. 178).—At the beginning the poet exclaims at the irreversible processes, the "gyres," of life and history. All that is held dear must perish until its time comes again: there is no alternative but to rejoice.—*Old Rocky Face*: this seems a kind of oracle, cherishing the best values but counseling joy in the face of their destruction. As Rocky Face inhabits a cavern, it may reside in the mountain-pit described at the beginning of *Man and the Echo* (p. 210). Notice that the latter poem at one point addresses the Echo as "Rocky Voice."

The Municipal Gallery Revisited (p. 193).—This is the gallery in Dublin; Yeats is describing his reactions to certain paintings by Sir John Lavery, Sean Keating, J. S. Sargent, his own father (the portrait of Synge in the final stanza), and others.

Last Poems and Two Plays (1939), pp. 199 ff.

Under Ben Bulben (p. 199).—*Calvert*, etc.: these artists of the sixteenth to eighteenth centuries are painters of integrity, still infused with the Quattrocento spirit if not with its revelatory power. But since them the modern "confusion" has been predominant.—*Cast a cold eye*, etc.: this final passage is cut on Yeats's gravestone.

The Black Tower (p. 202).—The refrain alludes to an ancient Irish custom of burying warriors standing, in a posture of combat.

Cuchulain Comforted (p. 203).—Yeats called this poem "a kind of sequel" to his play *The Death of Cuchulain*. (See Allan Wade, ed., *The Letters of W. B. Yeats*, p. 922.)

The Statues (p. 205).—Greek rationality, or measurement, is symbolized in the Pythagorean theory of numbers and in the measured proportions of Hellenic sculpture, which created standards of beauty and of the objects of desire. Against it are set Asiatic formlessness, symbolized in the relaxed inclusiveness of Buddha; the anti-aesthetic and self-indulgent sloth of Christianity grown decadent ("a fat dreamer of the Middle Ages"); and mere animality, perhaps demoniac, embodied in Grimalkin. The modern Irish have been flung by their struggles into a crucial moment of choice. "Pearse and some of his followers had a cult" of Cuchulain, wrote Yeats in a letter (*Letters*, 911). That clearly defined heroic image is a challenge to Ireland to combine passion with clear, measured vision in contrast to the formlessness of "this filthy modern tide." The final lines suggest that Ireland, wrecked by "formless spawning fury," must first grope in the dark to try to sense the right lineaments of an emergent personality to be created, as the Greeks created theirs, out of inspired calculation.

News for the Delphic Oracle (p. 206).—A Yeatsian reconstruction of the Earthly Paradise, inhabited by figures representing every variety of love—mystical idealism, mythical romance, and sensual passion. Divine love makes up the whole landscape and seascape and general atmosphere. It has a transcendent, joyous indifference like that of the Muses in *Two Songs from a Play*, and accepts the sufferings of the children slaughtered by Herod as "sweet and strange." The "intolerable music" that goes on endlessly is that of sexuality or the life force.—*dolphins:* See note on *Byzantium*, p. 243.

Man and the Echo (p. 210).—*that play of mine:* probably *Cathleen-ni-Houlihan*, performed in 1902; it had a tremendous political effect.—*that woman* and *that whereby a house lay wrecked:* there have been various speculations about these allusions. In any case, they reveal the poet's self-questioning about his responsibilities as man and artist.

The Circus Animals' Desertion (p. 212).—*I.* The "circus animals" are Yeats's body of motifs and symbols, which in this poem he says have deserted him so that he must use his own "heart," or self, for theme.—*stilted boys:* Oisin, Fergus, and other figures of Celtic legendry.—*II.* In this section the poet shows how, from the beginning, it was indeed the heart or self that he had meant to make this theme all along, but always in the past the dream, or symbolic world of the poem, has managed to engross his attention rather than "those things that they were emblems of."—*my dear:* Maude Gonne. Yeats alludes to his old quarrel with her about her immersion in political activity. He thus accounts for his writing *The Countess Cathleen*, in which she acted the title role. Here too "the dream itself" took over his attention.

THE DEATH OF CUCHULAIN (1939), pp. 215 ff.

This play contains references to a number of Yeats's earlier treatments of the Cuchulain legend, chiefly his poem *Cuchulain's Fight with the Sea* (p. 8) and several plays: (1) *At the Hawk's Well*, in which a being like the Morrigu appears and in which Aoife, a female warrior of the Sidhe (see Glossary) with whom Cuchulain both fights and makes love is a central if elusive figure; (2) *The Green Helmet*, in which Cuchulain's fellow hero Conal is a comic would-be rival; (3) *On Baile's Strand*, in which Cuchulain unknowingly kills his own son by Aoife in single combat (*Cuchulain's Fight with the Sea* deals with this story too, but presents Cuchulain's wife Emer as the young man's mother) and in which the Blind Man of the later play makes his first appearance; and (4) *The Only Jealousy of Emer*, a complexly symbolic work (like *The Death of Cuchulain*) in which Emer saves her husband from death by giving up hope for his future love and yielding him to his young mistress Eithne Inguba.

246

A major source for Yeats was Lady Augusta Gregory's *Cuchulain of Muirthemne* (1902). He made free, inconsistent use of Irish legend, especially in *The Only Jealousy of Emer*, *The Death of Cuchulain*, and the late poem *Cuchulain Comforted* (p. 203), and clearly came to treat Cuchulain as in part embodying certain of his own psychological crises and pressures. (See pp. xliii–xliv.) The essential materials derive from the *Tàin Bó Cuálnge* (*The Cattle Raid of Cooley*), the Irish epic of which Cuchulain is the hero.

Talma: François-Joseph Talma (1763–1826), famed French tragic actor, a favorite of Napoleon.—*Emain Macha:* ancient capital of Ulster.—*such a dancer:* An early draft specifies Ninette de Valois.—*The grey of Macha:* one of Cuchulain's chariot horses.—*Usna's boys:* In the legend of Deirdre (see Yeats's play *Deirdre*), her lover Naoise and his brothers, who helped him flee with her to Scotland.—*the Post Office:* Dublin site seized during the Easter Rebellion and surrendered after the rebels' defeat.—*living men* (Street Singer's song, p. 223): I have placed a comma here (end of line 12) because the "that"-clauses in the succeeding four lines parallel the "what"-clause beginning in line 10 and are equally the objects of the verb "recall." (The punctuation of all extant texts is incoherent.)—*Who thought Cuchulain:* Yeats wrote: "Cuchulain is in the last stanza because Pearse and some of his followers had a cult of him." (See Allan Wade, ed., *The Letters of W. B. Yeats*, p. 911.)

Purgatory (1939), pp. 225 ff.

See *A Vision*, Book III, Section XI, for some of the mystical and psychological implications of this play. See also p. xliii.—*the Curragh:* site of a famous racetrack, and of race-horse training and breeding, in County Kildare.—*Aughrim and the Boyne:* sites where William of Orange defeated Irish and Catholic forces in 1690.—*Puck Fair:* annual festival, especially of tinkers, in County Kerry.—*Tertullian:* Church father (A.D. 160?–230?) who wrote an *Apology* for Christianity. The Old Man proposes, ironically, that this work can help him cope with the degrading scene being reenacted in the house.

On the Text[2]

The text of the poems in this selection is a conflation based on *The Variorum Edition of the Poems* (1957), edited by Peter Allt and Russell K. Alspach, and *The Poems of W. B. Yeats: A New Edition* (1983), edited by Richard J. Finneran. The text of the plays is a conflation based on *The Variorum Edition of the Plays* (1966), edited by Alspach, and texts published in the Cornell Yeats series under David R. Clark's general editorship: namely, *The Death of Cuchulain* (1982), edited by Phillip R. Marcus, and *Purgatory* (1986), edited by Sandra F. Siegel. For complex reasons, we have no absolutely "right" text in many instances. I am grateful for what I have learned from the scholars, living and dead, just named, although of course none of them is responsible for textual decisions I have made.

I have taken advantage of a most important textual improvement in the *New Edition* over previous posthumous editions of Yeats's collected poems. The improvement consists of the proper sorting out (noted in my Foreword) of the groups of poems which those editions run together, without differentiation,

[2] See Bibliography for fuller notation.

as "Last Poems." After Yeats died his widow and Thomas Mark, his editor at Macmillan (London), set to work readying a "definitive" collected edition, including these "Last Poems." They agreed to combine, under this heading, the poems he had prepared for three separate publications: *New Poems* (1938) and the posthumous 1939 volumes *On the Boiler* and *Last Poems and Two Plays*. They also altered the order decided on by Yeats for *Last Poems and Two Plays*, mixing in poems from *On the Boiler* as well. The need to put all this right has been generally recognized by scholars for a number of years, beginning with findings published by Curtis Bradford in 1961.[3]

I cannot go much further here into the tangled history of Yeats's text, described in broad detail in Professor Finneran's *Editing Yeats's Poems* (1983) and argued over with some heat in the *Times Literary Supplement* and elsewhere. Finneran's edition of the poems is based primarily on the latest copytexts in manuscripts, letters, typescripts, proofs, or published versions seen by the poet before he died (28 January 1939). As a result, there are many tiny differences, and some important ones, between the *New Edition* and earlier established collections.

One set of differences has to do with punctuation. Yeats's was inconsistent and could be irrational by even the most sympathetic standards. He was aware of the problem and regularly depended on others—Thomas Mark especially— for help, although he did not always accept their suggestions. For the post-humous work that Mark repunctuated, reorganized, and apparently changed in other ways, we do not, naturally, have the author's imprimatur. At the same time, there is always a possibility that Yeats's editor and widow had access to proofs and other materials that have disappeared: something one has to bear in mind. Sometimes, too, they may well have chosen a superior version of a line or passage or even a whole poem. We have at least one striking instance of this last case in "John Kinsella's Lament for Mrs. Mary Moore." The text in what we might call the "Mark Edition" is based on one first published in the *London Mercury* of December 1938; the text in the *New Edition* is based on a letter Yeats wrote on 22 November 1938 offering emendations to make the poem "more suitable for singing." Never prepared for publication, this version— although I am sure one could learn to love it—has some awkwardness and does not match the harder wit and more sinewy rhythm of the other.

And yet, despite what I have just asserted, the *New Edition* version *may* be what Yeats would have preferred. As Professor Finneran notes in his Pref-ace to *Editing Yeats's Poems*, "any edition . . . will always be a provisional one, partly because not all manuscript material will be known or available, partly because many . . . decisions will have to be subjective and arguable." In general I have followed him whenever, from the standpoint of printing a coherent, superior, and justifiable text for readers, it has seemed possible to do so. Yeats obviously preferred a leaner punctuation, based on sound rather than syntax, than Mark did (although he also had a passion for the semicolon and sometimes forgot to round off a sentence with a period). As part of its scholarly scrupulousness, the Finneran edition respects this preference.

With the two posthumously printed plays, *The Death of Cuchulain* and

³ Curtis Bradford, "The Order of *Last Poems*," *Modern Language Notes*, 76 (June 1961), 515–516.

Purgatory, I am much indebted to the editions, by Professors Marcus and Siegel respectively, of these plays' "manuscript materials, including the author's final texts." I have followed the same procedure as with the poems. Where there are choices to be made one must make them, if hardly ever without a pang of regret. For the time being, all who go beyond a certain point in pursuit of Yeats's texts must make essential comparisons for themselves, using their own best critical judgment—which, in turn, will depend on a combination of textual responsibility and love and understanding of the work itself.

Glossary of Names and Places

Aengus (Oenghus MacOc)   The ancient Celtic "master of love" and god of youth, beauty, and poetry, who "reigned in Tir-Nan-Oge, the country of the young." Yeats's "Wandering Aengus" seems to be a mortal who ages, yet the incident he describes is based on the story of the god's love for Caer Ibhormheith, the faery girl.

Aherne, Owen   A fictitious character, to some extent Yeats's own spokesman. See Notes, p. 237.

Aillinn   Legendary princess, daughter of King Lugaidh. She and Baile, heir to Ulster's throne, "were lovers, but Aengus, the Master of Love, wishing them to be happy in his own land among the dead, told to each a story of the other's death, so that their hearts were broken and they died." (Yeats's note.) In original versions, not Aengus but a malicious spirit deceives them.

Anthony, St. (Anthony the Great), c. 250–350   Egyptian founder of Christian monasticism.

Armstrong   A military family in Yeats's paternal ancestry.

Artisson, Robert   "Incubus" of Dame Alice Kyteler, who was tried for practice of magic in 1324.

Aughrim   Site of second great defeat of James II's forces in Ireland (1691), consolidating the Protestant and Anglican ascendancy. (See **Boyne.**)

Baile   See **Aillinn.**

Ballylee   Near Coole. Mary Hynes, the beauty celebrated by Raftery the Gaelic poet and by Yeats in "The Tower," lived here. Yeats purchased Thoor Ballylee, his Norman tower and farmhouse, here in 1917.

Beauvarlet (Jacques-Firmin [1731–1797]?)   French painter.

Ben Bulben   Mountain in County Sligo, Ireland.

Berenice's Hair   The Constellation Coma Berenices.

Berkeley, George (1685–1753)   Irish philosopher; Bishop of Cloyne (1734), proponent of subjective idealism.

The Blind Man   Character in Yeats's plays *On Baile's Strand* and *The Death of Cuchulain.*

Boyne   Irish river; site of important battle in 1690 in which William III of England defeated the forces of James II.

Burke, Edmund (1729–1797)   Whig statesman and orator of Anglo-Irish descent admired by Yeats for his independence of thought and unconventional conservatism.

Butler   A family in Yeats's paternal ancestry dating from the marriage of Benjamin Yeats to Mary Butler in 1773.

Byzantium   see Notes, p. 240.

Calvert, Denis (1540–1619) Flemish painter, founder of Bolognese school.

Caoilte Legendary Irish hero (companion of Oisin).

Casement, Sir Roger (1864–1916) Irish Nationalist hanged by the British as a traitor in World War I because of his dealings with the German government to gain support for the Easter rising.

Cashel Site in Tipperary of chapel which Cormac MacCarthy restored in twelfth century.

Cathleen, the daughter of Houlihan Traditionally the symbol of Ireland. (See Yeats's play *Cathleen-ni-Houlihan*, in whose first production Maud Gonne played the title role.)

Chou, lord of A member of the Chou dynasty, which had the longest reign in Chinese history—possibly Wên Wang, Wu Wang, or Chou Kung, all idealized by Confucian scholars and later generations.

Claude (Claude Lorrain, 1600–1682) Landscape painter.

Clooth-na-Bare A faery who sought death in the deepest lake in the world, which she found in Sligo; hence, also a place name.

Conal (often spelled "Conall") **Caernach** Legendary hero-companion to Cuchulain. (see Notes, p. 246, to *The Death of Cuchulain*.)

Conchubar The king who reigned over Cuchulain and the Red Branch heroes after Fergus laid aside the crown.

Connolly, James (1870–1916) Marxian commander in chief of Easter Rebellion, executed for his part in it.

Coole; Coole Park Site of Lady Gregory's estate in Galway.

Cormac Cormac MacCarthy, twelfth century Munster King. See **Cashel.**

Cosgrave, William Thomas (1880–1965) Irish political leader; first president of the executive council of the Irish Free State (1922–1932).

The Countess Cathleen A play by Yeats produced in 1899.

Crazy Jane Character invented by Yeats, based on various folk and literary sources but also on an actual person whom he described but did not name (Cf. *Letters*, pp. 785–786).

Cuchulain (pronounced *Cuhoolin*) The great hero of the Red Branch cycle of Irish tales, chief warrior under Conchubar, who became in Yeats's later writing a symbol of his own values and problems and those of Ireland.

Danaan children Children of the magical world of Faerie, that is, of the Tuatha de Danaan. See Notes, p. 234.

Davis, Thomas Osborne (1814–1845) Irish poet, cofounder of *The Nation*, and leader of revolutionary Young Ireland party.

The Dean Jonathan Swift.

De Valera, Eamon (1882–1975) Irish political leader, for many years the most powerful figure in government of Ireland.

Diarmuid Hero of tragic love tale who eloped with Grania, the betrothed of the great chief Finn. He was killed by a magical boar through Finn's treachery.

Drumcliff Village in Sligo.

The Dutchman William III (William of Orange). See **James.**

Emer   Wife of Cuchulain; Yeats calls her "great-bladdered" in Rabelaisian appreciation of her triumph in a contest in the snow with other mythological ladies, but she is not a comic figure. See "Crazy Jane on the Mountain," p. 196.

Emery, Florence Farr (d. 1917)   Actress, fellow occultist, and friend of Yeats. She spent her last years, the "foul years" of his poem "All Souls' Night," teaching in Ceylon while suffering from cancer.

Emmet, Robert (1778–1803)   Leader of unsuccessful Irish revolt in 1803, hanged after capture and trial.

Fergus   "King of the proud Red Branch Kings" who, preferring less worldly pursuits, gave up his power to Conchubar, son of Nessa, as the price of marriage to Nessa. Yeats calls him "the poet of the Red Branch cycle, as Oisin was of the Fenian" cycle of mythical tales of ancient Ireland.

Ferguson, Sir Samuel (1810–1886)   Poet and lawyer much involved in reviving study of Gaelic antiquity and creating a new national literature.

Ferrara   Duke Ercole of Ferrara was renowned as a patron of art, letters, and the theater in the Renaissance.

Fitzgerald, Lord Edward (1763–1798)   Revolutionist who fought for Irish independence with the United Irishmen; died of wounds after being seized with other conspirators.

The Fool   Character in Yeats's play *On Baile's Strand.*

Fuller, Loie (1862–1928)   American soubrette and exotic dancer, admired by Mallarmé and others because of the similarity between her concept of dance and the Symbolist approach to poetry.

Giorgione, Giorgio Barbarelli (1478?–1511)   Venetian painter.

Glasnevin   The north Dublin cemetery in which Parnell was buried on October 11, 1891.

Goldsmith, Oliver (1728–1774)   Anglo-Irish poet, playwright, novelist.

Gonne, Maud (1866–1953)   British-born Irish revolutionary nationalist, the beauty who is "Helen," "My phoenix," etc., in Yeats's poetry but who refused him several times. She married Major John MacBride in 1903, and separated from him in 1905. See p. xxxiii.

Grania   The young bethrothed of the legendary Finn, whom she fled with Diarmuid. See **Diarmuid.** After Diarmuid's death she returned to Finn.

Grattan, Henry (1746–1829)   Orator and statesman who fought for Irish independence and Catholic emancipation.

Gregory, Anne   Granddaughter of Lady Gregory.

Gregory, Lady Augusta (1852–1932), née Persse   Irish playwright, one of the founders of the Abbey Theatre and student of Irish mythology and folk tales; Yeats's great friend and patron after 1896. Wife of Sir William Gregory (1817–1892), political figure who became governor of Ceylon.

Gregory, Major Robert   Son of Lady Gregory; artist, aviator; killed in action over Italy in 1918.

253

Griffith, Arthur (1872–1922) Founded Sinn Fein movement; first president of Irish Free State.
Guido Cavalcanti (c. 1255–1300) Italian poet, friend of Dante.

Hanrahan (Red Hanrahan) Protagonist of Yeats's *Stories of Red Hanrahan* (1904).
Horton, William Thomas (1864–1919) Artist and mystic.

Innisfree Island in Lough Gill, Sligo.

James James II, Catholic monarch decisively defeated by William III in two great battles in Ireland in 1690.
Johnson, Lionel (1867–1902) A leading poet of the 1890s.

Kiltartan Village near the estate of Lady Gregory.
Knocknarea Mountain in Sligo.

Lady Kyteler See **Robert Artisson.**
Lane, Hugh (1874–1915) Nephew of Lady Gregory; connoisseur and art dealer, collector of French impressionists which he wished to give to Ireland if they were housed in a special gallery to be built on a bridge over the Liffey. This offer, which was refused, and the public reaction to a Dublin exhibit of the paintings in 1908, became the subject of a bitter controversy. Lane died on the *Lusitania.*
Lapo Gianni Florentine poet, Dante's friend.
Lavery, Sir John and Hazel Irish painter (1856–1941) and his second wife (d. 1935).

MacBride, Major John (d. 1916) The "drunken, vainglorious lout" of "Easter 1916." Fought with Boers against England, and was executed for his part in the Easter uprising in Dublin. See **Maud Gonne.**
MacDonagh, Thomas (1878–1916) Poet executed for his part in the Easter Rebellion.
MacGregor "MacGregor Mathers" (1854–1918), translator of Rosenroth's *Kabalah Denudata.* A student of occultism with whom Yeats often stayed on visits to Paris. His real name was Samuel Liddell Mathers.
Maeve Queen of Connaught, Cuchulain's great opponent, who is supposedly buried on Knocknarea; her supposed invasion of Ulster is memorialized in "The Cattle-Raid of Cooley," central story of the Red Branch cycle; in folk tradition a queen of the faeries.
Mancini, Antonio (1852–1930) Italian landscape, genre, and portrait artist who painted Yeats and Lady Gregory.
Mangan, James Clarence (1803–1849) Romantic nationalist poet; adapter of Gaelic poems.
Mareotic Lake or Sea In Egypt: one site of the visions of the human soul and condition in Shelley's "The Witch of Atlas" (stanzas LVIII ff.); also, one of the regions in which Egyptian Christian monasticism flourished.

Meru Mt. Kailás (called Mt. Meru in the Mahabharata), the most famous Oriental dwelling place of gods and object of pilgrimages.

Mitchel, John (1815–1875?) Founder of United Irishmen.

Molay, Jacques de Grand Master of the Templars, burned for witchcraft in 1314. See Notes, p. 241.

Montashigi of Osafume Supposedly the maker of the Japanese sword which, with its silken sheath, Yeats called "my symbol of life."

Niamh (pronounced *Neeave*) Beloved of Oisin, whom she lures into the adventures described in Yeats's long early narrative poem "The Wanderings of Oisin." (See the Fenian tale *Oisin in the Land of the Young* for the original account.) Her name means "brightness and beauty." She is a "man-picker" because she is the wooer in "The Wanderings of Oisin."

O'Donnell, Hugh Roe (1571?–1602) Intransigent enemy of the English power in Ireland, one of the lords of Tyrconnel (modern Donegal).

O'Duffy, Owen (1892–1944) Chief of staff of Irish Republican Army (1921–1922) and of Irish Free State armed forces (1924–1925) who became leader of the fascist Blue Shirt Party and led a brigade in support of Franco in the Spanish Civil War.

O'Grady, Standish (1846–1928) Irish writer whose studies and popularizations helped create the Celtic Renaissance. His works are a basic source for Yeats's conception of Irish mythology and history.

O'Higgins, Kevin Christopher (1892–1929) Irish political figure who, as Minister for External Affairs, established the Civic Guard and restored order in Ireland. He was assassinated, his friend Yeats felt, because William Thomas Cosgrave had not been a decisive enough leader.

Oisin (pronounced *Usheen*) Son of Finn (central figure of the Fenian cycle of Irish mythological tales); a great poet as well as a warrior, he was chosen for lover by Niamh, the daughter of Aengus (god of poetry, youth, and love).

O'Leary, John (1830–1907) Fenian leader imprisoned 1865–1870 and then exiled for fifteen years, profoundly admired by Yeats for his qualities of personality.

O'Neill ("both O'Neills") Ulster chieftains, probably "Shane the Proud" (1532–1567) and his nephew Hugh (1540?–1616). Both stoutly resisted English encroachment and built Irish unity.

Ormondes Portraits of earls, marquises, and dukes of Ormonde—titled members of the Irish Butler family—hanging in the National Gallery, Dublin (part of the Hugh Lane bequest).

Oscar The "Oscar" of "A Statesman's Holiday" may well be the brilliantly witty Oscar Wilde. Alternatively, he may be the son of Oisin, a great warrior like his father in Irish mythology and considered a model of magnanimity. If so, the allusion is to the absence of aristocratic patronage of art and guidance to political principle in the modern world.

Palmer, Samuel (1805–1881) English painter and etcher, whose "The Lonely Tower" is one of the illustrations of "Il Penseroso" in *The Shorter Poems of John Milton* (Seeley and Co., 1889).

Parnell, Charles Stewart (1846–1891)   The outstanding figure of nineteenth-century Irish nationalism, extraordinarily effective in his parliamentary fight for home rule and for rights of Irish tenants. His career was ruined and his cause greatly damaged by exposure in a divorce suit of his adultery with Mrs. William O'Shea. Yeats viewed him as the ideal leader, committed but tough-minded, who was brought down less by his opponents than by the fickleness of his own followers.

Paudeen   Irish term for a petty-spirited, uncultivated fellow countryman.

Pearse, Patrick (1879–1916)   Author, teacher, commander in chief of Irish forces in Easter Rebellion, executed after surrender.

Pollexfen, George   Maternal uncle of Yeats, interested in astrology and magic.

Raftery, Anthony ("dark" Raftery), c. 1784–1835   Blind poet who composed in Irish.

Red Branch   House of the warriors celebrated in the Ulster (Uladh) cycle of Old Irish tales centering on Cuchulain and King Conchubar MacNessa.

Ribh   Fictitious character invented by Yeats as a mystical spokesman, a critic of Christian orthodoxy, "his Christianity coming perhaps from Egypt, and echoing pre-Christian thought." He speaks prophetically out of the same impulse that produced *A Vision*—that is, out of a conception of the subordination of man and his ideas and religions to the impersonal cyclical processes of warring opposites that constitute destiny. (Compare the Ribhus, celestial artists of the Veda.)

Robartes, Michael   Fictitious character, to some extent Yeats's own spokesman. See Notes, p. 237.

Sato, Junzo   League of Nations official who met Yeats in America and presented him with an ancient Japanese sword.

Sidhe (pronounced *Shee*)   The faeries, but with a more general implication of supernatural beings. See Notes, p. 234.

Sidney, Sir Philip (1554–1586)   Considered the very type of the Renaissance man because of his versatility—poet, soldier, statesman. (Yeats compares Robert Gregory to him because Major Gregory too was a gifted, versatile aristocrat killed in war.)

Strafford   Sir Thomas Wentworth, first Earl of Strafford (1593–1641). English anti-Puritan statesman, lord deputy of Ireland (1632–1638), chief adviser to Charles who plotted to coerce Parliament by force and was executed. A portrait by a member of the school of Van Dyck hangs in the National Gallery, Dublin.

Swift, Jonathan (1667–1745)   Dean of St. Patrick's, Dublin (1713). Yeats greatly admired Swift's savage wit and generally telling literary style, and emulated him as a great Anglo-Irish forerunner of the eighteenth century.

Synge, John (1871–1909)   Irish dramatist, author of *The Playboy of the Western World* and other works, associated with the beginnings of the Abbey Theatre and the Irish Renaissance.

Thebaid   The district about Egyptian Thebes, once associated with Christian monasticism.

Three Rocks   A Dublin mountain.

Timon   Greek philosopher, called "The Misanthrope," of the fifth century B.C. See Shakespeare's *Timon of Athens.*

Timor   The Mongol emperor Tamburlaine (1336–1405), who died while advancing to the conquest of China.

Tone, Wolf (1763–1798)   Founder of United Irish Club, leader of conspiracy to overthrow English rule with French help. Captured and condemned to death, he killed himself in prison.

Urbino   Site of the famous Renaissance court of Guidobaldo de Montefeltro, praised in Castiglione's *The Courtier.*

Usna's children   Naoise, Ainule, and Ardan, brothers beheaded by Conchubar. Naoise was the lover of Deirdre, whom Conchubar had planned to marry; they fled to Scotland with Naoise's brothers, but were tricked into returning to their death.

Veronica   St. Veronica, who wiped Jesus' face with a cloth ("napkin") as he was carrying the cross; the cloth took the impress of his face.

von Hügel, Baron Friedrich (1852–1925)   Author of *The Mystical Element of Religion* (1908), a Roman Catholic theologian who contrasted Homeric with Christian thought; founder of London Society for the Study of Religion.

Wadding, Luke (1588–1657)   Irish Franciscan friar and historian whose portrait by José Ribera (*Lo Spagnoletto*) hangs in the National Gallery in Dublin.

Wilson, Richard (1714–1782)   Landscape painter.

The Witch of Atlas   See Shelley's *The Witch of Atlas,* whose protagonist symbolizes the beauty of wisdom.

Selective Bibliography

I. WORKS BY YEATS

The Autobiography of William Butler Yeats (New York: Collier Books, 1965).

The Collected Letters of W. B. Yeats, Vol. I, 1865–1895 (Oxford: The Clarendon Press, 1986), ed. by John Kelly.

The Collected Plays of W. B. Yeats: New Edition with Five Additional Plays (New York: Macmillan, 1953).

The Collected Poems of W. B. Yeats (London: Macmillan, 1950; New York: Macmillan, 1956). These editions, based on *Poems* (London: Macmillan, 1949), are not quite identical.

The Death of Cuchulain: Manuscript Materials Including the Author's Final Text (Ithaca, N.Y., and London: Cornell University Press, 1982), ed. by Phillip R. Marcus.

Essays and Introductions (New York: Macmillan, 1961).

Explorations (New York: Macmillan, 1962).

The Letters of W. B. Yeats (London: Rupert Hart-Davis, 1954; New York: Macmillan, 1955), ed. by Allan Wade.

Letters on Poetry from W. B. Yeats to Dorothy Wellesley (New York: Oxford University Press, 1940, introduction by Kathleen Raine, 1964).

Memoirs (London: Macmillan, 1972; New York: Macmillan, 1973), ed. by Denis Donoghue.

Mythologies (London and New York: Macmillan, 1959).

The Poems of W. B. Yeats: A New Edition (London and New York: Macmillan, 1983), ed. by Richard J. Finneran.

Purgatory: Manuscript Materials Including the Author's Final Text (Ithaca, N.Y., and London: Cornell University Press, 1986), ed. by Sandra F. Siegel.

The Variorum Edition of the Plays of W. B. Yeats (New York: Macmillan, 1966), ed. by Russell K. Alspach assisted by Catharine C. Alspach.

The Variorum Edition of the Poems of W. B. Yeats (New York: Macmillan, 1957), ed. by Peter Allt and Russell K. Alspach.

A Vision: A Reissue with the Author's Final Revisions (New York: Macmillan, 1956)

Yeats's Vision Papers, 3 vols. (Iowa City: University of Iowa Press, 1992), ed. by George Mills Harper *et al.*

II. SECONDARY WORKS

Bjersby, Birgit, *Interpretations of the Cuchulain Legend in the Works of W. B. Yeats* (Cambridge, Mass.: Harvard University Press, 1951).

Bloom, Harold, *Yeats* (New York: Oxford University Press, 1970).

Bradford, Curtis B., *Yeats at Work* (Abridged Edition: New York: The Ecco Press, 1978).

Cross, K. G. W. and R. T. Dunlop, *A Bibliography of Yeats Criticism* (London: Macmillan, 1971).

Donoghue, Denis, *William Butler Yeats* (N.Y.: Viking Press, 1971).

Ellmann, Richard, *Eminent Domain: Yeats Among Wilde, Joyce, Pound, Eliot, and Auden* (New York: Oxford University Press, 1967).

———, *The Identity of Yeats* (New York: Oxford University Press, 1964).

———, *Yeats: The Man and the Masks* (New York: Macmillan, 1948).

Finneran, Richard J., *Editing Yeats's Poems* (New York: St. Martin's Press, 1983).

Gregory, Lady Augusta (trans.), *Cuchulain of Muirthemne* (New York: Oxford University Press, 1970).

———, *Gods and Fighting Men* (New York: Oxford University Press, 1970).

Henn, Thomas R., *The Lonely Tower: Studies in the Poetry of W. B. Yeats*, second edition (New York: Barnes and Noble, 1965).

Hone, Joseph M., *W. B. Yeats, 1865–1939*, second edition (New York: St. Martin's Press, 1962).

Jeffares, A. Norman, *A New Commentary on the Poems of W. B. Yeats* (London: Macmillan; Stanford: Stanford University Press, 1984).

———, *W. B. Yeats, Man and Poet*, second edition (New York: Barnes and Noble, 1966).

———, *W. B. Yeats: A New Biography* (New York: Farrar, Straus and Giroux, 1989).

Keane, Patrick J. (ed.), *William Butler Yeats* (New York: McGraw-Hill, 1973). Includes excellent bibliographical notes.

Kermode, Frank, *Romantic Image* (New York: Random House, 1964).

Kinsella, Thomas, *The Dual Tradition: An Essay on Poetry and Politics in Ireland* (Manchester: Carcanet Press, 1995).

——— (trans.), *The Táin* (New York: Oxford University Press, 1970).

MacNeice, Louis, *The Poetry of W. B. Yeats* (New York: Oxford University Press, 1967).

Moore, Virginia, *The Unicorn: William Butler Yeats's Search for Reality* (New York: Macmillan, 1954).

Parkinson, Thomas, *W. B. Yeats, Self-Critic and The Later Poetry* (Berkeley and Los Angeles: University of California Press, 1971).

Parrish, Stephen Maxfield (ed.), *A Concordance to the Poems of W. B. Yeats*, programmed by James Allan Painter (Ithaca, N.Y.: Cornell University Press, 1963).

Rosenthal, M. L. *Running to Paradise: Yeats's Poetic Art* (New York and Oxford: Oxford University Press, 1994).

———, *Sailing into the Unknown: Yeats, Pound, and Eliot* (London and New York: Oxford University Press, 1978).

———, and Sally M. Gall, *The Modern Poetic Sequence: The Genius of Modern Poetry* (London and New York: Oxford University Press, 1983).

Saul, George Brandon, *Prolegomena to the Study of Yeats's Plays* (New York: Octagon Books, 1971).

———, *Prolegomena to the Study of Yeats's Poems* (Philadelphia: University of Pennsylvania Press, 1957).

Stallworthy, Jon, *Between the Lines: Yeats's Poems in the Making* (Oxford: Clarendon Press, 1963).

———, *Visions and Revisions in Yeats's Last Poems* (Oxford: Clarendon Press, 1969).

Stock, A. G., *W. B. Yeats: His Poetry and Thought* (Cambridge, England: Cambridge University Press, 1961).

Tuohy, Frank, *Yeats* (East Meredith, N.Y.: New Amsterdam Press, 1976).

Unterecker, John, *A Reader's Guide to William Butler Yeats* (New York: Noonday Press, 1959).

———, (ed.), *Yeats: A Collection of Critical Essays* (Englewood Cliffs, N.J.: Prentice-Hall, 1963).

Vendler, Helen Hannessy, *Yeats's "Vision" and the Later Plays* (Cambridge, Mass.: Harvard University Press, 1963).

Wade, Allan, *A Bibliography of the Writings of W. B. Yeats*, third edition, revised by Russell K. Alspach (London: Rupert Hart-Davis, 1968).

Whitaker, Thomas R., *Swan and Shadow: Yeats's Dialogue with History* (Chapel Hill: University of North Carolina, 1964).

Wilson, F. A. C., *W. B. Yeats and Tradition* (N.Y.: Macmillan, 1958).

———, *Yeats's Iconography* (London: Victor Gollancz, 1960).

Index to Titles

Acre of Grass, An, 185
Adam's Curse, 28
After Long Silence, 153
Against Unworthy Praise, 33
All Souls' Night, 125
All Things Can Tempt Me, 36
Among School Children, 121
Ancestral Houses, 109
Apparitions, The, 209

Beautiful Lofty Things, 187
Beggar to Beggar Cried, 43
Black Tower, The, 202
Blood and the Moon, 133
Brown Penny, 36
Byzantium, 138

Calvary, 94
Cap and Bells, The, 24
Cat and the Moon, The, 75
Certain Artists Bring Her Dolls and
    Drawings, 66
Chambermaid's First Song, The, 185
Chambermaid's Second Song, The,
    185
Choice, The, 138
Chosen, 156
Church and State, 173
Circus Animals' Desertion, The, 212
Cloak, the Boat, and the Shoes, The,
    1
Coat, A, 49
Cold Heaven, The, 47
Collar-Bone of a Hare, The, 56
Come Gather Round Me, Parnell-
    ites, 188
Coole and Ballylee, 1931, 136
Crazy Jane and Jack the Journeyman,
    147
Crazy Jane and the Bishop, 145

Crazy Jane Grown Old Looks at the
    Dancers, 149
Crazy Jane on God, 148
Crazy Jane on the Day of Judgment,
    146
Crazy Jane on the Mountain, 196
Crazy Jane Reproved, 146
Crazy Jane Talks with the Bishop, 148
Cuchulain Comforted, 203
Cuchulain's Fight with the Sea, 8

Dawn, The, 59
Death, 130
Death of Cuchulain, The, 215
Death of the Hare, The, 124
Deep-Sworn Vow, A, 65
Delphic Oracle upon Plotinus, The,
    155
Demon and Beast, 88
Dialogue of Self and Soul, A, 130
Dolls, The, 49
Double Vision of Michael Robartes,
    The, 78
Down by the Salley Gardens, 5
Dream of Death, A, 14
Drinking Song, A, 34

Easter, 1916, 83
Ego Dominus Tuus, 68
End of Day, The, 67
Ephemera, 1

Faery Song, A, 12
Fallen Majesty, 47
Fascination of What's Difficult, The,
    33
Fergus and the Druid, 7
First Confession, A, 155
First Love, 124
Fisherman, The, 61

Folly of Being Comforted, The, 28
For Anne Gregory, 137
Four Ages of Man, The, 176
Fragments, 120

Girl's Song, 150
Great Day, The, 190
Gyres, The, 178

Hawk, The, 62
He and She, 175
He Bids His Beloved Be at Peace, 23
He Hears the Cry of the Sedge, 26
He Reproves the Curlew, 23
He Wishes for the Cloths of Heaven, 27
He Wishes His Beloved Were Dead, 27
Her Anxiety, 151
Her Courage, 68
Her Courtesy, 66
Her Friends Bring Her a Christmas Tree, 68
Her Race, 67
Hosting of the Sidhe, The, 20

'I Am of Ireland,' 153
I See Phantoms of Hatred and of the Heart's Fullness and of the Coming Emptiness, 114
Image from a Past Life, An, 82
In Memory of Eva Gore-Booth and Con Markievicz, 129
In Memory of Major Robert Gregory, 52
Into the Twilight, 21
Irish Airman Foresees His Death, An, 55

John Kinsella's Lament for Mrs. Mary Moore, 208

Lady's First Song, The, 183
Lady's Second Song, The, 183
Lady's Third Song, The, 184
Lake Isle of Innisfree, The, 12
Lapis Lazuli, 179

Last Confession, A, 156
Leaders of the Crowd, The, 86
Leda and the Swan, 121
Lines Written in Dejection, 59
Long-legged Fly, 207
Lover Pleads with His Friend for Old Friends, The, 26
Lover's Song, The, 184
Lullaby, 152

Magi, The, 48
Man and the Echo, 210
Man Who Dreamed of Faeryland, The, 15
Man Young and Old, A, 124
Mask, The, 35
Meditation in Time of War, A, 92
Meditations in Time of Civil War, 109
Memory, 63
Memory of Youth, A, 46
Meru, 177
Model for the Laureate, A, 191
Moods, The, 20
Mother of God, The, 140
Municipal Gallery Revisited, The, 193
My Descendants, 112
My House, 110
My Table, 111

News for the Delphic Oracle, 206
Nineteen Hundred and Nineteen, 115
Nineteenth Century and After, The, 135
No Second Troy, 32

Old Men Admiring Themselves in the Water, The, 30
Old Stone Cross, The, 192
On a Political Prisoner, 86
On Being Asked for a War Poem, 66
On Hearing That the Students of Our New University Have Joined the Agitation Against Immoral Literature, 34
On Woman, 60

[Pardon, Old Fathers], 38
Parnell, 191
Parnell's Funeral, 172
Paudeen, 40
Peacock, The, 45
People, The, 63
Phases of the Moon, The, 71
Pity of Love, The, 13
Politics, 213
Prayer for My Daughter, A, 90
Presences, 65
Purgatory, 225

Quarrel in Old Age, 143

Red Hanrahan's Song About Ireland, 30
Remorse for Intemperate Speech, 144
Ribh at the Tomb of Baile and Aillinn, 174
Ribh in Ecstasy, 175
Road at My Door, The, 113
Rose of the World, The, 11
Running to Paradise, 43

Sailing to Byzantium, 102
Saint and the Hunchback, The, 76
Scholars, The, 58
Second Coming, The, 89
Secrets of the Old, The, 125
September 1913, 38
She Turns the Dolls' Faces to the Wall, 67
Solomon and the Witch, 81
Solomon to Sheba, 56
Song of the Old Mother, The, 23
Song of Wandering Aengus, The, 22
Sorrow of Love, The, 13
Spur, The, 191
Stare's Nest by My Window, The, 113
Statesman's Holiday, A, 197
Statues, The, 205
Stolen Child, The, 2
Supernatural Songs, 174
Swift's Epitaph, 138

That the Night Come, 48
There, 175
These Are the Clouds, 36
Those Images, 193
Thought from Propertius, A, 64
Three Bushes, The, 180
Three Hermits, The, 42
Three Marching Songs, 204
Three Movements, 135
Three Things, 151
To a Child Dancing in the Wind, 45
To a Friend Whose Work Has Come to Nothing, 39
To a Poet, Who Would Have Me Praise Certain Bad Poets, Imitators of His and Mine, 34
To a Shade, 40
To a Young Beauty, 57
To an Isle in the Water, 4
To His Heart, Bidding It Have No Fear, 24
To Ireland in the Coming Times, 18
To the Rose upon the Rood of Time, 6
Tom O'Roughley, 58
Tom the Lunatic, 154
Towards Break of Day, 87
Tower, The, 103
Two Songs from a Play, 119
Two Songs of a Fool, 77
Two Trees, The, 17
Two Years Later, 46

Unappeasable Host, The, 21
Under Ben Bulben, 199
Upon a Dying Lady, 66
Upon a House Shaken by the Land Agitation, 35

Vacillation, 140
Valley of the Black Pig, The, 25
Veronica's Napkin, 135

What Then?, 186
When Helen Lived, 41
When You Are Old, 14
Whence Had They Come?, 176

Who Goes with Fergus?, 15
Why Should Not Old Men Be Mad?,
  196
Wild Old Wicked Man, The, 189
Wild Swans at Coole, The, 51
Witch, The, 44
Woman Homer Sung, A, 31

Woman Young and Old, A, 155
Words, 32
Words for Music Perhaps, 145
*Words Upon the Window-Pane,
  The,* 158

Young Man's Song, 150

Index of First Lines of Poems

A bloody and a sudden end, 208
A doll in the doll-maker's house, 49
A man came slowly from the setting sun, 8
A man that had six mortal wounds, a man, 203
A pity beyond all telling, 13
A speckled cat and a tame hare, 77
A statesman is an easy man, 192
A sudden blow: the great wings beating still, 121
All things can tempt me from this craft of verse, 36
Although crowds gathered once if she but showed her face, 47
Although I can see him still, 61
An affable Irregular, 113
An ancient bridge, and a more ancient tower, 110
An old man cocked his ear upon a bridge, 71
And thus declared that Arab lady, 81
Around me the images of thirty years, 193
As I came over Windy Gap, 43
As the moon sidles up, 175

Bald heads forgetful of their sins, 58
Beautiful lofty things: O'Leary's noble head, 187
'Because I am mad about women, 189
Because there is safety in derision, 209
Because to-day is some religious festival, 67
Because you have found me in the pitch-dark night, 174
Behold that great Plotinus swim, 155
Beloved, gaze in thine own heart, 17
Beloved, may your sleep be sound, 152

Between extremities, 140
Be you still, be you still, trembling heart, 24
Bird sighs for the air, 184
Blessed be this place, 133
Bring me to the blasted oak, 145
Bring where our Beauty lies, 66

'Call down the hawk from the air, 62
Civilisation is hooped together, brought, 177
Come gather round me, Parnellites, 188

Dance there upon the shore, 45
Dear fellow-artist, why so free, 57
Down by the salley gardens my love and I did meet, 5

Earth in beauty dressed, 151
Eternity is passion, girl or boy, 176

For certain minutes at the least, 88
For one throb of the artery, 92
From pleasure of the bed, 185

Had I the heavens' embroidered cloths, 27
Has no one said those daring, 46
Having inherited a vigorous mind, 112
He stood among a crowd at Dromahair, 15
He with body waged a fight, 176
Here is fresh matter, poet, 173
His chosen comrades thought at school, 186
How came this ranger, 185
How can I, that girl standing there, 213
How should the world be luckier if this house, 35

Hurrah for revolution and more cannon-shot, 190

I admit the briar, 155
'I am of Ireland, 153
I am tired of cursing the Bishop, 196
I care not what the sailors say, 146
I climb to the tower-top and lean upon broken stone, 114
I dreamed that one had died in a strange place, 14
I found that ivory image there, 149
I had this thought a while ago, 32
I have heard that hysterical women say, 179
I have met them at close of day, 83
I have old women's secrets now, 125
I have pointed out the yelling pack, 124
I hear the Shadowy Horses, their long manes a-shake, 23
I heard the old, old men say, 30
I know, although when looks meet, 147
I know that I shall meet my fate, 55
I lived among great houses, 197
I made my song a coat, 49
I met the Bishop on the road, 148
I ranted to the knave and fool, 144
I rise in the dawn, and I kneel and blow, 23
I saw a staring virgin stand, 119
I sought a theme and sought for it in vain, 212
I summon to the winding ancient stair, 130
I think it better that in times like these, 66
I turn round, 183
I walk through the long schoolroom questioning, 121
I wander by the edge, 26
I went out alone, 150
I went out to the hazel wood, 22
I whispered, 'I am too young, 36
I will arise and go now, and go to Innisfree, 12
I would be ignorant as the dawn, 59

If any man drew near, 31
If you have revisited the town, thin Shade, 40
In a cleft that's christened Alt, 210
Indignant at the fumbling wits, the obscure spite, 40

Know, that I would accounted be, 18

Locke sank into a swoon, 120
'Love is all, 146

Many ingenious lovely things are gone, 115
May God be praised for woman, 60
Midnight has come, and the great Christ Church Bell, 125
Motionless under the moon-beam, 94

'Never shall a young man, 137
Never until this night have I been stirred, 82
Nor dread nor hope attend, 130
Now all the truth is out, 39
Now as at all times I can see in the mind's eye, 48
Now that we're almost settled in our house, 52

'O cruel Death, give three things back, 151
O curlew, cry no more in the air, 23
O heart, be at peace, because, 33
On the grey rock of Cashel the mind's eye, 78
On the grey sand beside the shallow stream, 68
On thrones from China to Peru, 191
Once more the storm is howling, and half hid, 90
One had a lovely face, 63
One that is ever kind said yesterday, 28
Others because you did not keep, 65
Out-worn heart, in a time out-worn, 21

Pardon, great enemy, 68
Pardon, old fathers, if you still remain, 38
Parnell came down the road, he said
 to a cheering man, 191
Picture and book remain, 185
'Put off that mask of burning gold, 35
Pythagoras planned it. Why did the
 people stare, 205

Red Rose, proud Rose, sad Rose of all my
 days, 6
Remember all those renowned gener-
 ations, 204

Said lady once to lover, 180
Sang old Tom the lunatic, 154
Sang Solomon to Sheba, 56
Say that the men of the old black
 tower, 202
Shakespearean fish swam the sea, far
 away from land, 135
She has not grown uncivil, 67
She is playing like a child, 67
She lived in storm and strife, 48
She might, so noble from head, 64
She that but little patience knew, 86
'She will change,' I cried, 150
Shy one, shy one, 4
Speech after long silence; it is right, 153
Stand up and lift your hand and bless,
 76
Suddenly I saw the cold and rook-
 delighting heaven, 47
Surely among a rich man's flowering
 lawns, 109
Swear by what the Sages spoke, 199
Swift has sailed into his rest, 138

That civilisation may not sink, 207
That is no country for old men. The
 young, 102
That lover of a night, 148
The bees build in the crevices, 113
The brawling of a sparrow in the
 eaves, 13
The cat went here and there, 75
The Danaan children laugh, in cradles
 of wrought gold, 21

The dews drop slowly and dreams
 gather: unknown spears, 25
The fascination of what's difficult, 33
The gyres! the gyres! Old Rocky Face,
 look forth, 178
The Heavenly Circuit; Berenice's
 Hair, 135
The host is riding from Knocknarea,
 20
The intellect of man is forced to
 choose, 138
The jester walked in the garden, 24
The light of evening, Lissadell, 129
The lot of love is chosen. I learnt that
 much, 156
The moments passed as at a play, 46
The old brown thorn-trees break in
 two high over Cummen Strand, 30
The three-fold terror of love; a fallen
 flare, 140
The trees are in their autumn beauty,
 51
The unpurged images of day recede,
 138
There all the barrel-hoops are knit, 175
There all the golden codgers lay, 206
These are the clouds about the fallen
 sun, 36
They must to keep their certainty
 accuse, 86
This night has been so strange that it
 seemed, 65
'Though logic-choppers rule the
 town, 58
Though nurtured like the sailing
 moon, 124
Though the great song return no
 more, 135
Though you are in your shining days,
 26
Three old hermits took the air, 42
Time drops in decay, 20
'Time to put off the world and go
 somewhere, 43
Toil and grow rich, 44
Turning and turning in the widening
 gyre, 89

Two heavy trestles, and a board, III

Under my window-ledge the waters race, 136
Under the Great Comedian's tomb the crowd, 172

Was it the double of my dream, 87
We have cried in our despair, 41
We sat together at one summer's end, 28
We who are old, old and gay, 12
Were you but lying cold and dead, 27
'What do you make so fair and bright, I
'What have I earned for all that work,' I said, 63
What if I bade you leave, 193
What lively lad most pleasured me, 156
What matter that you understood no word, 175
What need you, being come to sense, 38
What shall I do with this absurdity, 103
What sort of a man is coming, 183
What's riches to him, 45
When have I last looked on, 59

When her soul flies to the predestined dancing-place, 68
When you and my true lover meet, 184
When you are old and grey and full of sleep, 14
Where dips the rockẏ highland, 2
Where had her sweetness gone, 143
Where, where but here have Pride and Truth, 34
Who dreamed that beauty passes like a dream, II
Who will go drive with Fergus now, 15
Why should I blame her that she filled my days, 32
Why should not old men be mad, 196
Wine comes in at the mouth, 34
With the old kindness, the old distinguished grace, 66
Would I could cast a sail on the water, 56

You say, as I have often given tongue, 34
You think it horrible that lust and rage, 191
'Your eyes that once were never weary of mine, I